STRENGTHENING AGING FAMILIES

STRENGTHENING AGING FAMILIES

Diversity in Practice and Policy

editors

Gregory C. Smith
Sheldon S. Tobin
Elizabeth Anne Robertson-Tchabo
Paul W. Power

SAGE Publications
International Educational and Professional Publisher
Thousand Oaks   London   New Delhi

For information address:

SAGE Publications, Inc.
2455 Teller Road
Thousand Oaks, California 91320

SAGE Publications Ltd.
6 Bonhill Street
London EC2A 4PU
United Kingdom

SAGE Publications India Pvt. Ltd.
M-32 Market
Greater Kailash I
New Delhi 110 048 India

Printed in the United States of America

Library of Congress Cataloging-in-Publication Data

Main entry under title:

Strengthening aging families: diversity in practice and policy /
    edited by Gregory C. Smith . . . [et al.].
        p. cm.
    Includes bibliographical references and indexes.
        ISBN 0-8039-5424-7. (alk. paper). — ISBN 0-8039-5425-5 (pbk. :
alk. paper)
        1. Social work with the aged—United States. 2. Family social
work—United States. 3. Aged—Family relationships. 4. Adult
children—Family relationships. 5. Family policy—United States.
6. Caregivers—United States. I. Smith, Gregory C., 1951–
HV1461.S875 1995
362.82'3'0973—dc20   94-45243

95 96 97 98 99 10 9 8 7 6 5 4 3 2 1

Sage Production Editor: Diana E. Axelsen

Contents

Foreword   vii
    NANCY K. SCHLOSSBERG

Introduction   ix
    GREGORY C. SMITH

PART I: Assisting Families With Normative Concerns   1

1. Supporting the Family in Elder Care   3
    RONALD W. TOSELAND, GREGORY C. SMITH,
    and PHILLIP McCALLION

2. Fostering Family Involvement in Institutional Care   25
    SHELDON S. TOBIN

3. Strengthening Sibling Relationships in the Later Years   45
    VICTOR G. CICIRELLI

PART II: Helping Families With Special Concerns   61

4. Confronting Maltreatment of Elders by Their Family   63
    JORDAN I. KOSBERG and JUANITA L. GARCIA

5. Assisting Older Families of Adults
   With Lifelong Disabilities   80
    GREGORY C. SMITH, SHELDON S. TOBIN,
    and ELISE M. FULLMER

6. Challenging Biases Against Families
    of Older Gays and Lesbians   99
    ELISE M. FULLMER

PART III: Recognizing Select Family Dynamics   121

7. Understanding Intergenerational
    Issues in Aging Families   123
    PAUL W. POWER

8. Facilitating Health Care Decisions
    Within Aging Families   143
    EVELYN J. BATA and PAUL W. POWER

9. Achieving Intimacy in Late-Life Marriages   158
    SUSAN KRAUSS WHITBOURNE and ERIN L. CASSIDY

10. Utilizing Culture in Work With Aging Families   175
    THOMAS W. JOHNSON

**PART IV: A Synthesis of Interventions
for Aging Families**   203

11. The Diversity of Direct Practice   205
    SHELDON S. TOBIN and PAUL W. POWER

12. Preventive Approaches to Building Competencies   221
    GREGORY C. SMITH

13. Critical Policy Issues   235
    ELLIE BRUBAKER and TIMOTHY H. BRUBAKER

References   248

Author Index   270

Subject Index   278

About the Editors   286

About the Contributors   287

Foreword

This book breaks new ground with a bold approach to working with aging families. Many books look at the topic from a single, limited perspective—presenting either a policy, an educational, or a clinical analysis. *Strengthening Aging Families: Diversity in Practice and Policy* approaches the topic differently by highlighting the needed interaction of clinical practice and education/enrichment with the larger view of policy.

Practitioners from a number of helping professions will read each chapter and come away with suggested ways to understand and intervene with aging families. For example, authors present a broad-based understanding of the particular family issue being discussed, whether it is elder care, elder abuse, or disabilities. Here the unit of analysis is the society, the very context in which the aging family exists. The authors also describe approaches that are presented in an educational or enrichment manner. And, of course, the authors examine the clinical ways in which the individual family members, or the family as a whole, can be helped to alleviate the presenting problem. This holistic approach makes good sense.

In order to ensure that each chapter touches on these various modes of intervention—counseling/therapy, education/enrichment, and policy—the chapters are organized similarly. Each chapter provides background information that defines the particular family being discussed, followed by theory and applied research relating to the family. Each chapter ends with a section on directions for practice and policy. This organization offers a consistent framework for the book, making it seem more like one voice than many edited books, with their fragmented approaches.

Congratulations are due also to the authors of this book for recognizing what Joe Glazer, the folk singer, portrays in his song, "Old Folks Ain't All the Same" (1986):

That's when I began to realize
That old folks come in different conditions and sizes
And shapes and situations,
And that's when I began to realize. . .
Old folks are not made on the assembly line,
They're as different as your mother is from mine.
Each one has an individual name,
And all old folks just ain't the same.[1]

The song mirrors what the book is about—diversity, heterogeneity, individuality. The chapters in the book reflect the only thing we know for sure about aging families—they are different, and consequently, they need to be understood and helped in diverse and complicated ways. The authors correctly warn against lumping groups together, whether they are siblings, families of gays and lesbians, elders being abused, four-generation families living together, or grandparents. In other words, there is no single category of the aging family; instead, there are aging families, with different constellations and combinations, no one of which may ever be repeated.

Those interested in and concerned about aging families need to understand the complexity, challenges, and problems of living longer. The authors bring a sensitivity to the subject that is illustrative of the forward-looking, future-oriented thrust of this book.

This book should receive attention from policy people, as well as those students and professionals in the helping professions. Too many works examine these issues by looking at them through one lens at a time. This book sets a new course.

NANCY K. SCHLOSSBERG
UNIVERSITY OF MARYLAND,
COLLEGE PARK

Note

1. Glazer, Joe, and Friends. (1986). *Old folks ain't all the same*. Silver Spring, MD: Collector Records. Used with permission. The complete song is available on cassette or LP recording from Collector Records, 1604 Arbor View Road, Silver Spring, MD 29815.

Introduction

GREGORY C. SMITH

Scholars and practitioners in the fields of gerontology and family studies have increasingly attended to the concerns of aging families. Many excellent practice-oriented books have described the application of specific family counseling and therapy techniques for work with older adults and their families (Bumagin & Hirn, 1990; Hargrave & Anderson, 1992; Herr & Weakland, 1979; Hughston, Cristopherson, & Bonjean, 1989; Neidhardt & Allen, 1993). There have also been numerous nonclinical books that describe the heterogeneity among aging families and the issues that confront them (for recent editions, see Brubaker, 1990c; Burton, 1993; Maddox & Lawton, 1993; Troll, 1986).

This book differs from all prior volumes on aging families in two important respects. First, unlike earlier works, this volume combines descriptions of diverse issues faced by various types of aging families, explanations of how these issues affect individual family members and the entire family unit, and the delineation of ways to strenghten family functioning. Second, the approaches to strengthening families extend beyond counseling and therapy with aging families to encompass prevention to build competencies as well as a consideration of how policy intersects with family practice.

However, this volume is not intended to be a "how to" book that instructs practitioners to use a particular kind of intervention or theoretical approach to practice and policy. Instead, the broader goal is to inform professionals involved with aging families as to when, how, and why direct practice, preventive strategies, and policy are appropriate in strengthening diverse types of aging families to meet the variety of challenges confronting them. It is assumed that the reader is already skilled in the use of interventions described, will obtain skills in these interventions through other sources if necessary, and will recognize when to refer families to more experienced practitioners.

Defining Aging Families

Later-life families are typically considered to be those with members who are beyond the child-rearing years and have launched their children. For couples who have been childless, or who have children with lifelong disabilities that require care throughout their adult years, living beyond the age of 50 years generally characterizes aging families. This definition, however, is not as straightforward as it appears.

Family scholars, for example, are quick to point out that there is no consensus on the definition of *family* (L'Abate, 1994; Levin & Trost, 1992). This lack of clarity results in an obvious question: Is the lay concept of "my family" the same as the helper's concept of *the family*? How, for example, does the helper proceed when a frail elderly woman refuses to recognize her daughter-in-law as a family member despite the daughter-in-law's willingness to serve as her primary caregiver?

Difficulty in defining the aging family also results from the increasing diversity found among these families, which necessitates an evolving definition of the aging family. Individuals are now aging in intergenerational families that are quantitatively and qualitatively different from those of their forebearers with respect to roles, relationships, and responsibilities. Today's elderly are more likely than those in the past to be part of a four- or even five-generation family, with fewer members in each generation. Moreover the length of time that older persons spend in family roles has risen considerably. Parenthood, for example, may continue for more than half a century, and grandparenthood and great-grandparenthood may last more than 20 years (Bengtson, Rosenthal, & Burton, 1990).

The contributors to this book offer readers an understanding of the aging family that includes classic family forms and newly emerging forms. Because of the many existing, nontraditional family structures, it is assumed in this volume that the meaning of the aging family must be truly comprehensive. The views expressed by the contributors, then, are consistent with those of Robischon and Smith (1977), who broadly defined the family as an interdependent group system that may consist of the biological or adoptive family and/or influential others.

Family practitioners, however, differ in their perception of the family as being either part of the problem, a resource, part of the helping team, the object of intervention, or irrelevant to the situation at hand (Hartman & Laird, 1983). Policymakers also hold differing views of the family's role in an aging society. Some of the interventions described in this volume are primarily targeted toward individual family members, with the expectation that they will benefit the entire family to some degree; others are directed at the family system, with the hope that a single family member will benefit the most; and still others are intended to enrich all members of the aging family equally.

Issues Confronting Aging Families

As noted above, one major goal of this book is to illustrate the diversity that exists with respect to the challenges and concerns faced by aging families. The three chapters in Part I, for example, illustrate an assortment of normative issues faced by the majority of aging families in our society (providing care to a frail elderly relative in Chapter 1, becoming involved with the institutional care of a loved one in Chapter 2, and relating to siblings in later life in Chapter 3). In contrast, each of the chapters included in Part II focuses on issues or circumstances that are unique to special populations of aging families (maltreatment of elders by their families in Chapter 4, adults with lifelong disabilities being cared for by aging family members in Chapter 5, and experiencing family life as an older gay or lesbian person in Chapter 6).

There are two caveats, however, regarding the organization of Parts I and II. First, the boundary between the normative concerns of aging families and issues confronting special populations of aging families is not as precise as this organizational structure might suggest. Not only do families differ widely regarding the particular manner in which they handle "normative" concerns (Bond & Wagner, 1988a), but many aging families facing "special" concerns must also deal with normative issues that arise during the later stages of their family life cycle. A second caveat is that the chapters included in these two sections are intended to be representative rather than comprehensive in nature. Not included in Part I, for example, are such normative late-life family issues as widowhood, retirement, and grandparenthood (for a recent review of these issues, see

Swensen, 1994). Similarly, Part II does not encompass a number of special aging family situations that have been increasingly encountered during the past several years, such as older parents caring for terminally ill HIV-infected offspring, grandparents caring for children of chemically addicted parents, or divorce in late life.

The chapters presented in Part III reveal that diversity exists even with respect to important family dynamics that transcend both normative and special issues facing aging families. Chapter 7 shows how families that provide care to a frail elderly relative vary in the quality of their intergenerational relationships; Chapter 8 reveals how the family engages in decision making regarding health concerns; Chapter 9 illustrates how the level of intimacy between marital partners can be related to family caregiving; and Chapter 10 considers how the family's ethnic/cultural heritage must be considered in all levels of intervention with the aging family.

Awareness of these dynamics is of obvious importance to all those who are interested in aging families.

The chapters in Parts I, II, and III follow a generic outline. First, a background is presented in which authors provide their conceptual groundwork by defining key terms, presenting relevant demographic information, and clarifying basic concepts. Second, there is an elaboration of family issues in which the authors review the literature on how the issue at hand affects the functioning of the aging family and its members.

Third, in discussing directions for practice and policy, the authors specify when, how, and why a variety of interventions may be useful for strengthening the types of aging families being discussed. Each of these chapters concludes with a case example illustrating key points offered in the chapter. The case examples are followed by discussion questions developed by the editors to enable students and trainees to obtain maximum benefit from the information presented.

The Diversity of Practice and Policy

Another major goal of this book is to inform professionals regarding the diversity of practice and policy for aging families. To this end, each chapter in Parts I, II, and III presents recommendations on the use of direct practice, preventive strategies, and policy for the given family situation at hand. In turn, the three chapters in Part IV synthesize and elaborate on these recommendations. Chapter 11 concentrates on direct practice with aging families and summarizes major issues and themes regarding advice giving, counseling, and therapy with aging families. Chapter 12 focuses on building competencies in aging families through various types of preventive strategies, using examples from previous chapters to illustrate what makes these approaches relevant and successful. Chapter 13 examines policy issues of importance to aging families. An emphasis on the family as provider of long-term care to its elderly members is appropriately placed in this chapter because policy research on the aging family focuses heavily on family caregiving to older persons (Tanenbaum, 1993). A key message throughout these final three chapters, as well as the entire book, is that all intervention programs can be viewed as having a common purpose: the strengthening of the aging family as a system and the improvement of the psychosocial well-being of each member of that family system.

Intended Audience

This book should be of interest not only to students but also to professionals from numerous disciplines who interact with distressed older persons and their families, including social workers, psychologists, psychiatrists, family counselors, rehabilitation specialists, nurses, and clergy. Professionals who are well versed in family practice, but who have negligible experience with *aging* families, will discover how their knowledge and skills may be applied to the variety of aging families. Conversely, those with expertise in applied gerontology, who work with and on behalf of aging families, will find relevance in our family interventions for meeting their clients' needs. The extensive use of case illustrations and the discussion questions at the end of each chapter make this book particularly well suited for classroom use by students.

℞ PART I ℘

ASSISTING FAMILIES
WITH NORMATIVE CONCERNS

Just as individuals have unique life histories that are shaped by multiple systems and factors, any family system has a unique developmental history that contributes to the variance with which families respond to transitions that arise at varied points across the life span. The transitions include both normative and nonnormative life events and nonevents. Generally occurrences that are shared by many individuals and that may be anticipated are considered to be normative. However, even normative events may, in some family systems, have unexpected or atypical elements. The three chapters in this section of the book offer examples of normative transitions encountered by aging families.

Toseland, Smith, and McCallion (Chapter 1) present a review of recent theory and research concerning the role of the family in elder care. They consider the prevalence and diversity of family caregiving arrangements and discuss how the family system may be affected by caring for a frail elderly family member. The case example of Mrs. A illustrates a primary caregiver overwhelmed by caring for her parents. In addition, the authors briefly describe the diverse range of effective interventions to support caregiving families, including educational programs, community-based services to alleviate the stressors of caregiving, psychoeducational support groups to facilitate adaptation of family caregivers, and family counseling/therapy to resolve serious family problems. This chapter points out the need to view informal caregiving from a family systems perspective. Moreover the authors point out that programs and services will continue to target the primary caregiver rather than the entire family system until

1

researchers, practitioners, and policymakers begin to conceptualize informal caregiving as a family matter.

Tobin (Chapter 2) considers ways to facilitate family involvement with an aging family member when the frail elderly person is institutionalized. Successful involvement of families by institutions should increase the general well-being of both the institutionalized older person and the family members. Institutionalization refers to a specific environmental transition in aging: relocation to a long-term care facility that frequently is the elderly person's last residence. Although at any one time approximately 5% of individuals age 65 years and over reside in a nursing home, there is a 50% to 60% probability of living part of one's life in a nursing home. Because so many families are involved at some time in placing an elderly family member in a nursing home, this topic is addressed in this section on normative concerns. Even after institutionalization of the older family member, strain on the family system is likely to continue. Family members feel guilty about placing their family member in a home, and nursing home residents initially may feel that they have been abandoned. Tobin summarizes ways in which nursing homes can involve families in the development and execution of a care plan for their family member that will increase the general well-being of both family members and the nursing home resident. The case example of Mrs. J illustrates the effects of various aspects of institutionalization on both the nursing home resident and on the family.

Cicirelli (Chapter 3) considers sibling relationships in adulthood. Most aging individuals have at least one sibling who lives close enough for occasional contact. Cicirelli's central thesis is that strengthening sibling bonds or relationships will help to promote life satisfaction, especially because siblings tend to be the last surviving members of their family of origin and because the general trend in sibling relationships in adulthood and old age is one of increasing closeness. It is important to recognize the similarities in issues between the literature on families and the literature on siblings. Just as there are varied definitions of family, Cicirelli considers definitions of siblings and points out that there is considerable variance in personal perspectives as to who is recognized as a sibling. Moreover the lack of a family systems perspective also is evident in sibling research. Cicirelli points out that most research into the sibling relationship is limited to sibling dyads, although in families with more than two children, the sibling group as a whole may be extremely important. The case study of a 60-year-old middle brother and his 51-year-old last-born sister illustrates the effects of sibling conflict.

1

🐚

Supporting the Family in Elder Care

RONALD W. TOSELAND

GREGORY C. SMITH

PHILLIP McCALLION

🐚

Families have been labeled the "backbone of long-term care" for the frail elderly in the United States (Kane & Reinardy, 1989), and caring for an elderly relative is now considered to be a normative family stress (Brody, 1985a). Indeed, about three quarters of elderly persons in need of long-term care receive informal support from family and friends exclusively, whereas most of the remainder use some combination of formal and informal supports (Doty, 1986).

Because family-based assistance is rendered chiefly by a primary caregiver, usually the spouse or an adult daughter (Brody, Hoffman, Kleban, & Schoonover, 1989; Rankin, 1990), practitioners and researchers alike have tended to focus narrowly on issues concerning the relationship between the primary caregiver and the care recipient (Brody et al., 1989). In fact, only recently have calls emerged in the gerontological literature to view informal caregiving from a family systems perspective (Gatz, Bengtson, & Blum, 1990; Sanborn & Bould, 1991). The goals of this chapter are to: (a) consider the prevalence, diversity, and demographics

3

of family caregiving arrangements; (b) address how the family system and its members are affected by caring for a frail elderly relative; (c) describe family-based interventions; and (d) discuss relevant policy issues.

Background

PREVALENCE AND TYPES OF
FAMILY CAREGIVING ARRANGEMENTS

Estimates of the number of frail older persons living in the community who require caregiving assistance vary from 1.8 million older persons who receive help from informal caregivers to meet their basic activities of daily living (ADLs), such as toileting and bathing, to as many as 5.1 million older persons who receive one form of aid or another from family, friends, and neighbors (American Association of Retired Persons, 1986; Gevalnik & Simonsick, 1993; Stone, Cafferata, & Sangl, 1987). In turn, estimates of the number of caregivers vary from 2.2 million to 13.3 million individuals, depending on how caregiving is defined (Stone et al., 1987; Stone & Kemper, 1989).

When an elder family member needs care, caregiving is most often provided by a spouse. If a spouse is not available, an adult daughter, an adult son, or other relatives such as daughters-in-law, the care recipient's siblings, granddaughters, or friends and other relatives are most likely to provide care (Shanas, 1968; Tonti, 1988). It has been estimated that spouses make up 42% of the population of primary caregivers (wives, 23%, and husbands, 19%), and adult daughters another 29% (Stone et al., 1987). However, even in families in which a primary caregiver has been designated, additional support is often provided by siblings (Townsend & Noelker, 1987), spouses of adult daughter primary caregivers (Kleban, Brody, Schoonover, & Hoffman, 1989), and even favorite nephews and nieces (Atchley & Miller, 1986).

DEMOGRAPHIC TRENDS
AND CAREGIVING FAMILIES

Several demographic trends are predicted to have adverse effects on caregiving families. Dramatic increases in single-parent families and lowered birth rates, for example, imply that older persons will have fewer spouses and adult children available to care for them (Crystal, 1982). Also, as women enter the workforce in growing numbers, conflict between work and caregiving responsibilities is expected to increase (Lang & Brody, 1983). This increased participation in the workforce also means that adult daughters are delaying childbearing, which creates the potential for future conflict between child care and elder care responsibilities. Another relevant demographic trend is that family caregivers are increasingly reporting incomes below the poverty level, making elder care even more burdensome on the entire family (Stone et al., 1987).

The combined influence of these demographic trends is predicted to yield a scenario in which (a) traditional divisions of caregiving roles by gender will be eroded, (b) adult children will be more likely to assume caregiving roles, and (c) all adult children will have some involvement in family caregiving (Kaye & Applegate, 1990b; Sanborn & Bould, 1991). As these events unfold, the circumstances of caregiving will have a growing impact on all involved family members. In turn, the need for family-based interventions can also be expected to rise significantly.

Elaboration of Family Issues

Caregiving is often experienced as a rewarding and fulfilling experience by family members (Lawton, Kleban, Moss, Rovine, & Glicksman, 1989). Even when caregivers are under considerable stress, the opportunity to demonstrate love and affection for the care recipient may offset negative circumstances and cause the caregiver to appraise the situation more positively (Lawton, Brody, & Saperstein, 1989; Toseland & Smith, 1991). Some adult daughter caregivers have even reported that the caregiving experience has improved their relationships with siblings and other family members (Brody et al., 1989). Other positive outcomes derived from family caregiving include increased family cohesiveness, altered perceptions of life's meaning, and personal growth (Gatz et al., 1990). Thus interventions for caregiving families should extend beyond a crisis orientation and encompass family enhancement as well.

Yet there are also many caregivers who either suffer from or are at risk for diverse psychosocial problems such as depression, anxiety, guilt, self-blame, psychosomatic symptoms, restrictions of social roles and leisure or recreational activities, and negative consequences for work situations and personal physical health (for review of research, see Gatz et al., 1990; Toseland & Smith, 1990). It is also likely that the entire family system is adversely affected by caring for a frail elder, although virtually no research has been conducted to examine this possibility.

Nevetheless, a number of variables have been hypothesized to influence how caring for a frail elderly relative affects family functioning (Ferris, Steinberg, Shulman, Kahn, & Reisberg, 1987; Gatz et al., 1990). These include:

1. The quality of the relationship between caregiver and care receiver
2. Family values and interaction processes
3. Shared versus independent living arrangements
4. Consequences of caregiving for work, family relationships, and finances
5. The availability of formal resources and other informal caregivers
6. The nature, extent, and duration of the illness

THE IMPACT OF CAREGIVING
ON INDIVIDUAL FAMILY MEMBERS

Caregiving Spouses

Even though caregiving spouses tend to be older and in poorer health themselves, they typically provide care for longer periods, in more physically demanding situations, and with fewer supports than other types of family caregivers (Montgomery & Datwyler, 1990). Moreover, they frequently choose not to ask other family members for appropriate help, and they are resistant to the idea of institutionalizing their husband or wife (Hess & Soldo, 1985; Montgomery & Kosloski, 1994). This makes care more burdensome and demanding, and it may precipitate the crisis spouses wish to avoid (Townsend & Noelker, 1987). It can also create family tension. Adult children, for example, are often left struggling with the choice of respecting their parents' independence or intervening before a crisis erupts (Parsons & Cox, 1989).

Adult Daughters

Adult daughters or daughters-in-law as primary caregivers face somewhat different problems than caregiving spouses. For example, there appears to be a direct relationship between family conflict and perceived burden and mental health problems among adult child caregivers (Strawbridge & Wallhagan, 1991). Thus, when wives argue with husbands about the care of a parent or parent-in-law, or when children resent a parent spending time caring for a grandparent, perceived caregiving burden increases. Conversely, it has been noted that adults who care for elderly parents perceive their effectiveness as caregivers to increase when other family members assist and cooperate with them (Townsend & Noelker, 1987). There is also evidence that adult daughter caregivers resent siblings who do not assist with care, become distressed by siblings who criticize them or who fail to give emotional or instrumental support, but feel rewarded when siblings offer support and understanding (Brody et al., 1989).

Caregiving can also affect job performance and career aspirations, which in turn influence family homeostasis. Caregiving daughters may need to rearrange work schedules, change from full-time to part-time work, or quit jobs entirely. Also, they may feel that they are missing important events in their children's and spouse's lives, and they may even be conflicted about whose life and care needs should be their priority.

Caregiving may also lead to redefinitions of parent-child relationships. For example, daughters may be forced to revisit old conflicts with the parent now in need of care, and caregiving may necessitate the redefinition of a valued relationship with the parent to reflect changed levels of dependency (Gatz et al., 1990; Hooyman & Lustbader, 1986; Tonti, 1988).

The Caregiver's Siblings

The results of recent studies suggest that siblings are involved with family caregiving in diverse ways. For example, in a study of caregiving families where an adult daughter was the primary caregiver, Matthews (1987) observed that at least one sibling either gave advice, provided personal services, or offered emotional and moral support. In his study of adult sibling networks, Cicirelli (1992a) found that in about half of the families, all siblings coordinated their efforts in providing care to parents, whereas in about one fourth of the families, there was partial coordination, and in the remaining fourth each sibling helped with care as he or she wished, independently of the others. There is also evidence suggesting that sisters are more likely to assist with homemaking, personal care, home health care, transportation, and psychological support, whereas brothers help more with doing home maintenance, identifying available services, completing applications, and negotiating access to formal services (Cicirelli, 1984).

However, despite their obvious contributions, many siblings experience distress related to family caregiving. This is particularly true among female siblings who, regardless of geographical distance from the parent needing care, often feel guilty about not helping more with caregiving and about their anger over the parent's increased dependency (Brody et al., 1989; Schoonover, Brody, Hoffman, & Kleban, 1988).

Female siblings also report social and emotional strains and problems resulting from these interactions identical to those of the adult daughter caregiver (Brody et al., 1989). For example, it has been reported that powerful feelings are unleashed among siblings as they become increasingly aware of their parent's loss of independence and realize that their parent's death is approaching (Tonti, 1988). Male siblings experience somewhat less guilt and strain and tend to provide less instrumental and emotional support than either the adult daughter caregiver or female siblings (Brody et al., 1989).

The Spouse of the
Adult Daughter Caregiver

The sparse literature that exists on the role of caregivers' spouses is controversial. Whereas some authors have suggested that husbands provide very little additional assistance (Brody & Schoonover, 1986), others have argued that emotional support from husbands is a significant factor mitigating the strains that adult daughter caregivers experience (George, 1986; Zarit, Reever, & Bach-Peterson, 1980).

The effect of the caregiving situation on the spouses of caregivers and on their relationship with their mate is even less understood. Many spouses are supportive of their wives' desire to care for their frail elderly parents. However, some are not supportive. Resentment can build because of the amount of time a wife is spending caring for a parent. Conflict can occur about when it is appropriate to institutionalize a parent or a parent-in-law. Others fear that their parents will be jealous of the attention being paid to an in-law.

In a study of 150 caregiving families, Kleban et al. (1989) found that 66% of the husbands reported strain from the caregiving situation. These husbands also reported disruptions in family vacation plans, family privacy, time spent with wives and children, and ability to work on projects around the house. They also perceived their wives' caregiving burden to be greater than did the wives themselves. It was concluded that spouses of primary caregivers are at risk for emotional burdens and are likely to perceive caregiving as having a negative impact on family relationships (Kleban et al., 1989).

The Care Recipient's Grandchildren

To date, studies regarding the impact of family caregiving on grandchildren have been rare. However, the findings reported so far suggest that social contacts are reduced, and grandchildren are torn between wanting to help and wishing to live their lives as their friends' families do (Kirschner, 1985). The attitudes and level of involvement of grandchildren in family caregiving varies by age (Hooyman & Lustbader, 1986). Although very young grandchildren are unable to assist with caregiving directly, their lack of inhibition about physical and cognitive impairments can enable them to relate to the care recipient (for example, by cuddling) in ways that adults cannot, offering substantial sensory and cognitive stimulation to a frail grandparent.

However, as grandchildren reach school age, they can become self-conscious around disabled grandparents and resist spending time with them. They may also feel apprehensive about being left alone with grandparents who may need help that the child cannot provide. For example, in a family counseling session, a couple expressed concerns about their 12-year-old daughter's recent behavior. They indicated that she had been sullen and withdrawn since her grandmother's death. After several individual sessions, the child revealed that she believed her grandmother died because of her failure to act quickly. Also, she blamed her parents for making her accept the responsibility of "baby-sitting" her grandmother. These beliefs had been formed when the 12-year-old was left baby-sitting her younger brother and her grandmother on the day the grandmother experienced a fatal stroke. The child explained that she had left her grandmother sitting in her usual chair in the family room while she made a snack in the kitchen for herself and her brother. When she returned to the family room, she found her grandmother lying on the floor unconscious. Although she called an emergency number, she expressed anguish that she had not done so quickly enough to save her grandmother's life. She also stated that she had told her parents before the incident that she did not want to be responsible for her grandmother, that she was afraid that something would happen. Her parents had responded by saying "Don't be foolish" and "Don't say such things."

During adolescence, teenagers' reactions to grandparents with disabilities can vary widely. Some ignore their grandparents. Others develop warm, close relationships. Some teenagers fear that a grandparent with disabilities will embarrass them in front of their peers. Others resent competing with their grandparent for their parent's time and attention. Also, teenagers have a strong desire to be included in family decisions about caregiving. This is particularly true when the decision affects their own living space, such as giving up their bedroom to a grandparent with disabilities.

The impact of caregiving on adult grandchildren can become extremely complicated. Because four- and five-generation families will become increasingly common in the future, some middle-aged grandchildren will no doubt be caring simultaneously for parents and grandparents. Moreover, the increase in divorces and serial remarriages may produce situations in which adult grandchildren are suddenly confronted with grandparents who are virtual strangers.

Regardless of age, the grandparent-grandchild bond is a special one, and the opportunity to contribute to a grandparent's well-being can be personally rewarding. Teenagers may be especially helpful when they share caregiving tasks with their middle-aged parents. The participation of grandchildren in family caregiving can provide a meaningful learning experience that can often help them to be more tolerant and understanding when they assume caregiving for their own parents in the future (Hooyman & Lustbader, 1986).

THE IMPACT OF CAREGIVING
ON THE FAMILY SYSTEM

It is apparent from the previous review of the effect of caregiving on individual family members that providing care to an elderly spouse or parent has a considerable impact on the entire family system. Indeed, families themselves perceive caregiving to affect family functioning. Strawbridge and Wallhagan (1991), for example, found that as many as 40% of the caregiving families they surveyed had experienced family conflict. Similarly, Smith, Smith, and Toseland (1991) found that primary caregivers identified family issues as problems they wished to work on in individual counseling.

Strain on the primary caregiver often radiates to other family members. Primary caregiver tasks that involve the entire family include:

1. Maintaining family communication and the exchange of information
2. Balancing the needs of the care recipient with the needs of other family members
3. Managing feelings toward the other family members who do not help
4. Maintaining the family as an effective decision-making group over a long period of time
5. Designating other responsible caregivers when necessary (Couper & Sheehan, 1987)

Strain on the entire family system results from such factors as conflict between caregiving obligations and other family tasks, disagreements among family members about the form or amount of caregiving, readjustments in family roles, and the emotional impact of caregiving on all involved family members (Gatz et al., 1990).

Caregiving families with the greatest risk for negative outcomes are those having poor communication skills, limited resources, many demands on their time and resources, suppressed or open conflicts, poor parent-child relationships, and high resistance to change (Moore, 1987). Conversely, the opportunity for engaging in social interaction for fun and recreation with family and friends helps to mitigate the burden of caregiving (Thompson, Futterman, Gallagher-Thompson, Rose, & Lovett, 1993).

The demands of caring for a family member with disabilities often require that previously developed relationships and structures within a family be renegotiated (Hansson et al., 1990; Kirschner, 1985). Prior to the onset of caregiving, families have typically advanced through the stages of formation: inclusion of children; resolution of the demands of work, home, and the raising of teenagers; the launching of young adults into independence; and the enjoyment of retirement and personal independence in old age (Masciocchi, Thomas, & Moeller, 1984).

The negotiation of these life stages results in diverse patterns of family relationships and structures that include extended families, dissolving families, isolated nuclear families, and modified extended families (Litwak, 1965). Existing structures and relationships may no longer be functional when the need for caregiving for a frail elderly member arises. Moreover, with the onset of caregiving, the family has entered a new life stage that will require new negotiations.

Several types of family renegotiations are of special interest to clinicians. Care of an older parent, for example, may result in power being transferred from the parent to an adult child (Kirschner, 1985). There may also be tension between maintaining the independence of elders and assuming a caretaker role (Hansson et al., 1990; Smith et al., 1991). Old family conflicts subdued by the maintenance of physical and social distance can be revived as family members are reengaged by caregiving roles (Hooyman & Lustbader, 1986; Townsend & Noelker, 1987). As noted earlier, the multiple demands of caring for parents, children, jobs, and spouses can also alter relationships within the primary caregiver's family (Kleban et al., 1989; Smith et al., 1991).

Directions for Practice and Policy

Effective interventions with caregiving families may involve diverse techniques such as educational programs to impart basic information, community-based services to alleviate the objective demands of caregiving, psychoeducational support groups to facilitate adaptation among family caregivers, family counseling/therapy to resolve serious family conflicts or problems, and policies to address the concerns of caregiving families at the societal level. Before considering these interventions in more detail, three fundamental concepts need to be addressed: (a) family empowerment, (b) family assessment, and (c) practitioner roles.

FAMILY EMPOWERMENT

Practitioners must realize that their overall goal is to empower family members and, therefore, they should strive to avoid taking over responsibilities and tasks that family members are capable of performing on their own. It is important, then, that practitioners assess the capabilities and capacities of the primary caregiver and other family members before deciding on what role to play in the intervention process. The practitioner empowers the caregiver and other family members by either reinforcing the notion that the family is handling the situation competently or by providing them with the necessary information and skills to handle the situation with increased competence.

FAMILY ASSESSMENT

The assessment process itself should focus on the ability and willingness of all family members to meet the care recipient's needs. As suggested by Rankin, Haut, and Keefover (1992), this is accomplished by assessing family functioning in four distinct areas.

First, it is important to assess contextual factors that may affect the caregiving situation. The practitioner should inquire, for example, about the availability and current use of formal and informal caregiving resources, family finances, the living arrangements of the caregiver and care recipient, family relationships, and the impact of caregiving on family and work.

Second, the practitioner should inquire about additional life crises that may have an impact on the caregiving family. Such problems as job loss, marital discord, or a child's illness, for instance, may tax the family's ability to provide care to a frail elder.

Third, it is also important to assess the coping styles of the caregiving family. For example, if the practitioner discovers that avoidance coping is commonly used by the family, this might explain why family members have not yet discussed what will be done if the elder's condition worsens.

Fourth, the practitioner should assess all family members' appraisals of the caregiving situation. In addition to assessing the extent of distress experienced by the primary caregiver, it is also helpful to assess the extent of distress of other family members and the extent to which they are aware of the primary caregivers' distress. It is also helpful to assess each family member's expectations of the helping process and each member's motivation, capacity, and commitment to improving the situation.

PRACTITIONER ROLES

The practitioner can play four roles, either singularly or in combination, when intervening with caregiving families: (a) consultant, (b) coordinator, (c) care manager, and (d) counselor/therapist. Each role requires the practitioner to use different combinations and types of family-based interventions, and occasionaly two or more of these roles must be performed simultaneously.

Consultation. This role is most appropriate when family caregivers are willing and able to take primary responsibility for the care of a frail older person, they are coping effectively with most aspects of the situation, and they feel able to enlist support from family members. As a consultant, the practitioner relies heavily on the family caregiver's assessment of the situation and addresses relatively specific and limited concerns.

Coordinator. This role is necessary when families are unable or unwilling to coordinate all services provided to the relative for whom they are caring. This may occur because of a care recipient's increasing disability or because family conflict prevents the primary caregiver from enlisting needed support from other family members. In such situations, the primary caregiver and other family members maintain day-to-day responsibility for the care of the elder, but they are aided in doing so by the support of formal services obtained and organized by the practitioner.

Care Manager. Practitioners assume this role when family caregivers are unable or unwilling to provide the day-to-day care needed by the frail older person. Care management activities include:

1. Comprehensively assessing the abilities and disabilities of caregiver, care recipient, and other family members
2. Developing a care plan to support the caregiver and the frail older person and to involve other family members in specific roles
3. Contracting with the caregiver, other family members, and other providers to carry out the plan
4. Implementing the care plan
5. Monitoring the implementation of the care plan to ensure that both care recipient and caregiver are receiving the services they need

Counselor/Therapist. This role becomes necessary when family caregiving provokes serious conflicts or problems within the family system that require some change in either how family members appraise the situation or in the nature of communication between them. The following brief example illustrates the need for the family counseling/therapist role:

Mrs. Pulkowski is an 86-year-old widow who has lived with her 57-year-old daughter, Anne, and her family since a stroke 2 years ago that resulted in paralysis on her right side. Mrs. Pulkowski's unmarried daughter, Joan, recently moved back to their hometown after being stationed overseas in the Army. As a result, Anne and her husband now feel that mom should live with Joan because Joan has no other family responsibilities. However, Joan strongly opposes this idea because she is finding it difficult enough to locate a new job and resocialize in the community. The bitter arguments that have occurred between the sisters has tarnished their once-close relationship and has left mom feeling both unloved and guilty.

TYPES OF INTERVENTIONS
FOR CAREGIVING FAMILIES

As described above, practitioners have a variety of interventions that may be useful, depending upon the particular stressors confronting the family and its resources to meet them.

Family-Life Education

Caregiving families often need and welcome the opportunity to learn more about the aging process; the nature and expected course of the care recipient's illness; related health, financial, housing, and legal issues; accessing formal services; and interpersonal communication and family dynamics processes (Couper & Sheehan, 1987; Masciocchi et al., 1984). Although family-life education programs represent an important means of assisting family caregivers with these particular informational needs (see, for discussion, Couper & Sheehan, 1987), "very few program descriptions or evaluations are published in family or gerontological journals" (Brubaker & Roberto, 1993, p. 218).

Community-Based Services

Among the diverse community-based services that assist caregiving families by relieving them of some responsibilities, case management and respite are two that have received the most attention in the family caregiving literature. Whereas case management is intended to help access available services for elders and their families, respite is intended to provide a temporary break in caregiving so that families can attend to other pending matters. Unfortunately, studies of the effectiveness of community-based services have not only produced controversial results but also have failed to examine the impact of services on the entire family (see, for reviews, Gatz et al., 1990; Zarit & Teri, 1991).

Noelker and Bass (1989) have suggested that the effectiveness of community-based services is likely to depend on how they interface with the family. In some families, for example, formal and informal helpers provide different but complementary forms of assistance to the elder. In other families, formal services may be relied upon to provide virtually all assistance. The scenario may also exist when families use few or no formal services. Indeed too many families seem to fall into this last category, and only recently have there been attempts to understand the reluctance of caregiving families to use available services (see, for discussion, Townsend, 1993).

Psychoeducational Support Groups

The primary emphasis in psychoeducational support groups is on "learning new skills or coping strategies for managing stressors and/or one's own emotions" (Zarit & Teri, 1991, p. 290). Unfortunately, the focus of this type of intervention has been on the primary caregiver rather than upon the family as a whole (Couper & Sheehan, 1987). Nevertheless, Toseland and Rossiter (1989) identified the following common themes of such groups, which could easily encompass a family perspective:

1. Providing information about the care recipient's condition and the aging process
2. Developing support within the group
3. Examining how to cope with the emotional aspects of caregiving
4. Learning how caregivers can care for themselves
5. Discovering how to improve relationships with the care recipient and other family members
6. Using formal services

In general, studies of the effectiveness of psychoeducational support groups indicate they have a moderately positive effect on caregiving burden and on improving the psychological and social well-being and perceived health status of caregivers (for reviews, see Gatz et al., 1990; Zarit & Teri, 1991).

Family Counseling/Therapy

This form of intervention is considered necessary when the circumstances of caregiving challenge the family's adaptive capacity or when unresolved conflicts resurface as a result of family caregiving (Greene, 1989). Yet compared to the other forms of intervention that were previously described, "less attention has been given to counseling and family therapy approaches, no doubt in part because of their cost and the limited third-party reimbursement available" (Zarit & Teri, 1991, p. 291). It has also been noted that the paucity of attention to family conflicts by gerontological practitioners may reflect their own discomfort with family strife (Couper & Sheehan, 1987). Our clinical experiences also suggest that caregivers are reluctant to ask other family members to become involved in counseling for many different reasons, such as long-standing family animosity, beliefs that involving other family members would be fruitless, and fear that care recipients may feel unwanted or that they have become a burden.

Although there has been some discussion of various theoretical approaches to multigenerational counseling/therapy (see, for review, Power, Chapter 7), their specific application to family caregiving issues has been largely ignored. An exception is Qualls's (1992) description of how four family therapy theories relate to the unique concerns of caregiving families. She maintained, for example, that family systems theory is useful for understanding how communication patterns and "family dynamics [may be] operating to further stress, or to buffer the stress, of a family member who is taking on a significant caregiving role" (p. 4). Behavior therapy, she argued, is well suited for "teaching families to label problems behaviorally, identify the contexts in which the behaviors occur, and measure effects of changes in contingencies" (p. 4), as well as for increasing the rate of pleasant events in caregivers' and care recipients' lives. Structural approaches to family therapy, which emphasize the roles, rules, and boundaries that define family structure, were said to be useful in addressing such questions as: How is it decided who becomes the primary caregiver? What determines if the family will seek formal assistance with caregiving? and How are family roles renegotiated as a result of caregiving? Finally, Qualls suggested that psychoanalytic theory is relevant to understanding how significant childhood experiences may effect adult family caregiving relationships. For example, a daughter who was sexually abused by her father is likely to struggle if expected to care for him.

FAMILY POLICY

Divergent goals have been associated with policy for caregiving families. These include engaging families in caregiving who would otherwise not do so, maximizing the amount and duration of family caregiving, enabling caregiving families to provide better care, making the job less burdensome to families, and ensuring that family caregiving is appropriate and equitable (Kane & Penrod, 1993). As a result, policies and programs for caregiving families have been divided into two somewhat contradictory philosophies: (a) Families need relief from their voluntarily assumed burden of care; and (b) incentives are necessary to ensure that families will fulfill caregiving obligations that they might otherwise attempt to escape (Kane & Penrod, 1993; Winbush, 1993). It has been further noted that this division "reflects a number of new and not-so-new controversies: family versus public responsibility, institutional versus community supports, men's versus women's issues, and young versus old, to name a few" (Winbush, 1993, p. 130).

In turn, these controversies point to three major questions that must be considered with respect to formulating policies for caregiving families:

1. What is the interface between caregiving families and formal services?
2. Do different caregiving populations require different programs and services?
3. Should family caregiving programs and policy be based on a model or perspective of family functioning?

Interface Between Families and Formal Services. It is important for practitioners to realize that the interface between informal and formal caregivers to the frail elderly involves both organizational and psychological aspects (Zarit & Pearlin, 1993). Noelker and Bass (1989) have suggested, from an organizational perspective, that the effectiveness of community services is dependent on the type and level of interaction between caregiving families and formal services. More recently Zarit and Pearlin (1993) have suggested that several psychological issues regarding the interface between formal and informal caregivers may also be related to service use and effectiveness. These include:

1. Assertiveness, because families may be forced to advocate for frail elders in an economic climate that seeks to control costs;
2. Control, because families should have a say about what services are available and how they will be provided; and
3. Trust, because to accept services, families must feel that the person making recommendations understands the situation and has the family's best interest in mind.

Diversity Among Caregiving Families. As eloquently stated by Kane and Penrod (1993), the problem of developing comprehensive policy goals for caregiving families

is complicated by the multitudinous patterns of family care involving different degrees of consanguinity in the family caregiver's relationship to the person needing care, differing life stages and competing obligations for family caregivers, and different demands of the job itself. (p. 276)

It has also been noted that family caregiving policies and programs should reflect racial, ethnic, socioeconomic, geographical, and cohort differences among caregiving families (Townsend, 1993).

A Model of Family Functioning. Of issue here is the fact that programs and services will continue to be focused mainly on the primary caregiver, rather than the entire family, until researchers, practitioners, and policy-makers begin to conceptualize informal caregiving as a family matter. A family life-cycle perspective, for example, would ensure recognition that family caregiving responsibilities can emerge at various points along the family life cycle (Winbush, 1993). Likewise, problematic interactions in caregiving families may be explained by adopting concepts from such frameworks as family systems theory (Couper & Sheehan, 1987) or the "Double ABC-X" model of family adaptation (Gatz et al., 1990). Finally, as noted at the beginning of this chapter, family caregiving to frail elders is a normative stress that may result in both positive and negative outcomes to the entire family. The goals of family-based interventions, therefore, should encompass family enhancement, as well as the alleviation of strain and distress.

CASE EXAMPLE

The following case example illustrates several points mentioned in this chapter.

Mr. J is a counselor in a large family service agency. He has been assigned the case of Mrs. A, who was referred to the agency by a local parish priest. Mrs. A is a 46-year-old married mother of two children, Rebecca, age 8, and Stacy, age 5. Mrs. A also works full-time as bookkeeper in the family dry cleaning business established by her parents. She has never received any prior counseling, and her presenting problem is anxiety, family conflict, and feelings of being "overwhelmed" by caring for her parents, Mr. and Mrs. T.

The following dialogue is taken from the first session:

Mr. J: Tell me about your situation.

Mrs. A: Well [hesitating] I don't know where to begin. I feel so tired and overwhelmed. I just don't know where to start.

Mr J: It's hard to talk with a complete stranger about the things that are bothering you. Just start anywhere. It really doesn't matter.

Mrs. A: Well, it's my parents—no, it's not them, they've always been there for me. It's the situation, my sister, my brothers, my family. They're driving me crazy! Sometimes I just want to run away and let someone else deal with it! But, no one else can do it. I'm so tired and overwhelmed. I feel like I'm gonna burst.

Mr. J: It must be really difficult. Although you may not think it's possible now, things can get better. Let's see what we can do to make things better for you. Tell me about your parents.

Mrs. A: They live in their own home, but Mom's becoming real forgetful and Dad's recovering from a stroke that's left him paralyzed on his right side.

Mr. J: So, they've started to need help to meet their daily needs.

Mrs. A: Yeah, and even though they live 25 miles away, it wasn't so bad at first. My husband didn't mind too much. He'd complain a bit but would take care of the kids when I was up there on a weekend, or in the evening. But when my father had the stroke, things changed. My mother is so forgetful, I was afraid to leave her up there by herself. She came to live with us until my dad got out of rehab. It was good because I could take her over to the hospital.

Mr. J: How did your family deal with that?

Mrs. A: My husband really didn't like having my mother at our house. They never got along well, and that made it a lot worse. But my girls loved having their grandma live with them. The three of them would spend hours talking together. Even so, they're too young to provide any help to me right now.

Mr. J: So it feels like it's all on your shoulders, huh?

Mrs. A: It sure does! My brothers don't do a damn thing, and my sister is jealous of my relationship with my parents. I'm constantly fighting with her about taking care of them.

Mr. J: Tell me about your brothers and sisters and how each of them is involved with your parents.

Mrs. A: Well, my older brother Bob and his family live about 70 miles north of my parents, so they don't come to visit much. My younger brother Jim lives closer to my parents, but he's single and too busy to spend time with them. Worst of all is that my younger sister Janice lives 3 hours away, and she hardly even talks to my parents.

Mr. J: Why do you say "worst of all" regarding Janice?

Mrs. A: Well, you know, her being another female and all. I really don't expect my brothers to help out too much, but I could really use some help from my sister. Also, Janice and I have felt bitter ever since she and her husband moved away and abandoned the family business. It really hurt us all financially and emotionally when they decided to sell their share of the business. But I suppose it was partly her way of getting back at my parents.

Mr. J: What do you mean?

Mrs. A: Well, being younger, she's always been a bit rebellious. My parents never forgave her for having a child out of wedlock, and she feels that I've gotten her share of their affection. So, even though I understand why she moved away, I'm still angry that she's not here to help me!

Mr. J: What kind of help would you like from Janice if she wasn't so far away and you were getting along better with her?

Mrs. A: All kinds of things, like listening to my parents' endless complaints, helping dad with his bath, and scheduling doctor appointments.

Mr. J: Tell me why you feel that your brothers can't help with these things.

Mrs. A: In our family, it's not a man's job to do that sort of thing. I just know they wouldn't want to get involved.

The following dialogue comes from the third session.

Mr. J: Last week we talked about your relationship with your sister. It's been strained for a long time.

Mrs. A: Yeah! Last week was really good. It helped me to see it from my sister's point of view. She's always had a rough time of it with my parents. Still, that's not my fault!

Mr. J: No, it isn't, but as we've discussed before, that's really not the point. The point is your sister gives you a hard time because you get the love she'd like to get from your parents.

Mrs. A: Yes, that's true.

Mr. J: I've got an idea. What about if you or I invite your sister to meet with us? I know she lives 3 hours away, but maybe she'd come for one or two meetings.

Mrs. A: She might. She always complains she's not included, but I'm just not sure. I don't think so.

Mr. J: What's the hesitation? You seem to be afraid that it won't go well.

Mrs. A: Every time we talk about my parents we quarrel.

Mr. J: Well, I know you don't know me very well yet, but you've got to trust me and this process. What's there to lose? Your relationship [with your sister] is terrible now. Right?

Mrs. A: Well, yes [expressing reluctance]. I wish I could get along better with my sister. I miss the closeness we had growing up.

The above dialogue illustrates some of the strategies Mr. J used to help overcome Mrs. A's resistance to involving her sister in counseling. It also shows how a counselor can point to the benefits of including other family members.

The following dialogue is from the next session, where Mr. J attempts to involve Mrs. A's sister, Janice, and explores the idea of including the brothers in a meeting as well.

Mr. J [to Janice]: During our last few meetings, your sister and I have been talking about your brothers and their involvement with your parents. Your sister thinks that they don't want to get involved.

Janice: I know she feels that way. But, you know, recently I talked with Bob. He said he'd help but he doesn't know what to do. He thinks Mary has the situation "under control." Maybe we've all relied a little too much on Mary.

Mr. J: Gee, I'm glad to hear you say that. Mary's feeling overwhelmed. Perhaps it's time we had a family meeting to see if we can figure out a plan to get Bob involved. What about Jim?

Janice: There I agree with Mary. He's hopeless. He's the youngest—spoiled rotten! [laughing]. Nice guy, but he hasn't a clue.

Mr. J: Well, maybe somebody should clue him in. He's not a kid anymore. Do you think he and Bob would come to a family meeting?

Janice: It couldn't hurt to ask.

Mr. J: Who should ask them?

Janice: Mary.

Mrs. A: Yeah, I guess I have to agree. When it comes to our parents, Bob and Jim seem to follow my lead.

Mr. J: OK then, will you call them and ask if they can make it next time?

Later in the same session, Mr. J assumes the consultant role by sharing a number of ideas about community services that could be used to assist Mr. and Mrs. T. For example, he suggests that Mr. and Mrs. T hire a part-time homemaker to help do some of the shopping and cleaning that neither of them can do anymore. He also suggests that Mrs. T be examined by a geriatrician to assess why she is so forgetful. He recommends two specialists, one of whom is a consultant to the Senior Services Program of the family service agency. He also mentions that the siblings might consider seeing if their father would enroll their mother in an adult day-care program, at least for a few days a week.

The following dialogue is taken from the next session, which Bob and Jim agreed to attend.

Mr. J: Bob, I'm glad to hear you say that you will spend Saturday afternoons with your mom and dad from now on. That will really help your sister. She won't have to be running up there both days on the weekend.

Bob: I'm looking forward to it. I didn't want to interfere, but I guess I should have offered to help before it got to this.

Mrs. A: Now I feel foolish. I should have asked for help, but I just figured that you would have offered if you had the time.

Bob: Well, I thought of it. In fact, I did, sort of, a couple of times. I just didn't know what to do, so I continued to call and to visit like always. I should have realized that after dad's stroke, you couldn't do it all.

Mr. J: What about you, Jim?

Jim: Sure, I'll help out. What do you want me to do?

Mr. J: What do you want to do?

Jim: Well [pausing], Mary was saying before that she spends a lot of time running mom and dad to the doctors. Mary's great with mom. I'm not sure I'd be comfortable taking her. But, how about I take dad to his appointments. I work the evening shift, so that shouldn't be a problem.

Mrs. A: That would be a big help.

Mr. J [to Mrs. A]: Can you help Jim with the information he needs about future doctors' appointments, addresses, and the like?

Mrs. A: Sounds good.

Mr. J: OK then. If that's settled, perhaps we should discuss the possibility of getting your mother and father some additional services to help them and to take the pressure off of Mary.

Mr. J saw Mrs. A for four more sessions. Mr. J's role continued to be one of coordination. To ensure that Mrs. A's husband remained supportive, he was invited to these sessions. The first two sessions were focused on ensuring that the care plan worked out during the family meeting was implemented smoothly. The remaining two sessions, which were spaced a month apart, were focused on ensuring that the plan was effective in reducing the overwhelming stress that Mrs. A had been experiencing as primary caregiver to her frail parents.

Discussion Questions

1. What practitioner roles were employed by the professional assisting the family?

2. How might the involvement of the two grandchildren be different if they had been teenagers rather than young children?

3. What gender differences in response to caregiving responsibilities are evident in this case example?

4. Which of the four theories of family counseling described by Qualls (1992) seems most appropriate to helping this family? Why?

2

Fostering Family
Involvement in Institutional Care

SHELDON S. TOBIN

The notion that families abandon their elderly to institutional care is a myth that was dispelled by gerontologists long ago. Indeed, institutionalization of an aging relative is usually a last resort that occurs only after the family has become exhausted from providing extensive home care (Chenoweth & Spencer, 1986; Morycz, 1985). It has also been documented that visits by family members to relatives in nursing homes are common (Moss & Kurland, 1979; York & Calsyn, 1977). What has remained less clear is how to promote family involvement with institutional care that encompasses more than just visiting.

Involvement by families is important because it affirms not only the ties that bind aging families together but also the concerns of families for their members, regardless of age. The intent of this chapter is to reveal how family involvement does not necessarily enhance the well-being of institutionalized elders or their families unless several specific objectives of this involvement are addressed. These include: lessening the apprehension and anxiety of family visitors; enhancing residents' sense of self, particularly those having Alzheimer's disease; sharing by family members in the caring for residents; facilitating cooperation and interdependence between family members and nursing assistants; and furthering an identification by family

25

with the facility as a caring community. Ways to foster these kinds of family involvement will also be discussed, following a description of why family programs must be based on an understanding of the psychological response to institutionalization by both elders and their families.

Background

The unwillingness of families to relinquish care to long-term care facilities explains why, of persons age 65 or older with the same frailties and incapacities, about three times as many live in the community as reside in nursing homes. Although the latter group represents only 5% of the entire U.S. population of adults 65 and older, those who reach that age have a 50% probability of living part of their lives in a nursing home, with the likelihood of entering a nursing home rising dramatically in the ninth decade of life. Therefore, despite the reluctance demonstrated by families toward institutionalization of their elders, it has become an inescapable fact of life for many families.

It is a nadir in family life, then, when institutionalization becomes essential to alleviate overwhelming burden experienced by family caregivers and to ensure the survival of an elderly family member. Although the family remains intact, care is now provided by an institution where the elder relative is merely one of many other frail, infirm, aged residents who need care. Family involvement with their elder, and with others in the facility, can facilitate the preservation of the elder's sense of self and reduce the family's feelings of guilt, shame, and anxiety over having abandoned their beloved relative.

A major cause for institutionalization of elderly family members is the profound and progressive deterioration caused by senile dementia. In fact, about two thirds of the residents admitted to nursing homes have senile dementia, with the majority (about 66%) being diagnosed with senile dementia of the Alzheimer's type (SDAT). Given that senile dementia is a "deselfing" disease, face-to-face contact with family members becomes of paramount importance for preserving the elder's sense of self. Yet, as described below, family strain is often at its peak when an elder is institutionalized due to dementia.

It is noteworthy that long-term care facilities often exacerbate the deselfing process and family strain, because of their propensity toward impersonal medicalized care. A nursing home, for example, is only euphemistically a "home" because it is more like a hospital and hotel than a

homelike environment. Indeed, current costs for care, whether by private
pay or by Medicaid, are primarily for hospital (e.g., medical) care and
secondarily for hotel functions, with little residual funds for creating a homelike psychosocial environment. Unless the scanty resources for creating a
home are used appropriately and include family involvement in diverse
ways, facilities become increasingly depersonalized and de-selfing of their
residents.

Elaboration of Family Issues

IMPACT OF INSTITUTIONALIZATION ON THE FAMILY

Even in the best of circumstances, and in the best of families, seeking
a nursing home and becoming a resident evoke feelings of abandonment
for those involved. The resident-to-be feels abandoned by a separation
from family, with an expectation of never returning to past family roles.
In turn, family members feel that they have abandoned their loved one,
and they often experience guilt and conflict (Brody & Spark, 1966; Spark &
Brody, 1970). Concurrent positive feelings, reflecting an existing ambivalence, are present when the nursing home is perceived as assuring that the
loved one will survive and that the separateness will not dissolve affectionate solidarity. When admission follows years of caregiving, there may
also be feelings that "it is best for everyone," with family members
relieved from an overwhelming home care burden.

As they visit after admission to the institution, however, the family's
feelings of abandoning, as well as the elder's feelings of being abandoned,
typically subside. According to Smith and Bengtson (1979), this pheno-
menom reflects the positive consequences of institutionalization. Nonetheless family members often continue to feel a sense of "caregiver burden."
Although the family is no longer strained by providing enormous amounts
of instrumental care, subjective burden continues because of persistent
concerns with the welfare of the institutionalized elder (Brody, Dempsey,
& Pruchno, 1990; Colerick & George, 1986; George & Gwyther, 1984;
Pagel, Becker, & Coppel, 1985; Pratt, Schmall, Wright, & Cleland, 1985;
Stephens, Kinney, & Ogracki, 1991; Zarit & Whitlach, 1992). Moreover,
although family members may no longer have day-to-day responsibilities
for direct care, they are uncertain of their possible role in institutional care
(Bowers, 1988; Brody, 1985b; Rubin & Shuttlesworth, 1983; Shuttlesworth,
Rubin, & Duffy, 1982).

In terms of the specific family stressors resulting from institutionalization of an elder, Stephens, Bridges, Ogrocki, Kinney, and Norris (1988) reported that more than a third of their sample of family members experienced stress from traveling to and from the nursing home, giving up activities to visit, having increased extra expenses, experiencing difficulties with staff, and facing problems related to the physical and mental status of their institutionalized family member. In their study, Pruchno and Kleban (1993) grouped stressors into perceptions adult children have of institutionalized parents, time pressures, hands-on care they provide, perceptions of staff, health of the parent, and the extent other people (primarily relatives) are involved in their parent's life.

Family strain, therefore, is likely to continue and even be exacerbated after institutionalization occurs. Stephens et al. (1981) observed family strain to be heightened when the institutionalized family member was afflicted with Alzheimer's disease. This increased strain was due to the need for more assistance with activities of daily living (ADLs), accelerated deterioration in the relative's cognitive and physical functioning, and lack of caregiving support from other family and friends.

IMPACT OF INSTITUTIONALIZATION ON THE ELDER

In order to foster family involvement in any meaningful way, it is essential to first examine how the elder family member who has entered an institution experiences the relinquishment of family life in the community. Knowledge of trauma to the elder precipitated by the relocation informs the development of family-oriented programs designed to offset this upheaval and promote adaptation of both the elder and family to institutional life.

As the new resident enters and lives in a foreign environment that is associated with what is labeled "the first-month syndrome" by Jerome Grunes, who was the psychiatric consultant for more than 3 decades at the Drexel Home for the Aged in Chicago (where I was a consultant for more than 2 decades). Unless psychotic, newly admitted residents will manifest behavioral changes. Some become quite disorganized, others become extremely depressed, and still others become both disorganized and depressed.

After the first-month syndrome, most residents in nursing homes of good psychosocial quality, in which there is individuation of care and greater encouragement of personal autonomy, are able to reestablish their self-pictures. Indeed, our later data suggested great stability in the self-picture from before to 2 months after admission (Tobin & Lieberman, 1976). The psychological portrait of residents by 2 months after admission approximated the portrait before admission. Adverse changes were limited to more hopelessness (less optimism about the future, but not more clinical depression nor less life satisfaction); an increase in bodily preoccupation and a perception of less capacity for self-care, suggesting the adoption of the role of patient among other old sick people; and a lessening of feelings of affiliation with other residents, reflecting an experience much like sibling rivalry.

Entering and living in the best of nursing homes, therefore, was not associated with changes that would support belief in the "destructiveness of institutions." However, there were subtle and less conscious changes. Reconstructions of earliest memories that disclose one's current sentiments, for example, revealed a significant shift by residents from feelings of abandonment to the introduction of themes of mutilation and death. This is not surprising, given that physical deterioration and death are encountered daily by nursing home residents. As noted earlier, although nursing homes may be called homes, they are more like medical facilities that are primarily focused on hospital and hotel functions.

What facilitates adaptation to institutions by the elderly? In a relevant study conducted by Lieberman and Tobin (1983), assessments were made of the possible psychological predictors of morbidity and mortality when residents-to-be were on waiting lists preceding admission to not-for-profit, sectarian homes for the aged. Measures were sorted into nine dimensions widely purported to be predictors of outcome to stress among the elderly: functional capacities, affects, hope, the self-system, personality traits, reminiscence, coping with the impending event, interpersonal relations, and accumulated stress. Two outcome groups (i.e., the intact "survivors" and the nonintact) were then contrasted on these measures. At the same time, these two institutionalized outcome groups were contrasted with two control samples of intact and nonintact elderly from the community. The purpose of this design was to see if the variables found to be associated with survival among the institutionalized group would be the same or different from those variables associated with survival in the community. In other words, the attempt was made to identify variables that uniquely predicted institutional survival.

Although several factors were found to predict survival among both the community and institutionalized groups (function capacities, affects, hope, self-system, coping, and interpersonal relations), only one variable was apparently a sensitizer to the stress of institutionalization: Passivity was associated with morbidity and mortality among those entering institutions but not with morbidity and mortality for those in stable environments within the community (see also Turner, Tobin, & Lieberman, 1972).

One factor that was obviously not relevant to the control samples was coping with the impending event of institutionalization. When those who were on waiting lists were assessed for how they were confronting the upcoming residential transition, it was found that those who perceptually transformed the situation to make the move totally voluntary and who visualized the relocation environment as ideal were those most likely to survive intact through 1 year following admission.

The kind of magical coping described above, along with aggressiveness and hopefulness, was also found to enhance adaptation in situations in which residents were facing relocation from one institutional setting to another (Lieberman & Tobin, 1983). Moreover, as a member of the Geriatric Consultation Team at a local hospital, I repeatedly observed how patients about to be transferred to nursing homes transformed the fear of their soon-to-be home to make it a welcomed place.

Not unexpectedly, the quality of the psychosocial environment (including family involvement) has also been found to predict survival after institutional relocation. This was most clear in one of our studies in which the en masse relocation of 427 state mental hospital patients to 142 nursing and boarding homes was examined. Whereas the relocated group of 427 had a death rate 1 year after relocation of 18%, a carefully matched non-relocated control group of 100 had a death rate of only 6%. Those who remained alive following the relocation were likely to have entered facilities of good psychosocial quality where family involvement was fostered.

The specific psychosocial qualities of the institution that facilitated resident survival were:

1. Warmth in both resident-staff and resident-resident interpersonal relations
2. Activities and other forms of stimulation
3. Tolerance for deviancies, such as aggression, drinking, wandering, complaining, and incontinence
4. Individuation, defined as the extent to which residents are perceived and treated as individuals in being allowed and encouraged to express individuality

This pattern of qualities reflects the acceptance by nursing home staff of residents' assertiveness and magical coping and also their concern for preserving the residents' selfhood. As described below, these same qualities are essential to develop effective programs that foster family involvement.

Chief among the personal characteristics fostered by survival-enhancing environments is a sense of control. The most impressive studies of control in nursing home adaptation have been carried out by Langer and Rodin (Langer & Rodin, 1976; Rodin & Langer, 1977). Langer, in her 1989 book *Mindfulness,* provides a full summary of their experiment on introducing control to nursing home residents. Experimental group participants were encouraged to make decisions for themselves. Langer (1989) wrote:

> Those in the experimental group were emphatically encouraged to make more decisions for themselves. We tried to come up with decisions that mattered and at the same time would not disturb the staff. For example, these residents were asked to choose where to receive visitors; inside the home or outdoors, in their rooms, in the dining room, in the lounge, and so on. They were also told that a movie would be shown the next week on Thursday and Friday and that they should decide whether they wanted to see it and, if so, when. In addition to choices of this sort, residents in the experimental group were each given a houseplant to care for. They were to choose when and how much to water the plants, whether to put them in the window or to shield them from too much sun, and so forth. (p. 82)

The effects of this control-enhancing intervention were dramatic. Three weeks after the experiment ended, residents in the experimental group participated more in activities, were happier, and were more alert. Eighteen months later, 30% of the residents in the comparison group had died, compared to only 15% in the experimental group. Not unexpectedly, the relationship that was found between control and survival for nursing home residents mirrors our finding of how aggression and magical coping are associated with intact survivorship for those entering homes: Clearly, what is lethal for the very old is passivity and the lack of a sense of control, of autonomy, and of mastery. Thus residents must not, if at all possible, be permitted to be passive and without control. It is essential that programs designed to foster family involvement bear this important fact in mind.

In summary, residents need to weather the disorienting first-month syndrome and maintain a preservation of the self; counteract the propensity toward hopelessness, toward becoming a patient focused on deterioration, and toward perceiving oneself as closer to death; and avoid passivity while feeling in control of the environment. To the extent that a nursing home individualizes care and promotes autonomy, its residents will be able to maximize their residual capacities and retain a preservation of self. It is family members, however, who can perhaps best attenuate the foreignness of the environment by maintaining face-to-face contact, who can enhance a sense of the persistence of self despite feelings of deterioration and closeness to death, and who can diminish passivity and mobilize control, or beliefs in control, of the institutional environment. Indeed, as described in the following section, families can both enhance the individualizing of care and foster the resident's sense of autonomy and control.

Directions for Practice and Policy

As noted at the outset, interventions designed to foster family involvement in institutional care should encompass the following elements:

1. Reducing apprehension and anxiety of family members
2. Face-to-face visiting that enhances the sense of self of residents, particularly of Alzheimer's victims
3. Sharing by family members in the caring for residents
4. Facilitating cooperation and interdependence between family members and nursing assistants
5. Furthering an identification with the facility as a caring community

In the remainder of this chapter, it will be shown that a variety of interventions are appropriate for meeting these objectives. These include: family counseling, family support groups, educational programs for family members, and fundamental changes regarding institutional staff and policy.

REDUCING FAMILY APPREHENSION

Perhaps the easiest and quickest way to reduce apprehension by family members is for administrators to say to them: "We give the best of care here, so you don't have to visit so much." Although their apprehension may be reduced if such simple-minded advice is followed, it will surely also result in harm to the institutionalized elderly relative. Unfortunately, this kind of advice is given too often, as the following example reveals.

I was asked to discuss my work on institutionalization at the annual meeting of the state proprietary nursing home association. My talk, and the discussion thereafter, seemed to reflect an acceptance by the administrators of the need for family involvement. But then at lunch, a cheerful man dressed in an expensive, well-tailored suit who owned several rural nursing homes said, "Let me tell you about families. I've been in the undertaker business all my life and what they want is for me to take over. You get them all upset if you involve them too much. I tell them I treat every resident like one of my own family and I tell my people to tell them that we are doing God's work and to let us do His work."

By not visiting, families avoid perceiving that their elder is "just another resident" whose uniqueness is easily overlooked by staff who are more oriented toward organizational efficiency than individualized care. Not visiting also permits family members to avoid witnessing the physical and mental deterioration of their loved one. These benefits to family members do not offset the potential harm to the elderly resident, who is left without meaningful family interaction.

What are institutions for the elderly doing to resolve this apparent dilemma? Montgomery (1982, 1983) sytematically examined staff-family relationships and nursing home policies. She reported subtle but noticeable differences in how policies create expectations of families. Some homes have no expectations of families, considering them outsiders, "visitors"; others view families as "servants" who should be available to assist in providing care to residents and when they do not do so, as neglectful; and still others perceive families as "clients" with whom the staff should spend time.

When families are viewed as clients, programs are developed to incorporate them into the life of the home, thereby reducing their apprehension. This process usually begins before admission by encouraging familiarity with the home through written materials and visiting and sometimes by having family members meet in groups. As evidenced by the following example, the content of such groups can become quite threatening to the home's staff and administration.

A New Resident Family Members group was developed at Drexel Home for the Aged, led by the newly hired Director of Social Services. After a meeting of one of these groups, the Director sought me out for my advice in my role as a consulting clinical psychologist to the Home. A recently admitted resident had told her son that her roommate chided her for leaving her watch on the bureau because it was likely to be stolen. Thievery became the topic of discussion at the Family Members Group, and the more the Director minimized the problem, the more angry the group became. One daughter even threatened to take her father out of the home. How to be honest about thievery and other problems without upsetting new family members became the content of the consultation.

After admission, families can continue to meet together in, for example, family support groups, family councils, programs that train families how to communicate to their residents who have dementia, and group counseling sessions. Individual formal and informal counseling of family members is also essential for maintaining involvement, assuring comfort, and alleviating apprehension.

We must not, however, overlook the fact that the more family members visit and become a part of the home, the more likely it is that their caregiving burden will continue. Effective programs to reduce apprehension require viewing each family individually, particularly with respect to family members' perceived burden. Each family, for example, brings its own unique, well-established, and persistent style of family interaction to the nursing home visit. Particularly destructive can be visits by a middle-aged daughter who has a long-term symbiotic relationship with her institutionalized mother. It is not uncommon for such a daughter to have been the primary caregiver at home before admission, having taken on this role to obtain the love from her mother that she feels has been denied her. At Drexel Home, for example, we often had to discourage these daughters from visiting because of their sometimes not so hidden abusive verbal behavior toward their mothers.

ENRICHING FAMILY VISITATION

Family visitors must be assured that their visits to resident relatives in the home make a difference. Otherwise, like my friend, Joan, in the following example, they may have doubts.

Joan visited her mother at Drexel Home almost every day, watching her mother's slow, progressive deterioration from Alzheimer's disease. Whenever I socialized with Joan, she would tell me about her mother's worsening condition and how hard it was for her to visit. She questioned whether the visits were doing any good. I stopped by one day to see her mother and chatted with a lovely nursing assistant. The assistant verified that Joan's mother sometimes did not recognize her during a visit; but a few hours after the visit, the mother was "bursting" to tell the nursing assistant that her daughter had been to see her.

Mothers may not recognize their daughters or may think their daughters are their mothers, but it is not unusual for mothers to later tell staff persons that their daughters visited them. Family members must be told so and assured that visits are important to confused, as well as nonconfused, residents.

Safford (1980) found, as we did at Drexel Home, that the amount of time spent with a resident whose cognitive functioning is deteriorating may lessen, but total time spent in the home remains about the same, with family members using the time to visit other residents. Visits to residents without family are particularly helpful.

Given the extent of senile dementia among nursing home residents, educating family members to communicate with residents becomes important for successful visits. Burnside (1981), a nurse with experience in long-term care settings, has discussed "bedside" helper techniques in communicating with residents who have senile dementia. These techniques include reinforcing reality, using touch, supporting denial if it is therapeutic, and helping to express feelings. As the first step, it is critical that staff are educated to these techniques so that they, in turn, can educate families.

Martico-Greenfield (1986) incorporated many of Burnside's recommendations into an exemplary family education program called Project CONNECT (Communication Need Not Ever Stop), which includes a series of lectures and small discussion groups for families whose resident relatives are confused. Families are specifically encouraged to (a) not speak for residents, (b) include residents in all discussions, (c) give residents choices and facilitate all decisions, (d) be a good listener, and (e) allow for reminiscence. Two obvious goals in this program are to encourage resident autonomy and to reinforce selfhood.

FAMILY SHARING IN INSTITUTIONAL CARE

Nursing homes can go beyond reducing family apprehensions and assisting good visits by developing ways that family members share in care with staff. However, role expectations need to be made clear. Shuttlesworth et al. (1982), for example, found that the primary responsibility for typical services in nursing homes was assumed by or assigned to staff. In a more controlled study, Schwartz and Vogel (1990) obtained similar findings, but they also found areas where families felt more responsibility than did staff. The task of encouraging others to visit the elderly resident, for example, was perceived by families to be their unique responsibility. Staff, on the other hand, perceived this as a task that they shared with families. This kind of discrepancy can and should be easily corrected by discussions with families.

More important, family members should be included in initial and follow-up treatment planning and then be active in delivery of care. It is most crucial for family members to provide biographical information to be used for individualizing care. Pietrukowicz and Johnson (1991), for example, used such information to develop short vignettes of residents for nursing assistants, which increased the assistants' individualizing of residents. Biographical data are also useful to professional staff so that they can understand the meanings of behavior, particularly bizarre behaviors that have meanings related to the striving for preservation of self. Sound biographical information makes it possible to see the continuity between bizarre postmorbid and premorbid personality traits and behaviors. When bizarre behavior becomes intelligible, family and staff can tolerate, or even encourage, seemingly aberrant behavior that helps the resident be herself or himself (Edelson & Lyons, 1985; Feil, 1993; Tobin, 1991). The following example illustrates this principle.

> Mrs. Gallagher, age 88, was admitted to the Dementia Care Unit of the local county nursing home. During her second day there, she began to jumble any loose objects (including her food) that she came in contact with. This very irritating behavior was understood by staff, after learning from a daughter that Mrs. Gallagher's favorite hobby for more than 50 years was to make bread at home.

Forming partnerships in care entails developing a role that is mutually agreed upon by staff and the family member. Spencer (1991) has discussed partnerships in care in specialized dementia care units as follows:

> Helping with meals is one of the common and obvious ways for families to be involved. Many people in the middle stages of dementia can still feed themselves, but they may need encouragement or assistance in becoming organized. If mealtimes are made a social, "family-style" affair, families can help in many ways. Simply sitting at the table chatting or serving people can be an enormous help to staff persons, but many family members will need encouragement from the staff to do this. Often they are afraid of interfering with routines, and the staff may be reinforcing this fear. To achieve relaxed, pleasant meals, families (and volunteers) should be encouraged to be present at mealtimes, to participate in meals if possible, or to bring their own food and join in. This relaxed, welcoming approach to meals is not the normal institutional style, but it can be a great asset when trying to create a homelike atmosphere for people with dementia. However, it may take some discussion with families and volunteers to establish a routine that is helpful rather than disruptive. (p. 199)

Families can also be very helpful in terms of either advising or assisting staff regarding their elder's ADLs. Bathing may be particularly stressful for residents, especially those who are paranoid or have dementia, and particularly dementia victims who are paranoid. Family members can advise on bathing habits, on preferences for baths or showers, on time of day their relatives usually bathed, and on other routines. In addition, if welcomed and encouraged, they can be present at baths for soothing or actual assistance.

But family members must make their own decisions regarding how to participate in the sharing of care. Some may not wish to be involved; others desire too much involvement. The right balance can only occur through discussions and participation. On dementia units, involvement often takes the form of participating in activities. Hansen, Patterson, and Wilson (1988) found that families evaluated their voluntary participation in activities as helpful to staff and therapeutic for their relatives. They welcomed having special roles on the unit. The staff, in turn, felt they were providing better care to the demented residents and were particularly appreciative of the assistance by families on weekends.

FACILITATING FAMILY-STAFF INTERACTION

A first step in facilitating interaction between family members and nursing home staff is to promote a mutual understanding and respect for the life experiences and social (especially family) context of both groups. In view of the fact that nursing assistants are the primary caregivers in nursing homes, the present discussion focuses on this particular group of staff. As described below, it is impossible to develop a "home" unless underpaid and often unappreciated nursing assistants are themselves individualized and are not only insulated from disrespect and verbal abuse by families, but become praised by families for their care to relatives. Families must learn how to relate to nursing assistants so that the latter feel rewarded and replenished rather than victimized and exhausted, feelings they already know all too well from their impoverished family lives.

Because they are usually underpaid and overworked, it is common to have a 100% turnover in nursing assistants each year. Even in better nursing homes, it seems that only half of the nursing assistants remain as employees for many years while the other half turns over about twice each year. Those nursing assistants who do remain for many years must be relied on not only for beneficial care to residents but also to indoctrinate newly hired nursing assistants.

It is important for family members to appreciate that nursing assistants, regardless of their tenure in the facility, are likely to live near or below poverty level and have personal problems related to limited economic resources (Tellis-Nayak & Tellis-Nayak, 1989). Given their personal lives and their onerous work as nursing assistants, Dobrof (1983) noted that nursing assistants have good reasons for feeling demoralized, helpless, and angry. Heiselman and Noelker (1991) identified the disrespect they feel from a lack of politeness, as well as lack of respect for their competence, individuality, and relationships with residents.

Often in my work as a nursing home consultant I have met with nursing assistants to hear their complaints and enhance their morale. Many times I have listened to their anger at and disappointment with families (e.g., "Don't they even care about that old man? He probably just sits there like that because they never visit him"); with other staff members and supervisors (e.g., "They leave all the dirty work for me. Nobody ever shows any appreciation around here"); and even residents (e.g., "After everything I have done for her, she doesn't even know who I am"). These kinds of negative feelings at work, together with frustrations at home in their personal lives, can lead to abusive behaviors toward residents. Indeed, maltreatment of residents by nursing assistants is quite widespread (Office of the Inspector General, 1990; Pillemer & Bachman, 1991; Pillemer & Moore, 1989, 1990).

Encouraging and exacerbating such abuse are vituperous, direct criticisms by family members of nursing assistants for dereliction in care of their relatives. Unfortunately, nursing assistants are often discouraged from talking to family members and may even be castigated for spending too much time on "emotional work" with residents (Foner, 1993). Given that residents come in sicker and more confused, the pressures are to complete work efficiently and quickly even when confronted by abuse from confused residents and racial slurs that are ubiquitous in those homes in which the assistants are Black or Hispanic women and the residents are White.

Family members who are unaware of these circumstances are likely to excoriate assistants when the root problem is actually the bureaucratic organization of contemporary facilities. To counteract the propensity to respond to bureaucratic demands by narrowly focusing on "crud" work, nursing assistants must be allowed and encouraged to do emotional work with residents, and they also must be insulated from unwarranted criticisms by family members.

Abuse by and toward nursing assistants can also be reduced by prevention programs (Pillemer & Hudson, 1993) and by creating a rewarding workplace milieu. One approach we took at Drexel Home was to insinuate a staff person between families and nursing assistants to reduce unwittingly critical comments and sometimes quite abrasive outbursts directed toward nursing assistants. Guiding our approach was the awareness of how families develop an institutional relationship, or transference, that includes both positive and negative projections. In this sense, the nursing home is perceived by family members as both the life-sustaining, all-giving other and the life-impeding other. Families consider the latter to be the cause of present as well as subsequent deterioration in their elderly relative.

To make this institutional transference useful for the resident, we deliberately encouraged a "split transference," whereby a unit worker became the all-giving, all-loving other and administrative personnel became the life-impeding others. Hiring unit workers was indeed a careful process in which persons were sought who were genuinely altruistic and giving individuals. This was to ensure that family members would feel more comfortable and confident in discussing concrete needs of the resident with the unit workers than with the nursing assistants.

An example of how this split-transference benefited all those concerned is revealed by one situation. A family became extremely upset when their elder's tattered but cherished sweater mysteriously disappeared. Although the sweater was very likely misplaced by the confused resident or accidently lost in the laundry process, the family insisted that it was stolen by a nursing assistant. The all-loving unit worker assured the family that "every possible means was being taken to recover the sweater." The family's sense of personal inadequacy and guilt thus was partially alleviated through projection onto the unit worker of feelings and actions of unconditional caring and loving for the family member in the home. This transference also permitted the family to relate to the nursing assistant without an angry outburst.

As noted earlier, one price to be paid for encouraging family involvement in nursing home care is the family's awareness that their relative is only one of many sick and deteriorating elderly for whom the home is providing care. To offset this family disillusionment, the unit worker's purpose was to enhance fantasies of the home's special concern and caring. The worker thus became perceived as different from all other workers in the home because of her or his special interest in the family member.

Many families explained the worker's special interest, concern, and care by thoughts such as "Mama after all is a special person," even when mama was actually only a shell of her former self and not very lucid. These kinds of thoughts echoed the concurrent rationalization by daughters and sons that "I am a special person because of all I have done for mama." In turn, as the unit workers became perceived as an extension of self, they became more like a family member who is believed to provide attention and caring out of unconditional love and certainly not because it is paid employment. Indeed, for some family members, although the unit worker became the perfect child while the daughter saw herself as the imperfect one, there was nevertheless a sense of satisfaction that the elder's needs were being met with tender loving care.

Underlying rage from anger toward oneself for abandoning the elder and toward the elder for provoking feelings of inadequacy, shame, and guilt were displaced onto the home and may have even diminished. However, these feelings were not completely extinguished. The unit workers assisted in containing the rage through actions and also through explanations regarding how good the home truly was. Yet can the displaced rage ever subside completely, having been generated by anger toward oneself for abandoning the elder and toward the elder for evoking feeling of inadequacy, shame, and guilt? The rage was purposefully redirected away from the all-loving and all-caring unit worker and toward an authority figure: the charge nurse, the chief of social service, the associate director, or the executive director, who became the "bad" other who was causing all their woes.

The main point to be made is that rage must be deflected from nursing assistants and toward authority figures. One kind of covert feeling regarding these authority figures is that "If they only cared enough, they would make her well again." Such projections often took the form of irrational tirades, particularly when a symbiotic relationship existed between daughter and mother. If the professional judgment is that interaction between daughter and mother is helpful for the maintenance of the mother's sense of self-identity, then such verbal abuse of staff becomes more tolerable. The staff can learn to understand and to appreciate that the irrational abuse is an expression of the daughter's internal state, expressing her own fear of personal dissolution when observing deterioration in her mother. This is not an easy task. It can only be accomplished by staff who are supported and nourished by administration so that they can withstand personal abuse.

CONTINUED IDENTIFICATION WITH THE FACILITY

All the efforts noted previously enhance the family's identification with the facility while the elder is still alive. Although often overlooked, it is also important to assist families in maintaining connectedness with the home after the resident's death. A resolution of the mourning process can be facilitated, for example, by becoming a volunteer. At Drexel Home we encouraged families to become members of the Friends of Drexel Home, which raised funds for special programs. Volunteers are often individuals who choose to volunteer in a home for the aged because of their past relationships with deceased parents or a dead husband or a wife. By giving to the home and to residents in the home, they can retain emotional connectedness with family members who are no longer alive. Especially for those volunteers who institutionalized a now-dead parent or spouse, residual feelings of having abandoned their family member to a facility can become lessened. Often at Drexel Home we asked volunteers to visit a resident who had no family visitors, to give the volunteer a special feeling of being like a family member to an isolated, abandoned resident.

In conclusion, it must be noted that nursing homes will not be successful in meeting the needs of residents and their families unless reimbursement formulas for care provide more resources for creating a home. Currently almost all costs are for medical care, for the hospital component, and for essential hotel functions. Without the necessary dollars for the psychosocial aspects of care, which include ensuring family involvement, nursing homes must struggle valiantly to counteract the medicalizing impetus. To do so they must develop in-house family policies that counteract prevailing reimbursement formulas, policies that can lead to less profit for proprietary facilities and the need for substantial subventions for not-for-profit facilities, but policies that will humanize their care and enhance the well-being of staff, residents, and families.

CASE EXAMPLE

Mrs. Jacklin was an 86-year-old widow who lived alone in a publicly sponsored senior citizen apartment and received instrumental and affect support from her 62-year-old only child, Donna. Shortly after Donna observed Mrs. Jacklin become quite confused and uncharacteristically negligent about her physical appearance and housekeeping, a compre-hensive physical and psychiatric evaluation indicated multi-infarct dementia. Because this disorder produces the same kind of insidious de-terioration of physical and mental well-being associated with Alzheimer's disease, Donna was advised by professionals to seek a nursing home placement on her mother's behalf. Yet Donna was extremely distressed by the thought of abandoning her mother to the care of strangers. However, no other choice seemed possible, because both she and her husband were working full-time. Also, past family situations requiring coresidence suggested that their present relationship should best remain as "intimacy at a distance."

Fortuitously, Donna had a close friend who was employed by St. Joseph's Home, a long-term care facility that was considered to be "one of the best" in the country. Donna visted St. Joseph's after hearing about its fine reputation and was so impressed that she immediately filed an application for her mother. This facility had three characteris-tics that seemed particularly appealing to Donna: (a) residents were allowed to bring their own furniture and decorations from home; (b) extended home visits (for example, weekends and holidays) were encour-aged; and (c) staff were outwardly referred to as the "St. Joseph family" by the administration. She was also pleased when the social worker who conducted the intake interview demonstrated consider-able interest in Mrs. Jacklin's personal background. However, this opti-mism was diminished soon after Mrs. Jacklin's admission. Both Donna and Mrs. Jacklin became upset that a private room was unavailable. Not only did this arrangement violate the privacy that Mrs. Jacklin desired throughout her lifetime, but it also meant that there would be insufficient room for her to bring her own furnishings from home. Donna also became extremely upset after observing a nursing aide make a disparaging statement to her mother. Mrs. Jacklin's difficulty in adjusting to these circumstances was evidenced by the fact that she phoned Donna up to 10 times a day during the first several weeks she was at St. Joseph's.

Therefore, even though Mrs. Jacklin was now in "one of the best" nursing homes, Donna felt considerable strain over such things as thoughts of abandoning her mother, apprehension about improper care from staff, visits several evenings per week, the constant phone calls from her mother, and the realization that her mother's health was progressively deteriorating. Donna was also upset that despite their own good health, her mother's siblings rarely visited. The constant phone calls provoked a family consultation with the interdisciplinary staff. Two things were decided at this meeting: (a) that Donna and her husband should attend a biweekly family support group run by the home, and (b) that Mrs. Jacklin would spend the weekends at Donna's house rather than receiving multiple visits at St. Joseph's. It so happened that these overnight visits were enjoyable to both Mrs. Jacklin and her family, in as much as they provided reminders of what family life had typically been in the past.

This plan turned out to be quite successful, and the next several months were uneventful, except for a few incidents. A private room became available, enabling Mrs. Jacklin to have her own furnishings, including the dressing table that she had used for the past 50 years. Mrs. Jacklin also developed a rash on her face that turned out to be due to her makeup. Donna was particularly helpful to staff—she was the only person who could convince her mother to switch from her cherished brand of facial cream. Also, although there were no major disagreements with staff, Donna clearly developed better rapport with some members of the nursing staff than others. She would often wait until her favorite staff were on duty before making special requests.

During Mrs. Jacklin's final year at St. Joseph's, her health deteriorated to the point that she was transferred to a higher level of care that was more like a hospital than her own bedroom. Once again, strain intensified for Donna and her family. No longer could Mrs. Jacklin visit them on the weekends, and their continual visits to the hospital-like atmosphere of dying patients was quite stressful. Adding to this discomfort was the fact that Mrs. Jacklin could no longer verbally communicate with them. Of great benefit to the family was the St. Joseph's "old-fashioned ice cream parlor": they could easily transport Mrs. Jacklin to this pleasant environment where the entire family enjoyed ice cream sodas. Each smile from Mrs. Jacklin as she drank her special treat was worth 1,000 words. Yet Mrs. Jacklin's health eventually worsened to the point where the family would repeatedly enter her room and find her unconsciously disrobing. Shortly after that, the home's Medical Director called Donna in the middle of the night to tell her that Mrs. Jacklin had been hospitalized. Two days later, she died from kidney failure. Donna was comforted not only by the doctor's concern for her own health, but also by follow-up phone calls from St. Joseph's social workers inviting her to attend their family survivors support group.

Now, several years after Mrs. Jacklin's death, her family is still involved with St. Joseph's Home. For example, they regularly attend the

annual family open house, and they make yearly charitable contributions. Donna not only remembers St. Joseph's as a caring home for
her mother, but she also now works as a volunteer in a long-term care
facility closer to her own home.

Discussion Questions

1. In what ways did Donna share caregiving responsibilities with staff
after her mother was institutionalized?

2. It is mentioned in the case example that Donna was upset over the
fact that her mother's siblings were such infrequent visitors to the nursing
home. What factors may have been responsible for the scarcity of their
visits?

3. It was noted that Donna felt more comfortable interacting with
certain staff members than others. How does this situation relate to the split-
transference intervention described in the chapter?

3

Strengthening Sibling
Relationships in the Later Years

VICTOR G. CICIRELLI

The central thesis of this chapter is that strengthening bonds or relationships between siblings in adulthood will help to promote a more personally satisfying life for individuals with siblings in their middle and old age, especially because elderly siblings tend to be the last surviving members of their family of origin. However, before suggesting any ways to strengthen sibling relationships, we will attempt to gain an understanding of the significance of the sibling bond in midlife and beyond by examining existing studies of sibling relationships in middle and old age.

Background

MEANING OF A SIBLING RELATIONSHIP

When we talk about a sibling relationship, we mean the total of the interactions (physical, verbal, and nonverbal communication) of two or more individuals who share common biological parents, as well as their knowledge, perceptions, attitudes, beliefs, and feelings regarding each other, from the time when one sibling first becomes aware of the other until the

45

end of life (Cicirelli, 1985b). A sibling relationship includes both overt actions and interactions between the sibling pair, as well as the covert subjective knowledge, thoughts, and feelings about the sibling and the relationship. The latter implies that the sibling relationship or bond is something more than the immediate behavior of siblings interacting and continues to exist over distance and time without continuous face-to-face interaction.

However, the above definition refers to a relationship between full siblings, that is, those who share a biological heritage from both parents. As a result of this heritage, full siblings have an ascribed relationship to one another. Such a relationship cannot be changed and exists for life, and potentially it has the longest duration of any human relationship. Also, it is a relatively egalitarian relationship in which the siblings have equal status and power (at least in adulthood).

However, the meaning of a sibling relationship may be different for half-siblings (who have one biological parent in common), step-siblings (who have no biological relationship but where a parent of one is married to a parent of the other), adoptive siblings (who have no biological relationship, but where a child is legally defined as a member of a family), or fictive siblings (who have no biological or legal relationship, but who are regarded as siblings). It is possible that the relationship between such siblings may depend more on frequent interaction to maintain its existence, regardless of its strength or quality. For example, full siblings may have a greater commitment to maintaining both the existence and quality of their relationship, regardless of strong disagreements or rivalries that may exist between them. Unfortunately the present chapter focuses almost exclusively on full siblings, as little existing research pertains to other than full siblings. (Hereafter, any reference to siblings means full siblings, unless otherwise specified.) It may be overgeneralizing to discuss strengthening sibling relationships beyond full siblings to siblings of other types.

The above definitions of siblings apply to individuals in most of the Western industrialized societies. However, in nonindustrialized societies, siblings tend to be defined by extension of the term to certain other types of blood kin or by classification on the basis of other criteria than blood relationship. Depending on the particular society involved, *siblings* also may include (a) the children of both parents' biological siblings; (b) the children of the parent's cross-sex siblings; (c) cousins of the same sex, the parent's siblings of the same sex, and even grandparents of the same sex; (d) children who were fostered in the same household; or (e) children of the same village or tribe who are of the same age range (Cicirelli, 1994). Siblings defined in these ways are taken seriously as true siblings, showing the sibling behaviors and feelings toward one another expected for that society, regardless of blood relationship.

One final point to be made is that most research into the sibling relationship is concerned with sibling dyads. This focus has considerable justification, because much sibling interaction takes place between just two siblings at any one time and because feelings, perceptions, and evaluations concern a particular individual and not a group. However, in families with more than two children, one may be concerned with the sibling group as a whole or with dyads, triads, tetrads, and so on. Coalitions of siblings exist in many larger families, consisting of smaller subgroups of siblings formed on the basis of age, gender, or common interests. The clinician, in particular, may wish to focus on interaction patterns and properties of these groups.

Elaboration of Family Issues

SIGNIFICANCE OF THE SIBLING
BOND IN ADULTHOOD AND OLD AGE

Existence of the Sibling Relationship in Adulthood. A first concern is whether it is meaningful to talk about sibling relationships in middle adulthood and old age. That is, do older adults even have surviving siblings and do they maintain some kind of contact with those siblings?

In our study of older people and their adult children in a Midwest city (Cicirelli, 1979, 1981), we found that 85% of the middle-aged adults had at least one living sibling (88% had siblings in their birth families), compared to 78% of those over age 60. Although somewhat higher percentages of 85% and 93% for older groups were reported in earlier studies (Clark & Anderson, 1967; Shanas et al., 1968), our sample contained a higher proportion of people in the older portion of the age range. Looking at each age range more specifically, those in the 60 to 69 age group reported an average of 2.9 living siblings, those in the 70 to 79 age group reported 2.2 living siblings, and those aged 80 and over reported 1.1 living siblings. These groups originally had averages of 4.6, 4.9, and 4.2 siblings in their family of origin. Some 26% of the elders had a sibling living in the same city, and 56% had a sibling within 100 miles. Thus most elders have living siblings, with the majority having at least one sibling near enough for occasional contact.

Some 17% of the older respondents saw their most frequently contacted sibling at least once a week, whereas 33% saw their sibling at least monthly;

the most typical frequency of visiting was several times a year. Although the remainder saw their siblings less frequently, very few respondents actually lost contact with a sibling. In addition, the frequencies of telephoning were similar to frequencies of visiting (Cicirelli, 1979, 1980b). These findings are supported by earlier work (Rosenberg & Anspach, 1973; Shanas et al., 1968). Step- and half-siblings, too, continue to keep in touch with each other in adulthood, although they see each other less often than do full siblings (White & Riedmann, 1992). Therefore it is clear that most older siblings do continue to communicate, either by talking directly to each other or indirectly through a third person.

Quality of the Sibling Relationship. Providing companionship constitutes an important function of sibling relationships in old age. Scott (1983) examined activities reported by siblings and others. Visits, reunions, and happy family occasions were the most frequent sibling activities reported, followed by various types of recreational activities (home, commercial, and outdoor) and by shopping, church attendance, and miscellaneous other activities. When proximity was controlled statistically, the frequency of these sibling activities compared quite favorably with elders' similar activities with children. Various authors have found that most sibling relationships in old age involve companionship to one another (Adams, 1968; Cicirelli, 1982, 1985a, 1985b; Johnson, 1982; Troll, Miller, & Atchley, 1978).

Early investigations of the quality of the sibling relationship centered around feelings of closeness and rivalry. Despite their reduced sibling contact, older adults report greater closeness with siblings than do younger cohorts (Cicirelli, 1980b, 1982, 1985b; Ross & Milgram, 1982). In our own work, 65% of older adults reported feeling close or very close to their most frequently contacted sibling (Cicirelli, 1979, 1980b). A similarly high percentage of respondents felt close or very close to their siblings in studies of young and middle-aged adults (Adams, 1968; Cicirelli, 1980b, 1985a). However, mean closeness to siblings increased from late adolescence through adulthood and into old age (Cicirelli, 1980b).

Sibling rivalry, as directly reported, appears not only to be low throughout adulthood but to decline throughout adulthood to old age, with rivalry greatest between pairs of brothers and least between brother-sister pairs (Cicirelli, 1980a, 1980b). However, investigators using clinical interview techniques or projective methods to identify rivalry (Bedford, 1989; Gold, 1989; Ross & Milgram, 1982) have found an incidence of sibling rivalry in adulthood of up to 45%. Although Ross and Milgram concluded that most rivalrous siblings seek to repair their relationships in later adulthood and old age, Bedford's work suggests that feelings of rivalry persist into old age. However, most older adults value their relationships with siblings and have developed ways of interacting that avoid conflict and overt rivalry. For example, two middle-aged sisters rarely talk about their children's career accomplishments, each feeling that to do so might revive their earlier rivalry in childrearing.

Other researchers (Gold, 1989; Matthews, Delaney, & Adamek, 1989; Scott, 1990) have attempted to classify sibling relationships in adulthood and old age into a few distinct types. Gold identified five types, based on patterns of psychological involvement, closeness, acceptance/approval, emotional support, instrumental support, contact, envy, and resentment. Intimate siblings are characterized by unusually high devotion and psychological closeness (affection, empathy, self-disclosure); they place the sibling relationship above all others. Congenial siblings are close and affectionate but place greater value on marital and parent-child relationships. Loyal siblings base their relationship on adherence to cultural norms; they support each other at special family events and crises and have regular but not frequent contact. Apathetic siblings have mutual lack of interest and see each other little but are not rivalrous or hostile; their lives have simply gone in different directions. Finally, hostile siblings have strong negative feelings toward each other, with considerable negative psychological involvement or preoccupation with the relationship. Gold found that 78% of the sibling relationships studied fell into the loyal, congenial, and intimate types, with the remaining 22% divided into the apathetic and the hostile types. This typology was given partial support by Scott's work, although she found that 95% of her sample fell into the first three types, with the remaining 5% apathetic. Matthews et al. classified the relationships between the middle-aged brothers they studied into four groups: the closely affiliated (very close to extremely close), the lukewarm (somewhat close to close), the disaffiliated (little or no closeness), and the disparate (disagreed about their level of affiliation).

In addition to feelings of closeness, siblings tend to serve as confidants for one another in middle adulthood and old age (Connidis & Davies, 1990).

Although the general trend in sibling relationships in adulthood and old age is one of increasing closeness, investigations of changes in the sibling relationship following various life events found that the relationship was not a static one but that it waxed and waned depending on the circumstances (Bedford, 1992; Connidis, 1992).

Effects of Siblings on Well-Being. Several researchers have attempted to answer the question: Do sibling relationships lead to greater well-being in old age? Studies have found that older people with living siblings, particularly sisters, had higher morale (Cumming & Henry, 1961); a greater sense of emotional security, stimulation, and social challenge (Cicirelli, 1977); fewer depressive symptoms (Cicirelli, 1989); and greater feelings of control over their lives (Cicirelli, 1980a). These positive effects on well-being did not appear to be the result of more frequent interaction with siblings (Lee & Ihinger-Tallman, 1980), but rather were due to merely knowing that a sibling existed and was available (McGhee, 1985).

Over all areas of research reviewed thus far, relationships with sisters appear to be particularly important in old age, whether it is a sister-sister or a brother-sister bond. One could attribute this to women's greater interest in initiating and maintaining family relationships; however, Gold (1986) found that brothers initiated sibling contacts with sisters about as often as sisters contacted brothers. What seems more likely is that women's emotional expressiveness and their traditional role as nurturers accounts for the importance of relationships with sisters (Cicirelli, 1989).

Sibling Help in Old Age. Despite the fact that most older people say that they want to help their siblings in time of need and also regard their siblings as a resource to be called upon if needed (Cicirelli, 1989, 1992b; Goetting, 1986; Hoyt & Babchuk, 1983), relatively few older people actually rely on a sibling for help (Cicirelli, 1979). Some 60% of the older people we interviewed said that they would help a sibling in a crisis, although only 7% regarded a sibling as a primary source of help. Normally, the spouse and adult children are the primary sources of support in old age. If they are unable or unavailable to help, siblings then tend to step in to give help. Elders regarded sibling help as most important when the brother or sister was ill, needed transportation, needed household repairs, or lost a spouse (Cicirelli, 1979, 1990; Goetting, 1986; Kivett, 1985; Lopata, 1973; Scott, 1983). In addition, those who were widowed or who never married tended to receive more help from siblings (Johnson & Catalano, 1981). Significantly fewer half- and step-siblings helped one another in old age than did full siblings (White & Riedmann, 1992).

In our recent study of support by family members to hospitalized elders (Cicirelli, 1990), we found that only about 20% reported receiving any kind of tangible sibling help, whereas about half wanted psychological support from their siblings, which they received in the form of visits and telephone calls. Psychological support is a type of support for which siblings may be uniquely suited by virtue of the bond of attachment between them and their common values and perceptions (Avioli, 1989; Cicirelli, 1988; Dunn, 1985). The sibling relationship's long history of shared experiences, coupled with similarity in age and values, makes a sibling better able to understand the other's problems and feelings. For example, when an elderly man was hospitalized for complications of diabetes, with the possible loss of a foot, his younger brother was able to understand how much that loss meant to him because both brothers had shared years of athletic activities together and admired active independent "macho" men. Because they had a close relationship, when the younger brother suggested that the brother would be able to handle the loss as a truly courageous man would, the older brother was able to feel better about the situation.

In an analysis of longitudinal data from the National Long Term Care Survey (Cicirelli, Coward, & Dwyer, 1992), only about 7% of impaired elders received help from siblings; help tended to be given in such areas as housekeeping, transportation, financial matters, and so on, rather than in areas involving direct personal care. Furthermore, sibling help tended to go to those elders who had neither spouse nor children. The majority of sibling helpers continued to help over the 2-year period; those who ceased helping appeared to do so either because the elder's health had improved or because they themselves were older and perhaps in poor health. Thus some siblings may not be able to give help to one another in the upper part of the age range, regardless of how much they might wish to do so. Gold (1989) similarly found that older siblings continued providing help until their own health declined.

Sibling Help to Elderly Parents. An important developmental task of adult siblings (Goetting, 1986) is to provide support to their parents in old age. If siblings can work together to accomplish this task, it provides not only an opportunity for increased interaction at midlife but also the potential for increased closeness as siblings share a major life experience. On the other hand, sibling help to elderly parents has the potential for reawakening old rivalries and leading to further estrangements. Discussion of the issue of sibling help to elderly parents is taken up by Toseland, Smith, and McCallion in this book (Chapter 1).

Siblings as Role Models. Still another way in which a good sibling relationship is important in later life is that siblings can serve as role models for each other in coping with problems of aging. The pioneering function of older siblings in childhood and adolescence is well-known, and it would seem to apply to old age as well. The first brother or sister to experience retirement, loss of spouse, or chronic illness would demonstrate coping behaviors to the others. For example, after an elderly woman's husband died, she sold her house and moved to a retirement apartment complex so that she would find plenty of daily companionship. Her younger sister was able to see how it worked out, and when her husband also died, she too decided to move into the complex. Here the sister's pioneering pointed out a way of coping that otherwise might not have seemed to be an attractive alternative for the younger sister.

Importance of a Good Sibling Relationship. From the brief review of sibling relationships in adulthood and old age presented above, one can conclude that a good relationship between adult siblings can enrich their lives. Siblings with a close and warm relationship can provide companionship for one another, enhance morale, and provide psychological as well as tangible support through major life events. This seems to be particularly true for sisters, who often seem to provide the glue that holds an entire family together. Not only are strong sibling ties rewarding in themselves throughout adulthood, but they lay the foundation for a more satisfying old age, in which the remaining siblings from the family of origin can assist and comfort one another's last years.

Sibling relationships may take on greater significance in the future. As the baby boom generation reaches old age, its members will have more siblings than members of the previous generation. They may need to depend on siblings for help to a greater extent, because they have had less stable marriages, more divorces, and fewer children of their own. Conceivably the sibling connection could become a central relationship in their lives.

TROUBLED SIBLING RELATIONSHIPS

Lest the reader come away from reading the last section with a too rosy picture of sibling relationships, it must be remembered that a minority of sibling pairs have either completely apathetic or very troubled relationships in adulthood and old age. Some 22% of the sibling relationships studied by Gold (1989) fell into the hostile and apathetic types, although Scott (1990) identified only 5%, all of which were apathetic. It appears that sibling relationships are more difficult for half- and step-siblings than for full siblings; a significantly greater proportion reported having a sibling with whom they did not get along (White & Riedmann, 1992).

Apathetic siblings may never have developed a very strong sibling bond in childhood, and in adulthood they simply drifted apart. Such factors as a wide age difference, little contact during the formative years, or general family disorganization can contribute to a weak bond. A hostile or conflict-filled sibling relationship in adulthood usually has its roots in childhood (Bank & Kahn, 1982a, 1982b; Dunn & Kendrick, 1982). Although some degree of conflict between siblings early in life can be considered a healthy experience in learning how to deal with disagreements, extensive or deep-seated conflict can have serious negative effects. Perceived unequal or unfair treatment by a parent, unfavorable comparisons to a sibling, spousal conflicts or divorce, parental violence or child abuse, sibling violence, and sibling sexual abuse can all have effects that persist in the form of poor sibling relationships throughout life or major psychological problems.

Even when early sibling rivalry and other problems have seemingly been transcended in adulthood, they can resurface when critical life events occur. Recent studies (Bedford, 1992; Connidis, 1992) found that for many siblings such events are accompanied by changes in the sibling relationship. Critical events influencing the sibling relationship involved such events as marriage or divorce, changing interests, employment change, relocation to a new area, illness and death, family arguments, and changing frequency of contact. Such changes may be positive for some sibling dyads and negative for others, depending on the circumstances. One sibling's marriage resulted in a less close relationship for a third of the sibling pairs studied by Bedford. This is understandable if the new spouse is not liked by the other sibling, but even if the spouse is liked, the marriage can disrupt the flow of a formerly close sibling relationship. On the other hand, marriage to a spouse who is well-liked can bring siblings closer together. Negotiating congenial relationships with a sibling's spouse is often difficult; this can be the source of bitter sibling conflict. Similarly, difficulties involving children of siblings can escalate into major family fights. Divorce and widowhood often bring siblings closer, but they also can lead to estrangement, particularly if one sibling feels that the other is somehow at fault. Employment stress or job loss can also affect the sibling relationship. Bedford cites the case of a sister who felt "stressed out" at work and asked her sister for help. The stressed sister was so appreciative of the help that she changed her behavior toward the other sister, who responded favorably, and the sisters drew closer. Often, severe medical problems or a brush with death will bring siblings closer, but they can do the opposite. Bedford reported the case of sisters in which one sister recovered from mental problems and drug dependency. The other sister was overtly happy for her but then felt unneeded, and their relationship deteriorated. The important conclusion to be drawn is that sibling relationships are not fixed and unchanging but can be influenced by events both internal and external to the relationship.

When siblings participate in family businesses together, the potential for conflict and acrimony is great because family issues are interwoven with business themes of power, control, and responsibility (Carroll, 1988); not only can disagreements disrupt the business partnership but they can damage the sibling relationship beyond repair.

Family issues such as inheritance also can threaten family relationships in midlife. Whether problems concerning inheritance involve such major issues as unequal bequests to adult children, failure to reward the sacrifice of a caregiving adult child, unusual bequests, or such minor issues as who should get mother's tea set or father's tie pin, they can lead to violent conflict and sibling estrangement.

In old age, too, lack of care or concern on the part of a sibling or lack of appreciation for help and support can lead to bitterness and withdrawal.

One can conclude that, no matter what the stage of life or what critical life event, the sibling relationship can be a stage for conflict, as old rivalries or dysfunctional family relationships are played out.

Directions for Practice and Policy

RECOMMENDATIONS FOR MAINTAINING
AND STRENGTHENING SIBLING BONDS

It must be recognized that sibling relationships change over the life span. In general, during infancy and childhood, siblings interact to form their basic relationship, one characterized by closeness, rivalry, or indifference. During adulthood, they begin to share their lives less as they become more involved in careers, marriages, and other interests, and a certain distance or indifference may predominate. But during middle age and in old age, there is a tendency to become closer again. One possible explanation is that the family of origin gradually erodes over time, as the parents and other family members die, with only fragments (e.g., certain sibling dyads) of the original family system remaining. After the whole is gone, it endures as memories and symbolic representations within the remaining members, who place increased value on sibling relationships

(Cicirelli, 1988; Gold, 1986). It is also possible that serious illnesses or brushes with death experienced by the siblings themselves can lead to a mellowing and desire to improve relationships. In general, closeness tends to predominate in later life, with only a minority of siblings maintaining rivalrous or indifferent relationships. Yet, for this minority, the possibility of repairing a damaged sibling relationship or strengthening a weak one offers an enriched life in the later years.

GENERAL RECOMMENDATIONS

Bonds between siblings in adulthood and old age can be strengthened in various ways.

First, appropriate parental treatment in early life will have long-range effects on sibling bonds over the entire life span. Parents should treat their children with love, caring, and responsiveness to their needs, without showing any favoritism. In addition, if parents can achieve strong and satisfying relationships with their own siblings and other family members, such a model can carry over into their children's adult lives. If siblings are raised to expect to care for each other, teach each other, and be models for each other, they will extend these positive feelings throughout their lives. Although inappropriate parental treatment cannot be changed after the fact, older siblings can come to an understanding of their parents' roles in shaping early sibling relationships, an understanding that will help them in their adult relationships.

Second, siblings who maintain communication and helping relationships with one another once they have left their family home will maintain their commitments to the relationship and stronger bonds to each other throughout adulthood and old age. Although sisters have traditionally assumed a primary role in maintaining family ties, brothers as well as sisters need to take responsibility for maintaining sibling relationships in adulthood through direct communication, not merely hearing about their siblings indirectly.

Third, because sisters seem to have a special effect on their siblings, understanding and encouraging their roles will facilitate the strengthening of sibling bonds for both brothers and sisters.

Fourth, because important life events (births, illnesses, deaths, marriages, divorces, retirements, geographic moves, and so on) seem to be times at which sibling relationships can either be strengthened or impaired (Bedford, 1992; Connidis, 1992), special attention needs to be paid to the course of the sibling relationship at such times. Maintaining communication, providing support, reaching compromises, and avoiding misunderstandings can all help to maintain good sibling relationships.

Fifth, strengthening sibling relationships in adulthood often depends on being able to establish and maintain good relationships with brothers-in-law and sisters-in-law. Siblings may need to make extra efforts to achieve harmonious relationships with one another's spouses for the sake of their own relationship.

INDIRECT INTERVENTIONS

Few organizations exist that offer support services for those with difficult sibling relationships. However, the Siblings and Adult Children Network, based in Arlington, Virginia, supports self-help for siblings of the mentally ill, and the Sibling Information Network, based in East Hartford, Connecticut, offers a clearinghouse referral service for self-help groups for siblings of the chronically ill.

Local organizations with memberships of older people could offer educational programs that might help elders repair and strengthen poor sibling relationships. Given the popular interest surrounding this topic, as well as the evident desire of many older people to repair poor relationships with siblings, such programs could be quite effective for sibling dyads who do not have deep-seated problems.

COUNSELING/ THERAPY WITH SIBLINGS

When siblings have persisting strong conflicts or rivalries, or when there has been a history of abuse or wrongdoing, sibling therapy can be used to attempt to mend the bond in adulthood or old age. There are a number of situations in which the sibling relationship becomes important in dealing with the mental health problems of the elderly (Cicirelli, 1988). Early conflicts and estrangements persisting from childhood or from the time of later critical incidents (Dunn, 1984), long-term sibling dependencies, or reactivated rivalries and aggressions can all come to necessitate therapy in old age.

However, it should be mentioned that in some cases, the damage done by an abusive sibling early in life was so great and long-lasting that it may be better to help the abused sibling escape the relationship and reach some understanding and peace of mind as an individual than to attempt to repair the sibling relationship. Few guidelines exist for treatment of the elderly client with problems involving siblings. Therapeutic approaches range from probing sibling relationships in the course of psychoanalysis (Rosner, 1985) to individual therapy (Bank, 1988; Bank & Kahn, 1982a, 1982b; Kahn, 1983) to inclusion of siblings in family therapy (Kahn & Bank, 1981; Palazzoli, 1985) and family counseling (Herr & Weakland, 1979). Therapy can include all living siblings or only a subgroup of siblings. If the siblings are close-knit, they can be seen as a group; otherwise it may be more effective to see a sibling individually (Church, 1986; Harris, 1988; Kahn, 1983; Kahn & Bank, 1981). Kahn and Bank recommend proceeding by attempting to transfer the emotional intensity from the difficulties in the sibling relationship to a context of parental failure, so that the siblings can see the parents' role in the genesis of the sibling problem.

The use of reminiscence as an approach to therapy with older people has gained favor in recent years with its use in the life review process. Whereas reminiscence in itself is simply talking or thinking about the past, in the life review past experiences are analyzed, evaluated, and reintegrated in relation to present events, values, and attitudes in order to resolve old conflicts, come to grips with past mistakes, and achieve integrity in the latter portion of life (Butler, 1963; Molinari & Reichlin, 1985; Osgood, 1985).

Reminiscence is an approach that could be used profitably with siblings. Because they share a long and unique history, reminiscing about earlier times together is an activity in which siblings spontaneously engage at many points in the life span, although it seems to become more frequent and valuable in old age. Indeed we found that most communication between elderly siblings centered around the discussion of family events and concerns and around old times (Cicirelli, 1985b), with old times discussed more frequently with siblings than with adult children. The fewer the remaining siblings in the family, the greater the extent of the reminiscing. As the surviving members of their families of origin, siblings can use reminiscences of old times together to clarify events and relationships that took place in earlier years and to place them in mature perspective. Ross and Milgram (1982) observed that sharing recollections of childhood experiences appeared to be a source of comfort and pride for the elderly, evoking the warmth of early family life and contributing to a sense of integrity that life had been lived in harmony with the family. Gold's (1986) elderly subjects reported that reminiscing about sibling relationships during the course of the interview helped them to put their current relationships with siblings into a meaningful context, to understand present events and the significance of sibling relationships in their lives.

Whether or not older siblings feel a need or desire to enter therapy to remedy a troubling sibling relationship, engaging in informal reminiscence together can help siblings come to a better understanding of their common past and an appreciation of their relationships. Certainly the persistence of the sibling relationship and its value for the individual should not be underestimated.

POLICY

Because most people regard sibling relations as secondary in importance to the spousal or parent-child relationship, and because most laws concerning property rights and responsibility for elder care pertain to spouses, parents, or adult children, a policy concerning adult siblings is considered unlikely to develop.

CASE EXAMPLE

Although I am not a clinician, I have encountered many adults with troubled sibling relationships in the course of my research work. One such memorable relationship involved a 60-year-old middle brother and his 51-year-old last-born sister. Coming from a three-child family, both got along well with their first-born older brother. Due to their age difference, they had relatively little contact or conflict with each other all through the sister's childhood. However, there may well have been a latent sibling rivalry based on differential treatment by the parents (primarily the mother) and competition for the mother's affection and attention. In adulthood, their relationship with each other changed to one consisting of sporadic verbal conflicts followed by periods of sometimes lengthy avoidance of one another.

A pattern developed where most of the information they had about each other was provided by their mother, who seemed to serve as a central switchboard for family interactions. When the siblings encountered each other, usually at their parents' home, what started as verbal sparring and needling escalated into angry and hurtful exchanges that usually ended in one or the other leaving the scene. Each learned well how to "push the other's buttons."

The brother had struggled through a lengthy period of completing a professional education and launching a career, whereas the sister had dropped out of college to marry and over time had achieved considerable social and economic standing in the community linked to the occupations of both her first and second husbands. Although she had carved out a public career of her own that continued after the end of her second marriage, her brother failed to recognize her achievements and felt that she flaunted her success and attempted to belittle his. On her part, she tended to ignore or belittle his professional expertise and achievements and frequently ridiculed him personally. Each of these siblings seemed to display a classic pattern of insecure attachment to the mother that was played out in their rivalrous sibling relationship.

Their conflict was exacerbated when their parents' health began to decline and they needed some help from the adult children in order to continue living independently in their own home. Although both the brother and sister helped, their mother began a pattern of complaining about one sibling's lack of help and caring to the other. Thus each sibling felt that he or she was carrying the main burden of help and that the other was remiss, and this became a further source of conflict between them. When the father died and the mother's health declined further, the mother went to live with her daughter.

The battle between the siblings continued on the sister's turf until the mother experienced serious illness accompanied by cognitive decline. The mother was exceedingly difficult to care for, and she refused care by other than family members. Despite their earlier differences, the siblings cooperated in caring for their mother. For the first time, the brother recognized the heavy caregiving burden that the sister was carrying, and the sister recognized and appreciated her brother's help and support. In the course of their caregiving, their hostilities gradually declined and they began to really talk to each other. They began a period of mutual reminiscing about their conflicted relationship, and they became aware of their mother's manipulative personality and her role in fueling their conflicts. At present, they maintain a civil and mutually supportive relationship for the most part.

This case history illustrates spontaneous moves in midlife toward repair of a conflict-filled adult sibling relationship, as various life events took their course. Considering the depth and long history of their conflict, intervention with family therapy at a much earlier point in life could have given this brother and sister many years of an enriched sibling relationship. Later, at the time they began their mutual reminiscence, a trained counselor might have helped to guide them toward a better relationship more effectively. Whether these siblings were sufficiently distressed either at that point or earlier in life to seek therapy is problematic. It is unclear at this point whether their rivalry has been truly defused or is merely lying beneath the surface. Whether their relationship can ever become truly close, given their history and the divergence of their life styles, I don't know, but it is encouraging that they seem to be trying.

Discussion Questions

1. What role did a major life event play in refueling the long-term sibling rivalry described in this case?

2. In what ways could gender differences influence the quality of this sibling relationship?

3. What kinds of family interventions offset the sibling rivalry documented in this case? At what point in the family life cycle should these interventions be offered?

℞ PART II ℈

HELPING FAMILIES
WITH SPECIAL CONCERNS

The three chapters in this section focus on helping families who have special concerns that must be addressed, in addition to the normative life events shared by all aging families.

Kosberg and Garcia (Chapter 4) explore one form of intrafamily adversity, elder abuse. They define elder abuse, describe possible causes of the problem, and suggest various methods of intervention. The case example of Mrs. Carson illustrates the complex situations that may be resolved through supportive services. The authors conclude that empowerment of older individuals themselves may be the best way to prevent elder abuse.

Smith, Tobin, and Fullmer (Chapter 5) address a population increasingly encountered by professionals: aging families in which older parents care for an adult child with a lifelong disability. The authors define the population of aging families of adults with lifelong disabilities, recognize that the majority of these families have a relative with mental retardation, indicate the salience of family-based care for such adults, examine cohort differences and future demographic trends, and discuss the impact of family caregiving for older mothers, siblings, and relatives. In addition, they advocate permanency planning as a family developmental task and discuss implications for practice and policy. The case example of Mrs. Kane, a 91-year-old widow who cares for her only child, Suzie, a 56-year-old woman with mental retardation, captures the issues to be addressed with this population.

Fullmer (Chapter 6) describes the families within which lesbians and gay men age. She outlines three major areas of family life for this population:

long-term relationships, social networks and social support systems in the gay community that provide family responsibilities and opportunities, and unique roles in the family of origin. Moreover, the author emphasizes that much of the family life of aging gay men and lesbians has been affected by social institutional bias. The case examples of Margery and Jay illustrate aging issues within the context of the gay and lesbian communities.

4

Confronting Maltreatment
of Elders by Their Family

JORDAN I. KOSBERG

JUANITA L. GARCIA

Adversity in contemporary society is a common theme. Crime in the streets randomly perpetrated by strangers makes us all vulnerable. However, offenses can also be perpetrated by those known to the victim; indeed, the perpetrator may be a family member.

This chapter focuses on one form of intrafamily adversity: elder abuse. The problem of elder abuse excludes no population in society, for it affects all racial, ethnic, religious, and socioeconomic groups. Elder abuse is found in rural areas, as well as in suburbia and metropolitan areas. The abused elderly person may live with, or separate from, the abusing relative.

Although such a problem may include abuse by any member of an older person's informal support system (family, friends, and neighbors), family members are the major abusers of elderly persons. Abusers may be elderly spouses, adult children, grandchildren, and siblings, among others; they can include a number of relatives who knowingly or unknowingly are involved in an abusing pattern of behavior. It is the intent of this chapter to define elder abuse, describe possible causes of the problem, and suggest various methods of intervention.

Background

Elder abuse by family members occurs for different reasons. Some abuse is a result of intentional malice, and the abuse is conscious and premeditated behavior against the older person. Other forms of family abuse result—inadvertently—from good intentions. Family members may genuinely wish to be good caregivers, yet the accumulation of caregiving stress and pressures, over time or given a particular incident, can result in elder abuse. As Garbarino (1977) has reminded us about abuse, given the wrong set of circumstances, anyone can be a potential child (or elder) abuser.

Elder abuse can also result from unintentional maltreatment by a family caregiver who is incompetent in the caregiving role. This inability to provide care may result from physical limitations or may be due to an inability to make correct decisions regarding meeting the needs of an older person. The caregiver (a spouse or child) may be old and, perhaps, as impaired and vulnerable as the elderly care recipient. In addition, as a result of improved medical advances, it is increasingly possible that children with certain forms of physical or emotional conditions (i.e., retardation, mental illness) will live into advanced years and, as their parents age, take on—for the first time—the role their parents took on for them: caregiver.

DEFINITIONS OF ELDER ABUSE

There has been a plethora of research and writing about elder abuse; yet findings may be at odds with one another, often because of differing definitions of the problem, research methodologies, and samples that are studied. Furthermore, the researcher and professional practitioner may not always agree on the definition of elder abuse. For example, although agency personnel often include self-abuse as a form of elder abuse, researchers are reluctant to include a form of adversity that does not involve a perpetrator and victim (Stein, 1991).

The following definitions of elder abuse are believed to be representative of elderly maltreatment by members of their families.

Passive Neglect. This is exemplified by situations in which the elderly person is left alone, isolated, or forgotten. The abuser is often unaware of the neglect or the consequences of the neglect, due to the abuser's lack of experience as a caregiver or because of certain deficits in mental functioning (diminished cognitive or emotional capacity). This form of abuse reflects a lack of intentionality. A depressed caregiver, for example, may simply "forget" to give medication or to take groceries to an elder parent.

Active Neglect. This is characterized as the intentional withholding of items necessary for daily living, such as food, medicine, companionship, and bathroom assistance. As such, the abuser is aware of the consequences of the neglectful behavior. An angry spouse may be actively "paying back" for earlier affronts. "You never cared about my needs, now you can just wait!"

Physical Abuse. This occurs when the older person is being hit, slapped, bruised, sexually molested, cut, burned, or physically restrained. The family member who engages in this form of abuse is aware of the adversity; it may result from a spontaneous burst of emotion or may be premeditated. Such behavior may be an accepted familial pattern and the typical response to stress or a malicious example of getting even by a hostile personality.

Psychological Abuse. This type of abuse arises when the older person is called names, insulted, infantilized, frightened, intimidated, humiliated, or threatened. Such behavior may actually be characteristic of the caregiver, but it is no less harmful. A grown but mentally challenged son may not be aware that his behavior humiliates or insults a parent he wishes to aid. On the other hand, the caregiver may very well know what is being done.

Material or Financial Misappropriation. This includes monetary or material theft or misuse (when money or property is not being used for the benefit, or with the approval, of the elderly person). Need or greed, when combined with poor impulse control or underdeveloped conscience, can be translated into misappropriation of funds or actual theft.

Violation of Rights. This is characterized—most dramatically—by efforts to force an elderly relative from his or her dwelling and/or to force the person into another setting (most often an institutional setting) without any forewarning, explanation, or opportunity for input or against the relative's wishes. Being "at the end of one's rope" does not necessarily mean the caregiver will take the proper precautions in addressing caregiving responsibilities.

Self-Abuse. The previous definitions included interpersonal dynamics involving, at least, the dyad of abused and abuser; as mentioned earlier, there is some disagreement as to whether or not to include self-abuse (or self-neglect), as well.

Although the majority of U.S. states include self-neglect as a form of elder abuse, researchers often omit it in their definitions of elder abuse. A group of researchers assembled by the Administration on Aging in 1990, for example, excluded such behavior from its definition of elder abuse (Stein, 1991). The clinically oriented book on elder abuse by Breckman and Adelman (1988) also excluded such behavior from consideration: "Since this form of neglect is not inflicted by another family member, but rather is self-imposed, it will not be addressed in this book" (p. 14).

However, Kosberg (1988) has indicated that although such behavior might not involve others, on occasion there are family members, neighbors, or friends who know of the adversity and choose not to intervene (and call the dangerous behavior to the attention of the professional community). In such cases, this is perceived as an example of neglectful abuse as much as it is of self-abuse.

In addition, members of the family might very well aid in the self-abusive or self-destructive behavior by purchasing alcohol, medication, and so on, which are then abused by the older person. In such cases, this is perceived as an example of active physical abuse as much as it is of self-abuse. It becomes evident, then, that self-abuse needs to be addressed, until such time as it is determined to be a personal choice made by a competent older person.

THE INVISIBILITY OF ABUSE

There have been many estimates of the extent of elder abuse in North America. Podnieks (1992) estimated that 4% of all elderly Canadians are abused in one way or another. Pillemer and Finkelhor (1988) estimated the figure to be 3.2% in the United States. The Canadian study used phone calls to determine the existence of abuse, and the U.S. study was conducted in Boston and used a limited definition of the problem. Still, other studies have used these figures to indicate that the problem—although unfortunate for the abused person—is not widespread.

The elderly living in private dwellings in the community (possibly with family members) may well be the most invisible, voiceless, and dependent population in the United States. Elder abuse may well be the most invisible social problem in the country. Indeed, a U.S. Congress Select Committee on Aging (1980) estimated that whereas one out of three cases of child abuse was uncovered, only one out of six cases of elder abuse was detected. The Attorney General of Massachusetts, Scott Harshbarger (1993), has estimated that "only one out of 14 cases of violence against elders is reported" (p. 43). There are several explanations for the invisibility of elder abuse.

Family Affair. Elder abuse is invisible because it is generally a family affair. Neighbors and professionals alike are somewhat reluctant to intervene in a problem that occurs within a family. The members of the family, abused and abuser, often seek to keep secrets of intrafamily violence from outsiders. It can be a matter of pride; protection of the family name has been a common theme.

Abuse Occuring Within the Home. As stated elsewhere (Kosberg, 1988), elder abuse is invisible because it occurs within a private dwelling. Quite unlike abused children, who can be detected by outsiders when they go to school, play outdoors, or see a physician as part of a required medical regimen, older people remain within their dwellings. In fact, because of a physical infirmity, they may be unable to leave the dwelling and thus abuse of older persons goes unnoticed. Such abuse will remain hidden and can continue undisturbed by outside interventions.

Failure to Report. Professionals and others should not assume that elder abuse can be identified because the victims will report their adversities. There is evidence that this generally does not happen. First there is the possibility of fear—that the solution to the problem (institutionalization) or retaliation by the abuser will be worse than the problem itself. There is also the possibility of embarrassment—at the acts of a child or at the possible identification and arrest of a child. The older person may also reflect resignation—believing one is getting paid back for early behavior against the abuser (i.e., child abuse) or another family member (i.e., spouse abuse) or that one is the cause of the problem (because of the inability to live independently). And finally, it may be that there is a lack of knowledge—being unaware of resources that are available, not knowing who to turn to, not realizing that others face similar problems.

Inadequate Detection. Finally, it is believed that elder abuse is invisible because professionals and others incorrectly interpret the true cause of the problems faced by an older person. Often, in answer to why an elderly relative shows physical signs of maltreatment, a family member will refer to the advanced age of the elderly person (or the fact that there may be problems with vision, balance, etc.). These explanations for the poor condition of the older person may be accepted at face value with little or no effort made to pursue alternative explanations (including abuse) for the condition of the older person.

Elaboration of Family Issues

Various social scientists and practitioners have sought to identify the causes of elder abuse in different ways. Although the vulnerability of older persons is related to various physical, social, economic, and psychological characteristics (Kosberg, 1990), elder abuse also has been associated with high-risk profiles of older persons, family members, and family situations (Kosberg, 1988). Families that might pose problems in care provision to (especially dependent) elderly persons are those who already have major caregiving burdens (i.e., problem-drinking spouse, delinquent child, etc.) and who live in overcrowded dwellings, face economic hardships (perhaps unemployed family members), have a history of intergenerational conflict, and/or are otherwise dysfunctional.

CAUSES OF ELDER ABUSE

Focusing on understanding elder abuse within a family context, several reasonable explanations can be given. The following explanations of elder abuse are suggestive of the efforts to understand why family members would engage in such abusive behavior.

Pathological Caregivers. Elderly persons can be maltreated by family members who exhibit abnormal or deviant behavior, including drug dependencies, alcoholism, mental illness, and cognitive problems (Quinn & Tomita, 1986). Persons who are ill-suited to provide care may be conscious of their behavior and its impact on the elderly relative; others are less aware and/or have little control over their actions. Although the consequences for older persons may be the same, the distinction between the motivations of abusing caregivers has important practice implications.

Life Crisis Model. Justice and Duncan (1976) discussed stress resulting in child abuse and focused on life-changing events that require readjustment in the lifestyle of a person or family. When an excessive number or magnitude of such life-change events occur, a "state of life crisis" may be said to exist. Holmes and Rahe (1967) have developed an index of events (including physical illness, accident or injury, and personal, social, economic, or interpersonal changes) requiring some readjustment by family members. According to this view, a series of such events in the life of a person (or in a family system) may result in a life crisis. "[The] end state of the life crisis is a stage of exhaustion, or decreased ability to adjust, and increased risk of losing control" (Justice & Duncan, 1976, p. 112). Within such a climate, it is reasonable to believe that elder abuse may occur.

Socialization of Aggression. According to this view, children who are punished severly by their parents become more aggressive than children who are not punished in violent ways. Such transmission of intrafamily violence (including elder abuse) from one generation to another has been used to explain "cultures of violence."

The socialization of violence within families is characterized as occurring more frequently in families from lower socioeconomic backgrounds and from certain cultures and geographic locations (rural mountain areas or densely populated urban areas). Although there is some suggestion of the validity of such a theory of intrafamily aggression, more research is needed.

Intergenerational Conflict. There may well be intergenerational problems existing between the elderly and their grown children. Tensions between them may be based on personality conflicts or past disagreements or hostility that can worsen with the passing of years. Furthermore, failure to define or redefine family roles over time has been seen to result in either disappointment or anger over the incongruities in expectations between generations—as related to the giving and receiving of care, as well as rights and responsibilities.

Dependency. The dependent relationship of one member of the family with others can explain intrafamily violence. Although using dependency as a cause for elder abuse has been criticized (Fulmer, 1990), dependency is a fact of life. Such dependency might be economic, social, or psychological. Certainly some elderly relatives have found themselves in such dependent roles. Their relatives, faced with the "costs" of providing care to the elderly person, can become angry with the perceived (and actual) source of problems: the older person.

However, another likely scenario can be the dependency of a family member on the older person, whether as a result of addiction, mental illness, unemployment, or other problems (Greenberg, McKibben, & Raymond, 1990; Pillemer, 1985). As an example, an adult son might be living in his mother's home or be economically or psychologically dependent on her. Given such a possibility, the son might be angry at himself for being dependent or angry with his mother (because more is expected than received). Elder abuse can result from the dependent child's anger, frustration, or embarrassment. The point is that dependency, as an explanation for elder abuse, can go either way.

Relatedly, a change in the nature of the normal intergenerational relationship may cause conflict, anger, and tensions (Edwards & Brauburger, 1973). Such incongruities with past exchange relationships within the family can result in abuse and maltreatment directed at the person who is seen as no longer able to maintain or provide the usual intrafamily tasks. Quoting Barusch (1987): "The power reversal which accompanies incapacity in old age may be more painful and difficult to live with than the incapacity itself" (p. 54).

Human Ecological View. Garbarino (1977), in his human ecological view of child abuse, has discussed the "incompetent" family caregiver. Extrapolating from this work, maltreatment of the elderly can result from caregiver incompetence for at least three reasons:

1. Lack of experience or background to "rehearse" the role of caregiver
2. Lack of knowledge regarding health problems, as well as unrealistic expectations
3. Inability to reorder priorities concerning the gratification of personal needs

Abuse results (in the ecological view) from incompetence, not deviance or abnormalities. Furthermore, the isolation of an older person and caregiver can be seen to be a "catalytic agent" for abuse, and the privacy from kinship intrusion and neighborhood surveillance can result in the lack of detection and thus the continuation of elder abuse.

LEGAL/CLINICAL ISSUES

There are several issues in working with and for abused older persons that challenge those in the helping professions. Certainly some types of elder abuse are crimes, and actions against these can be taken through the legal/judicial system.

Whether through formal or informal means, it may be possible to circumvent the judicial system in cases of clearly defined and confirmed abuse by giving the abusing family members the option of seeking individual or family therapy. It is often important to include the abused elderly person in the helping process, if the older person is a part of the problem and is physically and cognitively able to be involved in the therapeutic process. However, other forms of adversity are not so clear and are defined by moral, legal, or religious standards. As such, the interpretations by the abused, the abuser, other family members, and professionals are much more idiosyncratic and less absolute. Accordingly those in the helping professions must address the issue of proper standards of behavior. The following are issues to be considered.

Family Responsibility. Placement of an elderly person in the care of family members is often preferred by professionals for several reasons: It may be the easiest placement decision, alternatives may be unavailable or more difficult and time-consuming to achieve, and professionals may believe that families should provide care for their elderly relatives on the basis of ethical and/or religious dictates.

An important issue to consider is whether or not professionals should automatically turn to families for the solution to the problems of an elderly relative when, in fact, it may be that the family is a part of the problem (or might become the problem in the future). Relatedly, there is a question of how persistent a professional should be in "pushing" family care of an especially frail and vulnerable older person onto a resistant family. As child abuse has been associated with unwanted (or unexpected) responsibilities for a child (Garbarino, 1977), so too might unwanted care of an elderly relative result in elder abuse.

Reconceptualization of Client. A practice issue to be considered pertains to the need to reconceptualize who should be the center of a practitioner's attention. The professional (with an elderly client or patient) can attempt to meet the needs of the older person by implementing—as far as possible—the wishes of the older person. This effort at self-determination, although understandable, may result in problems for the older person and for family members as well.

For example, placement of an older person with an adult daughter and her family might be in keeping with the parent's wishes, but it might result in an overcrowded household and/or force the daughter to go from (needed) full-time employment to part-time employment. The placement might require the use of savings (for the education of the children) to meet the needs of the older parent. Ultimately, the placement could result in excessive demands on the daughter for care, adversely affecting her, the children, and the elderly parent.

Self-Determination. It is often difficult for a professional to turn away from an abused older person who refuses to acknowledge the existence of a problem or refuses the offered assistance. However, it is important to differentiate between the abuse of a child and the abuse of an elderly relative. In the former, the abused child has no rights of self-determination, and intervention occurs regardless of the child's preferences. For the competent elderly person within an abusing situation, there is a choice to be made by the individual (as an adult).

Indeed, considerable attention has been given to the involuntary intrusion into the life of an older person who is abused (Regan, 1983). It is reasoned that such individuals have a right to refuse services and assistance and that such a right supersedes all other considerations. "Doing good for the adult at risk may mean not just providing help when needed, but also knowing the limits of one's power to help" (Regan, 1983, p. 291).

In such situations, following an assessment of the cognitive ability of an older person to determine what is in his or her best interest, a professional needs to be certain of several things prior to withdrawing from the situation. First, the older abuse victim needs to understand that cooperation with the professional does not necessarily mean removal from one's dwelling, institutionalization, and/or incarceration of the abusing relative. Indeed, such actions would be the last, not first, resort for the professional. Second, the abused person needs to be aware of alternatives. These may include professional counseling for the abusing person and family therapy, alternatives to family caregiving (i.e., housing for the elderly), and supportive services to assist family members in caregiving responsibilities (i.e., day care, respite services, home care workers).

Acknowledging the importance of self-determination and nonintrusion into the lives of individuals, some oppose the mandatory reporting legislation of suspected cases of abuse (which exists in many states). Although some helping professionals (such as attorneys, physicians, social workers, and nurses) believe that their client/patient communication is privileged, waiving mandatory reporting legislation, this is not the case. Accordingly, the social worker who learns of possible elder abuse, in the course of family counseling or individual therapy, is required to report such adversity (should such requirements exist).

Competency. The determination of an older person's competency is a process that has been criticized, both in terms of the procedures taking place and of the rights lost by an individual who is declared incompetent (Pepper, 1989). It is necessary to closely assess the motivations of family members who seek the declaration of incompetency for an older relative, inasmuch as the family member may gain control of the resources of the older person who has been declared incompetent. For example, a wealthy widow's son tried to "drive" her crazy so that she would be declared incompetent and he would gain access to her possessions.

Should a person be declared incompetent and assigned a guardian, there is still reason to be concerned about whether the guardian is acting in the best interest of the older person and making appropriate use of the older person's financial assets (Iris, 1990). A special issue of the *Journal of Elder Abuse and Neglect* (Dejowski, 1990) was devoted to "Protecting Judgement-Impaired Adults: Issues, Interventions and Policies." The issue focused on legal issues related to guardianship for older persons. Additional writings have focused on accountability of lawyers (Schmidt, 1993) and the judicial evaluation of guardians (Zimny & Diamond, 1993).

Influence. The use of influence by a professional, in cases of intrafamily elder abuse, is another issue that can have widespread implications. There are those who question the use of influence by professionals through the use of positive or negative inducements and threats or use of selective information (Abramson, 1991; Moody, 1992).

For example, professionals have the power to influence an elderly person's decision to formalize a charge of abuse against a family member. With this power comes a responsibility to safeguard the older person, because retaliation by an abuser is not unknown. Clearly, if the problem of abuse is to be formally acknowledged (and labeled), a prompt and effective intervention is necessary to safeguard the abused individual.

Summary. The research findings and practice experiences on family caregiving and consequent burden are too numerous to ignore. The adverse consequences can include:

1. The possibility that family caregivers (adult children, spouses) may become clients or patients as a result of the physical, social, and psychological "costs of care" (Kosberg & Cairl, 1986)
2. Ineffective care by those who are unable to meet the needs of the elderly relative
3. At its worst—elder abuse

Accordingly, there is a need to view the family as the "client," whether the family is a dyad (elderly parent and adult child, elderly couple), a nuclear family (three generations), or a multigenerational extended family.

Directions for Practice and Policy

There are practice ramifications from the discussion of the dynamics of elder abuse and its prevention, detection, and intervention (Quinn & Tomita, 1986).

PREVENTION

Prevention at the microlevel means that those in the helping professions should screen potential family caregivers for suitability. Such assessments have been developed and include not only objective measurement of physical, psychological, economic, and social dimensions, but also measurement of the perception of anticipated consequences of providing care to an elderly person (Kosberg & Cairl, 1986). Furthermore, attention to the characteristics of an elderly person or a family caregiver can permit the identification of high-risk situations (Kosberg, 1988).

Prevention also involves meeting with those who are considering taking on the caregiving role. Such family contacts should include the identification of present as well as future caregiving needs of the older relative. Because an older person's health is unlikely to improve dramatically over time (it will probably worsen), the family needs to acknowledge this fact and—with the assistance of the professional—weigh its ability to provide such assistance and anticipate the consequences of providing the projected level of care.

Prevention at the macrolevel of intervention mandates eliminating conditions that give rise to elder abuse, as well as trying to preclude the placement of an elderly person in a potentially abusive situation. Prevention at this level also pertains to the elimination of ageism and violence, as well as poverty, unemployment, and other broad conditions that cause problems for family members and place vulnerable elderly persons at risk.

DETECTION

Detecting abuse after it occurs is an important role for those in the helping professions who function in settings in which the problem can be observed (i.e., emergency rooms or clinics, service centers, private dwellings). As mentioned, the first step in detection is a sensitivity to the possible problem of elder abuse.

Detection protocols are increasingly being developed for use within health and social service settings (Quinn & Tomita, 1986). Generally speaking, there are two areas for detection: physical and/or behavioral symptoms (Kosberg, 1988). The former refers to obvious physical signs of maltreatment, such as bruises, abrasions, burns, and so on. The latter pertains to the demeanor of the older person, such as withdrawal, embarrassment, depression, vigorous denial, and so on. Although there is no assurance that these symptoms are necessarily related to elder abuse (rather than an accident, fall, or a general personality trait), the existence of such symptoms should necessitate an exploration of possible abuse by the professional.

INTERVENTION

Various direct and indirect forms of intervention can be used with families of abused and abusing individuals. Direct interventions include counseling and therapy, community-based interventions, and family life education. Indirect methods of confronting elder abuse in aging families include planning, policy development, and professional education.

Counseling/Therapy. Counseling and therapy can focus on the individual, a dyad, or a family system. In some ways, such direct practice in abuse is no different from direct intervention with any form of intrafamily problem. For example, it may represent a general inability of individuals or families to cope with problems (Garcia & Kosberg, 1992). Elder abuse may represent the continuation of a long-term problem in interpersonal dynamics (such as spouse abuse or hostility between family members).

Depending on the assessment of the problem, intervention may include short-term or long-term treatment of the abused, abuser, and family system

(Quinn & Tomita, 1986). Educational and environmental therapies have been found to be effective in working with elder abuse cases.

Clearly, the first task to be undertaken is the protection of the abused individual from continued harm. Working with abuse cases necessitates great sensitivity, understanding, and support (Breckman & Adelman, 1988; Quinn & Tomita, 1986). It is important to identify reasons for the abuse as quickly as possible. Some abusers are not bad individuals, but they are driven to abuse because of excessive and unrelenting demands and pressures. Others abuse willfully or because of an inability to curb a habit (i.e., substance abuse) that contributes to the abuse of an older person.

Family counselors and therapists who work with abusing families and family members are likely to encounter a variety of affects that can range from anguish to anger (Garcia & Kosberg, 1992). Although the initial response to abuse is often either denial or excuses, it is necessary to understand the abusers' perceptions of the causes of the problem and to determine the authenticity of their embarrassment or regret. Genuine feelings of remorse and concern for avoiding repetition of the adversity should motivate the professional to provide intervention to the family member. The abusing family member's denial, hostility, or lack of remorse should alert the professional to seek a solution to the problem that will safeguard the older person from further abuse (and perhaps to seek alternate placement for the older person away from the abusing family members).

As mentioned earlier, the characteristics of older persons may contribute to their problems. This may refer to the level of impairments or other conditions that influence the nature and extent of needed caregiving. Although it in no way excuses the behavior, this may also mean that the older person is not sensitive to the pressures on caregivers, is unrealistic in expectations, and may have a provoking nature (Kosberg, 1988).

Community-Based Interventions. Community awareness of the potential problem of elder abuse is a preventive effort at a broader level than individual helping approaches. Both elderly relatives and their families should become aware of the possibility of abuse and the factors associated with abuse. Thus, they can make decisions that might result in a family not taking on the caregiving responsibility or in an elderly person realizing the possible adverse consequences of a decision to live with a family member. Another cause and result of community awareness can be the development of multidisciplinary and multiprofessional collaboration (Eisenberg, 1991), such as between the legal and social service professions.

Also imperative is the availability of community resources to provide alternatives to family care for the elderly. Such resources may include housing for the elderly, foster care, and group living among others. The existence of institutions as the only alternative to family care is unacceptable, for this forces both the family and older person to make a very difficult choice when independent living by an elderly person is no longer possible.

In addition, there is a need to provide supportive services for those family members who wish to take on caregiving responsibilities for elderly relatives. These resources can include day care, senior citizen centers, respite care, and homemaker and home health services, among others. Such services can make the difference in the ability to continue to provide care, often to avoid institutionalization for the older person, and very possibly to reduce the occurrence of elder abuse.

Education. Family life education and the education of professionals are two important methods of dealing with elder abuse in aging families. Family life education refers to helping families identify and solve problems before the problems escalate into more serious situations (Garcia & Kosberg, 1994). Such education will help families clarify both structural pressures within the family (such as role ambiguities, changes in interpersonal roles, competing demands on one's time) and emotional pressures (such as attitudinal and behavioral changes, mood changes, and cognitive impairments) (Springer & Brubaker, 1984).

With respect to professional education, not only is there a need to introduce content on the possibility of elder abuse into professional school curricula, but training should include attention to the detection, prevention, and mediation of the causes of the problem, as well as to the problem itself. For those already working in the field, in-service training and staff development can supplement their professional education.

Conclusion

It seems unlikely that the problem of elder abuse will soon disappear; indeed, it is suspected that the problem will likely increase. Reasons for such a dire projection include:

1. The growth of the number and proportion of the elderly (especially the oldest of the old—those who are the most impaired and in greatest need of care)

2. The fact that social changes are resulting in a decrease in the desire of families to take on caregiving responsibilities for the elderly

3. The decrease in the availability of family caregivers, given an increase in the likelihood of women working outside the home

4. The economic conditions in society that result in high levels of poverty and unemployment

It seems apparent that those in the helping professions face a difficult challenge in seeking to reduce the existence of elder abuse. Certainly efforts at prevention, detection, and intervention are vital. Yet, in the final analysis, the solution to the problem may well be the opportunities for older persons to retain their independence in the community, living within their own dwelling for as long as possible, through the assistance of supportive services, volunteer efforts, and financial support. Generally family members do not want to have intensive and extensive caregiving responsibilities for their elderly relatives. Neither do their elderly relatives want to become burdens on their families. In providing assistance to the elderly, professionals are not only helping them and their family members, they are also avoiding the likelihood of elder abuse.

CASE EXAMPLE

Mr. Block, a caseworker for the local family service agency, was sent on a home visit to 82-year-old Mrs. Carson, in response to a phone call from her indicating that her family was "freezing" because the utility company had turned off the heat due to repeated failures to pay utility bills. When Mr. Block arrived, he found Mrs. Carson sitting by the front door with a butcher knife at her side for protection. In another room, a frantic argument was taking place between Mrs. Carson's son, Jim, a 52-year-old man with chronic paranoid schizophrenia, and his 25-year-old girlfriend, who has moderate mental retardation. The content of the argument vacillated between who had failed to pay the monthly utility bills and why the girlfriend had allowed herself to become pregnant.

After employing crisis intervention techniques to solve the family's immediate heating problem, Mr. Block interviewed them in-depth to uncover more about this current situation. He found out, for example, that Mrs. Carson had become blind during the past 5 years and had a foot amputated due to not taking medication prescribed for her diabetes. Without transportation of her own, she relied on her son to purchase this medicine. Now, with her blindness, Mrs. Carson sometimes went for days without food when Jim "goes on one of his binges" and doesn't come home at all for long periods of time. When asked why she hadn't called sooner for help, Mrs. Carson replied, "I'm just afraid they'll want to take either Jim or me away from our home. After all, we only have each other, you know."

Mr. Block proceeded to assure Mrs. Carson that the family could remain intact if they would allow a case manager from the local department of social services to arrange a number of supportive services. Comforted by the notion that she would not be separated from her son, Mrs. Carson and Jim eventually received a number of services including visits from a public health nurse to monitor Mrs. Carson's diabetes, a homemaker service to assure a clean household, Meals on Wheels, and outpatient psychotherapy for Jim.

Discussion Questions

1. What type(s) of elder abuse does the case example illustrate?
2. Describe some of the reasons why Mrs. Carson and Jim had remained unknown to service providers until Mr. Block's visit.
3. What possible causes may have contributed to the elder neglect revealed by this case example?

5

Assisting Older Families
of Adults With Lifelong Disabilities

GREGORY C. SMITH

SHELDON S. TOBIN

ELISE M. FULLMER

Such trends as deinstitutionalization, decreased mortality rates, improved health care, aging of the baby boom generation, and expanded community services have combined to produce an accelerated increase in the numbers of individuals with lifelong disabilities surviving to later adulthood and in the numbers of their elderly parents, who in many instances function as their primary caregivers (Jennings, 1987; Lefly, 1987). As a result, families in which older parents care for an adult offspring with a lifelong disability are now increasingly encountered by professionals from the aging, developmental disabilities, and mental health networks. Yet, despite the many needs confronting these families, little information currently exists regarding how to best assist them (Smith & Tobin, 1993c).

The goals of this chapter are:

1. To define the population of aging families of adults with lifelong disabilities, recognizing that the majority of these families have a relative with mental retardation
2. To indicate the salience of family-based care for adults with lifelong disabilities
3. To examine cohort influences and future demographic trends among these families
4. To discuss the impact of family caregiving on older mothers, siblings, and the relatives with disabilities
5. To portray permanency planning as a family developmental task
6. To describe interventions and policies designed to assist these aging families

Background

In the context of this chapter, a lifelong disability is synonymous with the term *developmental disability,* which, according to Public Law 95-602, refers to a severe and chronic condition that (a) is attributable to a mental or physical impairment (or a combination of impairments); (b) manifests before age 22; (c) is likely to continue indefinitely; (d) results in substantial functional limitations in three or more areas of major life activity; and (e) reflects the need for a combination and sequence of special individualized services that are lifelong or of an extended duration.

In terms of diagnostic categories, developmental disabilities encompass the following disorders: mental retardation, cerebral palsy, autism, sensory or neurological impairments, multiple disabilities, and various other debilitating conditions (Lippman & Loberg, 1985). Many persons with chronic mental illness also meet the functional criteria specified in PL 95-602 (Jennings, 1987; Walz, Harper, & Wilson, 1986). However, despite this heterogeneity, data regarding life expectancy and age-specific prevalence rates reveal that the vast majority of people with lifelong disabilities surviving to later adulthood are those with mental retardation (Lubin & Kiely, 1985). As a result, attention has been mainly focused on this disorder, and little is known at this time about the impact of other developmental disabilities on aging families.

Despite the nuances associated with specific diagnoses, older families of adults with lifelong disabilities of any kind are similar in that they share nonnormative caregiving responsibilities, as well as the ensuing benefits and stressors. Thus, even though this chapter focuses chiefly on families of adults with mental retardation, several of the issues presented here may apply equally to families encountering other lifelong disabilities.

However, generalizations to older families facing lifelong disabilities other than mental retardation are merely speculative, given the present lack of research on these families.

The potential stressors facing older parents of offspring with lifelong disabilities include the following: a state of "perpetual parenthood" caused by the adult offspring's unending dependency, chronic sorrow from the realization that the offspring has not experienced a normal life, age-associated decrements in parents and their offspring that adversely affect caregiving, unavailability of formal resources to relieve their burden, social isolation, and financial concerns (Greenberg, Seltzer, & Greenley, 1993; Jennings, 1987; Lefly, 1987). In turn, because the majority of aging parents can now expect to be survived by their disabled son or daughter (Janicki & Wisniewski, 1985), the two primary issues faced by these families are providing care for as long as possible and making plans for when they can no longer care due to their disability or death (Heller & Factor, 1993; Smith & Tobin, 1989).

THE SALIENCE
OF FAMILY-BASED CARE

Family care at home has been the residential arrangement of choice for parents of persons with developmental disabilities (Heller & Factor, 1993; Seltzer, Krauss, & Heller, 1991). Apparently, about 85% of the caregivers for persons with mental retardation, as well as mental illness, are parents (Greenberg et al., 1993). Family caregiving is thus widespread, and many families even play an exclusive and unassisted role in the lives of their relatives with lifelong disabilities (Jennings, 1987; Krauss, Seltzer, & Goodman, 1992). Indeed, as discussed below, a substantial number of families exist who have shunned the aid of formal services altogether (Horne, 1989).

Unfortunately the situation of those older parents whose offspring with a lifelong disability has already moved away from the family has been ignored in the literature. An exception is the recent study by Smith and McClenny (1994), in which a sample of these parents reported less subjective burden, higher stages of residential planning, greater optimism regarding the offspring's future, and more ease in asking for assistance from offspring than did older parents still caring for a son or daughter with a disability at home. Yet those parents with offspring already living away from home experienced enough concern to participate in a parental support group.

COHORT INFLUENCES
ON CAREGIVING FAMILIES

Practitioners and policymakers intending to assist these families must have an appreciation for parents from the oldest cohorts, particularly those in their 80s and 90s, whose children were born prior to the 1970s, when community-based day services originated. Before then, only institutional care was available, forcing many caregiving families to rely entirely on support from relatives, friends, and neighbors. In turn, they feared that contacting service providers would induce a placement outside the home (Lippman & Loberg, 1985; Tymchuk, 1983). For many, the subsequent development of day services did not dispel their belief that using these services would lead to institutionalization of their son or daughter.

Without the availability of day services during most of their parenting, many in the oldest cohorts developed coping skills that enabled them to handle problems on their own with great self-assurance. As a result, they now regard professional help as unnecessary and intrusive, even when the objective circumstances of their aging suggest otherwise (Engelhardt, Brubaker, & Lutzer, 1988). Many elderly parents also find it inconceivable that younger professionals could possess the same level of patience, understanding, and competence that took them a lifetime to achieve. As one older mother commented: "My son's daily needs are taken care of by me. We don't need help from anyone."

Older parental cohorts also may avoid services because of earlier unfavorable interactions with professionals resulting in mistrust and a lack of confidence. As a mother in her 80s said: "The doctor told me to throw my son away like an old dishrag." Practitioners must realize that today's older parents conceived their children during a historical period when the predominant view of the mentally retarded was one of worthlessness and inferiority (Tymchuk, 1983). This stigmatization produced feelings of shame, low self-worth, and even nonacceptance of the disability, all of which may have inhibited these parents from seeking professional help (Nadler, Lewinstein, & Rahav, 1991). Now, in that these parents are in their later years, such feelings are likely to be reinforced by ageism within the mental retardation service system (Janicki, 1988; Seltzer & Seltzer, 1985; Smith & Tobin, 1993a).

Parents from the oldest cohorts may also be less able than younger parents to access needed services because of their own increasing physical and cognitive impairments, as well as their generally lower levels of educational attainment. Because contemporary aging and disability service systems are highly complex bureaucracies (Seltzer, 1992), very old parents may require considerable assistance in dealing with them (Smith, Fullmer, & Tobin, 1994; Smith & Tobin, 1989).

DEMOGRAPHIC TRENDS

Several demographic trends have implications for providing support to aging families of persons with lifelong disabilities. Due to increased life expectancy of most persons with retardation, for example, the period of family involvement is now prolonged. In turn, this means that the ratio of older to younger caregiving families is rising, necessitating a differentiation of the supportive services required by families at various stages of the family life cycle. Whereas the greatest family needs of younger families are related to the education and socialization of children, older families typically require services oriented toward health maintenance and long-term care in order to support aging parents in their caregiving role (Seltzer, Krauss, et al., 1991).

Demographic trends also suggest that additional stress and caregiving demands may be experienced apart from those associated with parenting an offspring with a disability (Seltzer, Krauss, et al., 1991). For example, because there will be considerably fewer members of the younger generation available to care for aging family members, older mothers of adults with retardation are likely to have additional responsibilities, such as caring for a frail parent or spouse. Also, as a result of both the increasing divorce rate and the tendency among wives to outlive husbands, increased numbers of older mothers will be caregivers in single-parent households (Seltzer, Krauss, et al., 1991).

Elaboration of Family Issues

The impact of the caregiving arrangement on individual family members will be reviewed in this section, followed by a discussion of why planning for the future well-being of an offspring with a lifelong disability should be recognized as a family task by practitioners.

IMPACT ON OLDER MOTHERS

Our focus in this chapter is limited to older mothers because they, rather than fathers, have assumed the role of primary caregiver (Seltzer, Krauss, et al., 1991). Moreover, in the only study comparing older mothers and fathers, gender was unrelated to attitudes and concerns about caring for an adult offspring with a lifelong disability (Brubaker, Engelhardt, Brubaker, & Lutzer, 1989). Yet, because studies of younger family caregivers have consistently shown that the burden of caregiving adversely affects the psychological well-being of females more than males (Avison, Turner, Noh, & Speechly, 1993), it seems premature to dismiss totally gender differences between older parents.

Unlike women who provide care to frail elderly relatives (see Chapter 2 of this volume), older mothers of adults with mental retardation appear to be generally well adjusted and satisfied with the caregiver role. Seltzer and Krauss (1989), for example, described their sample of older mothers of adults with mental retardation as being "resilient, optimistic, and able to function well in multiple roles" (p. 309). These mothers were also found to be more similar to than different from their age peers with respect to self-reported health status, depressive symptoms, life satisfaction, social support networks, and their ability to respond to stressful life events unrelated to caregiving (Seltzer, Krauss, Choi, & Hong, in press).

There are several reasons why these older mothers endure so well despite the additional stressors and demands in their lives brought on by caregiving. Not only may they have developed special personal competencies as a result of their unique caregiving responsibilities (Seltzer & Ryff, in press), but also they may have received companionship and instrumental assistance from their son or daughter with a disability (Grant, 1986; Heller & Factor, 1993). Moreover, parents with better coping skills may have been more disposed to remain in the caregiving role into their later years (Krauss & Seltzer, 1993), while deriving satisfaction and self-esteem from confronting its challenges (Heller & Factor, 1993; Wood & Skiles, 1992). Also, gratifications derived from "perpetual parenthood" may offset any sense of failure these parents experience regarding nonconformity to cultural norms of family development (Seltzer & Ryff, in press; Todd, Shearn, Beyer, & Felce, 1993). Furthermore, because about 90% of older mothers have at least one other nondisabled offspring (Seltzer, Begun, Seltzer, & Krauss, 1991; Smith et al., 1994), normative family events encountered through these children may attenuate nonnormality associated with parenting a child with a disability (Seltzer et al., in press).

However, it should not be concluded from the above review that there is neither risk nor diversity within the population of aging parents of adults with lifelong disabilities. Of particular relevance to family practitioners are recent findings that aspects of the family's social climate are important predictors of well-being among older mothers of adults with mental retardation. Seltzer, Begun, et al. (1991), for example, found that older mothers with nondisabled children who provided support to their disabled sibling had better well-being than mothers with either no other children or children not involved with their sibling. They concluded that "the family social climate, including the relationships among family members, the value orientations of the family, and the organization of the family, may be more salient for the older [mothers of adults with mental retardation] than for their age peers" (p. 310). More recently, Smith and Tobin (1993b) found both lower levels of family cohesion and the perception of becoming adversely affected by one's own aging to be associated with feelings of burden among older mothers of adults with mental retardation.

It also appears that risk among older parents may be related to the particular disability of their offspring. Greenberg et al. (1993), for example, found older mothers of adults with mental illness to report higher levels of subjective burden, poorer relationships with the offspring, greater behavioral problems by the offspring, more caregiving responsibilities to other family members, smaller social support networks, and less positive family environments than older mothers of adults with mental retardation. Also, nearly all of the families involved with mental retardation used some type of day programming, whereas less than half of the families confronting mental illness had done so.

In summary, survey studies of older mothers of adults with retardation suggest that these parents are typically well adjusted, satisfied with their role as family caregiver, and without overt pathology. However, the finding that older parents of adults with a chronic mental illness may not fare as well suggests that important differences may exist among aging parents of offspring with diverse kinds of lifelong disabilities. There is also recent but limited evidence suggesting that aspects of the family's social environment may differentiate older parents who are at risk.

IMPACT ON SIBLINGS

Although it is believed that siblings of young children with lifelong disabilities are at risk for emotional morbidity (see, for discussion, G. Seltzer, et al., 1991; Seltzer, 1993), no longitudinal studies of the long-term effect of developmental disabilities on sibling relationships have been reported. However, a small number of recent cross-sectional studies have addressed the relationships between adults with lifelong disabilities and their nondisabled siblings. It has been found that nearly all adults with mental retardation who reside with aging parents have at least one living sibling who could potentially provide them with support (G. Seltzer, et al., 1991; Smith et al., 1994).

In examining the assistance actually provided, G. Seltzer et al. (1991) found that siblings tended to limit their involvement to affective support, leaving the older parents to provide the bulk of instrumental aid (such as help with daily tasks and self-care) to the offspring with mental retardation. It was also discovered that one sibling, who was more likely to be a sister, was usually identified as being "the most involved." Nevertheless, the typical pattern of involvement by siblings without disabilities was best characterized as "caring at a distance."

Despite the apparent disinclination among siblings to provide instrumental support to their brothers and sisters with disabilities, it has been repeatedly observed that older parents expect another family member, most often a sibling, to take over the caregiving responsibility when parents are no longer able to fulfill this role (Grant, 1986; Heller & Factor, 1991, 1993; Kaufman, Adams, & Campbell, 1991; Seltzer, 1993; Tobin, Fullmer, & Smith, in press; Wood & Skiles, 1992). Yet, in reality, researchers (Krauss, 1993) and clinicians have observed that siblings perceive their future involvement as being far less extensive than what is envisioned by parents. As described below, these unconfirmed parental expectations often lead to a family crisis that threatens the well-being of the offspring with a disability (Heller & Factor, 1991).

IMPACT ON THE OFFSPRING
WITH A LIFELONG DISABILITY

Ironically, those who are most neglected in the literature on aging families of adults with lifelong disabilities are the offspring themselves. Yet they encounter several risks within their families that practitioners need to be aware of.

The greatest peril involves the failure of their aging parents to plan for the time when they can no longer continue as primary caregivers. An unfortunate but consistent finding has been that most older parents have not made definite plans for their son or daughter's future (Heller & Factor, 1991, 1993; Kaufman et al., 1991; Roberto, 1988; Smith, Tobin, & Fullmer, in press; Wood & Skiles, 1992). Instead, they typically resort to a "one day at a time" attitude or, as noted above, mistakenly presume that a sibling will become the "successor caregiver." As one 96-year-old mother of a daughter with mental retardation said: "The time has not yet come for me to plan."

In the absence of adequate planning, the offspring with a disability is not only left unprepared to face emotional upheaval caused by the sudden illness or death of a parental caregiver, but he or she is also at risk of receiving an inappropriate residential placement on an emergency basis (Heller & Factor, 1991; Janicki, 1988; Kaufman et al., 1991; Seltzer & Seltzer, 1985; Wood & Skiles, 1992). As an illustration, a case manager from the developmental disabilities service network said he had an elderly woman client who refused to plan, apparently hoping she would live as long as her child (see Smith & Tobin, 1993a). When she became institutionalized, her 60-year-old son was angry and resentful, living in the hospital with his future placement unresolved.

Adults with lifelong disabilities are also at risk because their personal wishes and preferences are often either overlooked or disregarded, especially when they are incompatible with the older parent's own attitudes, fears, and anxieties (Smith & Tobin, 1993a). One frail mother in her 80s, for example, refused to consider eventual placement in a group home that her daughter with mental retardation was fond of, because the staff had failed to replace a button on the younger woman's sweater during a prior respite stay. Another 80-year-old woman told a case manager that she would kill her 47-year-old daughter before placing her, a sentiment that unfortunately is common among older parents.

Many older parents also prefer not to talk to their offspring with a disability about plans for the future, even when such discussions could be readily comprehended (Smith & Tobin, 1989; Wood & Skiles, 1992). They also tend to inhibit the offspring's developmental progress (Smith & Tobin, 1993a). Whereas young parents of children with lifelong disabilities are generally optimistic about their children reaching maximum performance potential, older parents seem to focus more on maintenance of current abilities (Seltzer & Seltzer, 1985; Todd et al., 1993).

FUTURE PLANNING AS A FAMILY TASK

As noted above, a primary developmental task for these families is to plan for the time when aging parents can no longer remain in the caregiver role. Known as "permanency planning," this entails the making of future arrangements within three life domains: residential, legal, and financial (Smith & Tobin, 1989). Although planning in all three areas is crucial, it is safe to assume that making arrangements for an offspring's future residence is the most essential and arduous responsibility for aging parents because it forces them to recognize that their son or daughter may someday reside in a setting that is not as beneficial as the one they have provided (Smith & Tobin, 1989).

Without the assurance of continued family care, elderly parents facing the likelihood of outside placements are deeply concerned about such issues as potential abuse of their offspring, uncaring staff, uncleanliness, sexual permissiveness, poor quality of meals, lack of supervision, unsafe neighborhoods, fear of facilities being closed, and negative community attitudes toward those with disabilities (Heller & Factor, 1987). Even when aging parents are able to suppress these concerns, they are likely to face waiting lists due to the unavailability of appropriate residential options (Smith & Tobin, 1993a).

In our study of 235 older mothers of adults with mental retardation, nearly one half had not made concrete residential plans (Smith et al., in press). Indeed, 20% reported not having any discussions about this matter, whereas another 30% or so either were in early discussions or were still considering alternatives. Because this sample participated voluntarily, our findings may actually overestimate the true extent of planning among older parents.

The major purpose of our study was to test a theoretical model of residential planning based on the prominent "double ABCX" model of family stress and adaptation (McCubbin & Patterson, 1982). In our proposed model:

A = the objective stressors of the caregiving situation (impairment demonstrated by the offspring, the mother's disability level, and the extent of caregiving tasks performed)

B = mediators, specifically resources (use of formal services and help from offspring without disabilities) and coping behaviors (escape avoidance)

C = appraisals of the caregiving situation (perceived need for services, subjective caregiver burden, and awareness of adverse age-related changes in the self)

X = a crucial family outcome (stage of residential planning)

"Double" = the accumulation of additional problems secondary to caregiving, such as changes in the mother's functional ability, that impact family adaptation

A further assumption of our model was that the objective stressors of caregiving would affect residential planning indirectly through their influence on appraisals, resources, and coping skills.

With structural equation modeling, we found that this representation of the double ABCX model fit the data from our 235 older mothers well (Smith et al., in press). Four variables were observed to influence stage of residential planning directly: nonuse of avoidance coping; the mother's awareness of being adversely affected by age-related changes (i.e., increasing disability); use of family support services; and assistance from offspring with no disabilities.

The relationship that we found between avoidance coping and residential planning is consistent with the above discussion of how many older parents prefer to deny or postpone planning for as long as possible. As noted by Heller and Factor (1993) older family members often "neglect to plan for their relative's long-term care, put it off for years, or give up in frustration" (p. 110). Yet our findings also suggest that many parents encounter the need to plan for the first time when confronted with the awareness of their own impending disability or death. This is exemplified by the following remark made by one older parent in a support group: "I didn't realize that I was growing older until I retired. Then I became aware of some physical changes that I'd previously ignored. Suddenly, it struck me that I needed to begin planning for my daughter's future!"

Practitioners therefore face the difficult task of assisting those who have not planned to engage in honest self-exploration of the growing limitations associated with aging.

Our finding that use of family support services had a direct effect on stage of residential planning is understandable given the recurrent speculation that formal service use fosters planning by reducing older parents' apprehensiveness toward community residences (Seltzer et al., 1991; Smith & Tobin, 1993a; Wood & Skiles, 1992). Another possibility is that older parents seek out and rely on service providers more intensively as they initiate permanency planning arrangements (Dobrof, 1985).

Finally, it is noteworthy that we found assistance from offspring without disabilities to have a direct effect on stage of residential planning that was independent of formal service use. It may be that if older parents perceive either of these resources as being unhelpful with planning, they turn to the other for assistance. It may also be true that service providers are not sufficiently encouraging other family members to become involved in the planning process. Thus we concur with the conclusion by G. Seltzer et al. (1991) that "practitioners may be able to ease the stress associated with the inevitable separation of the mother and the child with retardation by reinforcing the involvement of the siblings with the brother or sister" (p. 316).

In summary, our model of residential planning (Smith et al., in press) supports the belief that "families with more internal resources and stronger interpersonal and community support systems cope more successfully with stressful events" (Slater & Wikler, 1986, p. 387). It also reveals to practitioners that family members' perceptions, resources, and coping are more important than objective stressors in determining the extent to which aging parents have made residential plans for an offspring with a lifelong disability. Clinicians should not only confront older parents' tendency to engage in avoidance coping, they should also enable parents to accept their age-related limitations with equanimity. Finally, the use of formal services and the involvement of nonhandicapped siblings in permanency planning should be encouraged.

Directions for Practice and Policy

The inability of older parents to remain as caregivers unceasingly has profound implications for both policy and clinical practice. Policymakers, for example, must ensure that appropriate residences and services will be available when parental care is no longer possible (Heller & Factor, 1987; Rose & Ansello, 1987). Clinicians, on the other hand, must help older parents to acknowledge their own mortality (Smith et al., in press) and to accept that the provision of care in the future will not be as loving as the care they have provided (Dobrof, 1985; Goodman, 1978). Interventions are also needed to minimize the emotional trauma faced by adults with lifelong disabilities upon separation from their parents (Heller, 1985), as well as to support siblings regarding their involvement with family developmental tasks and crises (G. Seltzer, et al., 1991).

Before considering specific interventions to aid older families, it should be noted that both the aging and developmental disabilities networks have been somewhat unresponsive to their needs (Kaufman, DeWeaver, & Glicken, 1989; Sison & Cotten, 1989). It is evident that too few community resources and viable residential placements exist for aging families, that relationships between older parents and practitioners are often characterized by avoidance and mistrust, that ageism exists among developmental disabilities professionals, and that there has been a lack of counseling for families regarding permanency planning (Smith & Tobin, 1989, 1993a, 1993c).

POLICY

The shortcomings just noted indicate that the service system must become more meaningful to aging families. This meaningfulness must develop more from policy changes than through the modification of practice by individual clinicians. A family policy focused on aging families should encompass making the *family* the client rather than only the adult offspring, ensuring home care until residential placement is necessary, and having sufficient community residences avaliable for future placement (Heller & Factor, 1993; Smith & Tobin, 1993a, 1993c). As noted by Seltzer and Krauss (in press):

> It is also necessary to develop viable alternatives to the dominant community-based system of group homes, supervised apartments, and foster homes. Many family members want to create options that mirror conditions in which their adult children have lived most of their lives. (p. 14)

The service system can also become more meaningful to older families by recognizing that their most pressing needs are different from those of younger families. Professionals from the developmental disabilities network need to know more about aging issues if they are to understand the age-related changes and transitions confronting these families. They must also know how to make appropriate referrals to professionals and programs within the aging services network (Smith & Tobin, 1993a). The cultivation of geriatric specialists within the developmental disabilities service system has also been proposed (see, for example, Sutton, Sterns, Schwartz, & Roberts, 1992).

There also is a strong tendency within the developmental disabilities service system to regard family members as merely resources for the client, rather than recognizing that the family itself has needs that must be met (Slater & Wikler, 1986). Fortunately, the proposed 1992 amendments to the Older Americans Act of 1965 call directly for the provision of services to "older individuals who provide uncompensated care to their adult children with disabilities, or counseling to assist such older individuals with permanency planning for such children" (U.S. House of Representatives, April 9, 1992, p. 2606).

A final policy issue pertaining to aging families of adults with lifelong disabilities concerns identifying gaps in services to these families. For example, outreach efforts are needed to locate those families who are served either inadequately or not at all by the formal service system. This will not only demand increased resources and expenditures to conduct the outreach, but a parallel increase in available services may be required to support newly identified families (Smith et al., 1994).

FAMILY INTERVENTIONS

Because two central issues facing aging families of adults with lifelong disabilities are how older parents can remain in the caregiver role and what will happen to the offspring when they can no longer do so, the interventions reviewed in this section will be considered both in terms of how they stabilize the current caregiving arrangement and how they assist families in dealing with the eventual relinquishment of caregiving. Three major categories of intervention for this population are described, including family support services, educational programs, and family counseling.

Family Support Services

Although a wide variety of support services are available to families of individuals with lifelong disabilities, day services and case management have received the most attention in the literature on aging families.

Day Services. These services may be defined as "any focused and purposive activity of a full day duration that involves work or habilitative tasks, or sociorecreational, avocational, and stimulatory activities" (Janicki, Otis, Puccio, Rettig, & Jacobson, 1985, p. 295). Day services consist of competitive employment or sheltered workshops for those with minimal impairments, whereas a combination of clinical services and habilitation activities are typically involved for more severely impaired clients.

These services benefit adults with lifelong disabilities by promoting skill development (personal, interpersonal, and vocational), socialization, recreation, creativity, self-esteem, educational enrichment, and ancillary support from the community (Barbero, 1989). When caregivers are elderly parents, day programs often assist them in coping with the care and supervision of their disabled offspring, especially when coupled with various ancillary support services. Thus day services not only provide socialization opportunities for the offspring outside the realm of the immediate family environment, but they may also abate the kind of parent-offspring inter-dependence thought to hinder permanency planning by older parents (Grant, 1986). Recent evidence confirms the importance of day services to aging families of adults with lifelong disabilities. For example, Greenberg et al. (1993) concluded that one reason why older mothers of adults with mental illness report lower well-being than mothers of adults with retardation is because offspring with mental illness are far less likely to use day services. Similarly, Smith et al. (1994) found that aging families of adults with mental retardation who were uninvolved with day programs were at greater risk regarding potential disequilibria, had fewer resources to facilitate the accession of other needed services, and were less likely to have made future legal or residential plans for the offspring than families who were using day services.

Case Management. Case management may be defined as "an attempt to reach out to persons in need of service, promote service awareness, provide a needs assessment, develop a service plan, and finally, ensure that the prescribed services are received" (Seltzer, 1992, p. 66). Kaufman et al. (1989) proposed a case management model that encompasses six profes-sional roles thought to be important to effective intervention with aging families of adults with lifelong disabilities: outreach worker, advocate, teacher, therapist, enabler/facilitator, and broker/coordinator.

Such models are useful in illustrating the diversity of issues that confront case managers who work with aging families, but there is reason to suspect how realistic they are in practice. For example, although case managers may be cognizant of the six roles specified by Kaufman et al. (1989), they are unlikely to see themselves as being able to perform each of them on their own. This is so either because their caseloads are pro-hibitively large or because they feel that others are more apt at certain tasks (Smith & Tobin, 1993c). Rather than assuming the therapist role, for example, case managers are inclined to refer aging families with consid-erable emotional difficulties to appropriate mental health professionals.

Further limitations of professional case management models, including high turnover among case managers and a reluctance by many older parents to have their family affairs managed by strangers, were described by Seltzer (1992). She found that training families to be case managers for adults with a disability eliminated these concerns by empowering them to act on their own behalf, while simultaneously reducing the caseloads of professionals and ensuring continuity of care.

Yet another limitation of the professional case management model is that it focuses primarily on maintaining the relative with disabilities in the home by helping the family to effectively access and use available resources and services. This narrow focus obscures the important task of assisting aging parents with planning for their offspring's future. Indeed, practicing case managers often report frustration over having too little emphasis placed on permanency planning by administrators (Smith & Tobin, 1989). In reality case managers are faced with the opposing tasks of maintaining existing family stability and initiating the inevitable parent-offspring separation.

Educational Programs

Given the shortcomings of the case management model noted above, various educational programs may be effective alternatives for assisting older families with permanency planning, as well as informing them of available resources and services.

Psychoeducational Support Groups. Heller and Factor (1991) found unmet needs for a family support group in more than one fourth of their sample of older families of adults with retardation; they suggested that such groups should be facilitated by parents who have already completed the permanency planning process. Recently, Smith and Kirchner (1994) reported a case study of a psychoeducational support group that encompassed the following objectives: informing parents of the residential, financial, and legal aspects of permanency planning; promoting acceptance of the inevitable relinquishment of care to others; teaching coping skills relevant to the impact of age-related changes on caregiving; encouraging use of formal services; and instilling solidarity among participants. They found that the program was rated to be the most useful by participants (as well as by the professional leaders) in terms of providing planning information and allowing parents to express mutual concerns.

Permanency Planning Workshops. For some families that may either be reluctant to become involved with support groups or consider them superfluous to their need for information alone, permanency planning workshops may be an appropriate intervention. Ruth Roberts (personal communication,

April 1992), for example, found that a considerable number of older families who were previously unknown to formal service providers attended permanency planning workshops that were conducted outside the auspices of the developmental disabilities service network. The value of permanency planning workshops was further suggested by Heller and Factor's (1991) finding that nearly half of the older families they surveyed lacked information on residential programs and that more than one third needed information on establishing guardianships and making future financial arrangements for their family member with disabilities.

Family Counseling

Demand for counseling with this target population was clearly revealed in a study by Caserta, Connelly, Lund, and Poulton (1987), in which 20% of older caregivers of adults with lifelong disabilities reported a need for family counseling, and a third of the sample expressed a need for personal counseling. As Jennings (1987) noted, the counseling needs of aging families "most often involve providing for the future care and protection of dependent adult children as they face their own issues of decreasing health and eventual death" (p. 432). However, some families may also require counseling regarding the maladaptive behavior of the relative or the poor health of family members (M. Seltzer, et al., 1991). Counseling with older families should also "include an assessment of the parents' informal social network resources to identify the type and degree of potential future assistance that might be available to the child from family members, friends, and neighbors" (Kaufman et al., 1991, pp. 299-300).

Family counseling may be especially valuable in enabling aging families to

> accept the reality that a secure, residential placement may be impossible to insure absolutely, and, instead, to motivate family members to remain involved with their elderly mentally retarded relative on an ongoing basis to monitor the quality and appropriateness of the residential placement. (Seltzer & Seltzer, 1985, p. 105)

Even when it is impossible to involve all relevant family members, friends, and neighbors in counseling directly, it is still important for counselors to recognize their significance to the family system at hand. It is especially crucial for the counselor to ascertain, as straightforwardly as possible, the views of the family member with a lifelong disability. In this manner, family practitioners can truly support the growing belief that the needs of people with disabilities can be met more effectively when their unique personalities, skills, and personal choices are an integral part of plans to improve their quality of life or secure their future (for a relevant intervention, see Sutton, Heller, Sterns, Factor, & Miklos, 1994).

Finally, in helping these families, counselors must be cognizant of personal feelings regarding both their own aging and the reluctance of older parents to let go of their son or daughter with a lifelong disability. Through in-depth interviews with case managers, for example, we observed overt hostility toward older parents because of a perceived selfishness for not making future plans. As one practitioner caustically remarked: "I'll be ready to leave the office late Friday afternoon when a son or daughter is dropped off after the death of the last parent." Unless counselors can be patient, appreciate the plight of these families, tolerate their pain and anger toward the service system, and cope with their own negative feelings toward parents' reluctance to make plans, they cannot act in their best interest.

CASE EXAMPLE

A college graduate and former teacher, Mrs. Kane is a 91-year-old widow who lives with her only child, Suzie, a 56-year-old woman with severe mental retardation. Because the family moved from Maine to Florida 10 years before Mr. Kane's death, this mother and daughter have no relatives nearby to assist them.

After giving birth to Suzie, Mrs. Kane had to choose between rearing her at home or placing her in a large, dismal residential facility. She chose to quit teaching and to devote herself to her daughter. Suzie never went to school nor did she use any of the day care programs that finally became available when Suzie was in her 30s. Mrs. Kane feels that Suzie may be too set in her ways to now start attending day programs, and she is very uncomfortable about any potential sexual behaviors that Suzie might experience there. Also, as Mrs. Kane often says: "What can day programs offer my child that I haven't already taught her?"

Mrs. Kane's only contact with the formal service system is with a case manager from the county social service agency who arranged for a homemaker service to assist with daily chores that are becoming increasingly difficult for her to perform. As a first step toward the inevitable separation, the case manager has brought up the benefits of Suzie attending a day program. But this worker knows all too well that, because Mrs. Kane has become so dependent on Suzie for companionship, the discussions must go slowly and trust must be firmly established before day programming becomes a real possibility. To date, Suzie continues to stay at home watching TV and occasionally helping with simple housework.

During regular chats with Mrs. Kane in her home over coffee, the worker gently steers the conversation whenever possible toward Mrs. Kane's aging. However, this has been difficult because Mrs. Kane thinks of herself as being "middle-aged" and refuses to acknowledge having become old. Also, as Mrs. Kane says: "My whole life is centered on my daughter and she couldn't survive without me. Mental retardation is God's true test of my love."

On one occasion when the worker mentioned the possibility of participating in a support group with other older parents, Mrs. Kane vehemently said: "I don't need anyone telling us how to live. Let them take care of their children and I'll take care of Suzie." Yet, on a recent visit, the worker was surprised when Mrs. Kane expressed sudden concern over an incident where she passed out in her bathroom. "What would have happened to Suzie if I had died in there," she exclaimed. Recognizing this as an opportunity to bring up permanency planning arrangements, the worker mentioned an upcoming one-day planning workshop for older parents. Although initially resistant to the idea of attending, Mrs. Kane asked the worker several weeks later for more information about the workshop.

Discussion Questions

1. What cohort influences are obvious in the case example?
2. In what ways has Mrs. Kane's behavior put Suzie at risk?
3. What do you think Mrs. Kane's reaction would be if the case manager were to suggest that she seek personal counseling to face her own death and plan for Suzie's future?

6

Challenging Biases Against
Families of Older Gays and Lesbians

ELISE M. FULLMER

Demographic changes in the United States in the 1980s and 1990s have required that society recognize and embrace the reality of multicultural diversity. There is increasing attention to cross-cultural factors, which include differences not only of ethnicity (see Chapter 10, this volume), but also of gender and sexual orientation. As stereotypes about sexual orientation are challenged and as increasing diversity in family forms is accepted, perceptions of the family are expanding to include the interpersonal relationships of older lesbians, gay men, and bisexuals. The purpose of this chapter is to describe alternative definitions of family and the parameters of family membership from the perspective of older lesbians and gay men and to point out the implications for practice and policy.

Background

Thought regarding the nature of the family has undergone a metamorphosis during the last 30 years. Establishing and recognizing forms of family among older lesbians and gay men has been complicated by oppression. Services for older lesbians and gay men are still in their infancy. Until recently, information about the history of the lesbian and gay communities, and various cultures within them, generally has not been available to most gay and lesbian people except through sources that were clearly antihomosexual. Particularly for the oldest lesbians and gay men, few if any positive role models for coupling, aging, or creating alternatives to traditional family structures have been available. Gay or lesbian individuals may be the only gay or lesbian person in their family of origin, and they may have had to resolve their identity issues in isolation from others like themselves. Furthermore, because heterosexual models of family have predominated, and because of overt and legally sanctioned discrimination, lesbians and gay men have had to be creative in establishing their own social networks. Often these social networks, particularly for the oldest gay and lesbian people, have been close knit and shrouded in secrecy (see, for example, Adelman, 1986; Clunis & Green, 1988). This is one reason that representative samples of gay and lesbian people have been difficult to obtain and that research on coupling and the formation of families among older lesbians and gay men is noticeably lacking.

Elaboration of Family Issues

DEFINING FAMILY WITHIN
THE LESBIAN AND GAY COMMUNITIES

The definition of family and who is considered a family member in the gay and lesbian community is very diverse. In general, what must be stressed about the intimate relationships, families, and social networks of older lesbians and gay men is that there is no single pattern in the formation and composition of lesbian and gay families. For lesbians and gays of all ages, "family" has come to mean a variety of arrangements, from networks of people not biologically related who provide emotional and/or tangible support to one another to same-gender couples who have children through adoption, a previous heterosexual marriage, or natural or artificial insemination. Although many people identify themselves as lesbian or gay as early as preadolescence, other people may not identify themselves as lesbian or gay or seek same-sex partners until their 40s, 50s, or later (see, for example, Kehoe, 1989). People coming out in later life must integrate themselves into a new culture and may be faced with some of the same tasks in later life that are typical of adolescents and young adults, including issues related to expressing sexuality, dating, and forming relationships. The age and life stage at which a person identifies as gay or lesbian will likely influence family structure and support networks. Gay or lesbian individuals probably will be one of the only gay or lesbian people in their family of origin, and are likely to depend on supports outside of the biological family for validation.

Nevertheless Kimmel (1992) has identified the three most typical family types within which lesbians and gay men grow older. These include (a) long-term committed relationships or "companionships"; (b) social networks of friends, significant others and selected biological family members who provide mutual support of various kinds; and (c) special roles in their family of origin that reflect their unique social position.

Patterns in forming intimate relationships also vary, but typically in all age groups and with both men and women, a preference for a long-term committed relationship with one other person is expressed (see, for example, Bell & Weinberg, 1978; Kehoe, 1989), and long-term committed relationships seem to be more common than is typically assumed (Kimmel, 1992). This is not surprising, given that a committed relationship with one other person is the accepted norm in the dominant culture. Some lesbians and gay men have maintained long-term heterosexual relationships with an opposite sex spouse and at the same time balanced single or multiple relationships with same-sex partners (Berger, 1982; Humphreys, 1970; Kehoe, 1989).

Kimmel's categories generally describe some aspects of family life among lesbians and gay men, but there are probably substantial differences between men and women in the nature of their intimate relationships, their support networks, and the roles that they play in their families of origin because of gender role socialization and socially prescribed gender role stereotypes and economic differences between women and men. For this reason it does not make sense to generalize across lesbian and gay populations. For example, women in our society are socialized and encouraged to remain connected and interdependent with their family of origin and are more likely to have raised children (see, for example, Turner, Scadden, & Harris, 1985), whereas males are socialized and encouraged to be more independent from biological family. Furthermore, responsibilities for caregiving are more likely to be assumed by women rather than men (see, for example, Kazak & Marvin, 1984; Wilkin, 1979).

Also, because women generally make less money than men, they may be more economically dependent on family and likely to be poorer as they age. Gay men, on the other hand, may on average be in a better position to provide occupational and financial support to biological family members and to support themselves independently because of higher occupational status and earning ability and generally higher levels of retirement income.

The nature of long-term relationships also differs by gender. Researchers and family therapists working with lesbian and gay couples have reported some differences in the intimate relationships of lesbians and gay men. Women, for example, may merge identities (Chodorow, 1978) and may be more likely to equate the expression of sexuality with love (Decker, 1985). Male couples, on the other hand, may be more inclined to emphasize independence, competitiveness, and self-control more than relationship skills and to be able to express their sexuality without legitimation (see, for example, Chodorow, 1978; Decker, 1985; McCandlish, 1985; Peplau, 1981). Older lesbians, who are probably more dependent on combined incomes for support, may be more tied economically as well.

The social networks of lesbians and gay men are somewhat different. There is some evidence that the attitude toward intergenerational association is more positive among lesbians. Moreover, the frequency of interaction between older and younger lesbians may be higher than intergenerational contact between older and younger gay men (Fullmer & Eastland, 1993). Furthermore, because women are more likely than men to raise and care for children, it makes sense that older lesbian families are more likely to include or to have contact with adult offspring. With increasing opportunities for gay couples to adopt children and for men to gain custody of children from a previous marriage, this family form may be even more common among gay male couples and will probably affect the composition of aging gay families in future generations.

In addition to taking into account gender differences within Kimmel's descriptions of aging lesbian, gay, and bisexual families, it is also important to make a distinction between issues related to family of origin and issues of families that include offspring. Both of these family forms are included in Kimmel's descriptions of family of origin, and yet the two family compositions are fundamentally different in terms of the role that a gay, lesbian, or bisexual family member might play. Lesbians, gay men, and bisexuals with offspring become grandparents and may devote more of their time and resources to their offspring and grandchildren or may be more dependent on these family members for support. Older lesbian, gay, and bisexual people with offspring may have felt a greater need to conceal their identity in order to protect their offspring from social stigma, a factor that could influence their connectedness to the lesbian, gay, and bisexual community, which could affect their involvement in and knowledge of the community as they age. For these reasons, it makes sense to make a distinction between families that include offspring and relationships with family of origin.

Perhaps one of the most salient questions concerning the families of older lesbians and gay men is how their needs differ from heterosexual families. In many ways the families of older lesbian and gay people possess the same strengths and deal with the same issues and challenges common to most families with older members. Most older lesbians and gay men, like most elderly people, live independently and do not become incapacitated and dependent. Older gay men and lesbians also must face the life changes and events generally common to aging individuals: declining income; changes in role status; retirement; death of parents, siblings, and friends; changes in physical health status; and other issues related to grief and loss. Like other stigmatized minorities, gays and lesbians also must face prejudice and discrimination based on sexual orientation. Unlike racial and ethnic minorities, gay or lesbian individuals probably will be one of the only gay or lesbian people in their family of origin; for this reason, it is impossible to consider older homosexuals and the usual problems associated with aging outside of the biased social context and unique social position in which they live. The special problems and concerns that the families of older lesbians and gay men face are primarily due to a social and institutional bias against a same-sex sexual orientation rather than to deficiencies in the families of older lesbians and gay men.

In general, social and institutional bias against homosexuals and their families has implications throughout the life span development of both the individual and the family, and the effects of this bias can be compounded in old age when a reliance on formal social service agencies may become more necessary and when people are most likely to become isolated due to illness and the death of partners and friends.

Older gays and lesbians have learned through a lifetime of experience that they will likely be discriminated against if it is known that they are homosexual. It is common in our society to typify older gay men and lesbians as pathetic and lonely "dirty old men" or "child molesters," as "old maids" or as "drag queens." In addition, service providers for the aged in organizations such as nursing homes, hospitals, and senior citizen centers make the assumption that their clients are heterosexual and may be blind to the significant relationships that form the families of lesbians and gay men. Elderly lesbians and gay men may be unwilling to correct misconceptions because they fear stigmatization. In this way older lesbians and gays and their families become invisible within the service system, and these families may avoid using the formal service system (see, for example, Kehoe, 1989) because their invisibility makes it impossible to take into account their significant interpersonal relationships and to give them the support they need.

Another important influence on the families of older lesbians and gay men is loss and grief that take place in an environment of fear. Identifying oneself as homosexual has implications at any stage of life, and this process of coming out has been written about by a number of authors (see, for example, Coleman, 1985; Moses & Hawkins, 1982). People coming out later in life must integrate themselves into a new culture and may be faced with some of the same tasks in later life that are typical of adolescents and young adults. But unlike adolescents, older lesbians, gay men, and bisexuals who are coming out must integrate their past lives into the coming out process. This process may involve giving up a part of their previously held identity as a heterosexual and coping with their own resulting grief and the grief of heterosexual family members. The process is complicated by the stigma attached to homosexuality, because the person coming out and his or her family may be inhibited from sharing their grief with others and so grieving can become a solitary process. Older people who are "coming out" for the first time also may risk being ostracized from offspring and family of origin at a stage in life when these supports may be needed most.

Another type of loss an older lesbian or gay person may face is the illness or death of a partner or other family member. Our culture has built-in mechanisms to help people cope with the loss of an intimate relationship. Typically, a spouse and other significant family members are involved in making funeral arrangements, and a formal period of grieving is socially acknowledged during which church, family, and friends help the survivors to cope with their loss. These supports may not be in place for lesbian and gay survivors or their families.

First, biological families may take the primary responsibility for making funeral and other arrangements because the relationship between same-sex companions is not acknowledged and, therefore, there is little public recognition of the relationship that existed or the extent of the loss experienced by the surviving companion. In some instances the surviving companion of a same-sex relationship may be prohibited by the biological family from attending the funeral of his or her partner. The surviving companion has no formal mechanism for grieving and may not even be able to express grief openly. Second, in heterosexual communities, churches and family of origin members, in particular, may be a source of emotional comfort and tangible help to a survivor. Gay and lesbian couples and their families may be alienated from institutions such as churches because many religious organizations have been very vocal in their condemnation of homosexuality; individuals and families may be alienated from family of origin. Also, some older homosexual couples live in isolation, even from the lesbian and gay community (Clunis & Green, 1988; Lyon & Martin, 1979), and therefore help from formal and informal sources may be lacking altogether.

LONG-TERM COMMITTED RELATIONSHIPS

One of the myths about lesbians and gay men is that the most important aspect of their personality is their sexuality. This myth leads to an assumption that gays and lesbians are promiscuous and unable to maintain stable relationships. At the same time, we prefer in our society to think of older people as not sexual, which leads to stereotypes of older gay men and lesbians as pathetic and lonely. Although the effects of these stereotypes on older lesbians and gays are subtle, when internalized they are likely to influence self-concept and decrease the value that gay and lesbian couples place on their own relationships (see, for example, Decker, 1985).

Contrary to popular stereotypes of the instability of gay and lesbian relationships, lesbians and gay men do have long-term committed relationships, and relationship quality is not different than with heterosexual couples (see, for example, Kurdek & Schmitt, 1986). Long-term relationships for many older lesbians and gay men can provide nurturance, support, acceptance, a shared sense of history, and memories; for some, such relationships are a buffer against a condemning world (see, for example, Clunis & Green, 1988). However, the nature of these relationships may differ by the gender of the same-sex couple. Women are socialized to be less aggressive sexually, to be monogamous, and to be nurturers, whereas men are socialized to be aggressive sexually, to be independent and autonomous, and to be competitive. When two people of the same gender are involved in an intimate relationship, the dynamics between them may be different from opposite-sex couples. For example, some therapists report that among gay and lesbian couples seeking therapy, women may find themselves overinvolved in each other's lives, whereas men may have problems with competitiveness in their relationships (see, for example, McCandlish, 1985).

In later life, gender socialization may also have differing implications for men and women in terms of their ability to socialize and to form intimate relationships. Among both lesbians and gay men, age stratification has been observed within some segments of the lesbian and gay communities (Berger, 1982; Lee, 1988; Lyon & Martin, 1979; Poor, 1982), and authors discuss the apparent invisibility of older gays and lesbians at community functions and meeting places. Furthermore, lesbians may be more willing than gay men to socialize and form intimate relationships intergenerationally (Fullmer & Eastland, 1993). Regardless of willingness, studies suggest that intimate relationships are usually formed between people who are within 10 years in age (Bell & Weinberg, 1978; Berger, 1982; Harry & Devall, 1978; Kehoe, 1989). Older lesbians and gay men who do not have a companion and who wish to find a partner may have few options for meeting people their own age, so they are limited to the people whom they already know, a group that will diminish as the individual ages. Furthermore, age stratification within the community probably becomes self-perpetuating because older people are not represented and do not feel welcome at community meeting places and so do not return.

There are a number of legal issues that directly affect the well-being of older gay and lesbian couples. Acting on a same-sex sexual orientation is illegal and punishable by law in many states, and there is no equivalent of marriage for same-sex partners. The criminal status of homosexual behavior and the unavailability of a legal bond between same-sex partners makes gays and lesbians vulnerable.

Retirement Income and Housing. Most organizations do not allow homosexuals to include their partners on health policies. Furthermore, employer-purchased life insurance policies often exclude "unrelated" people as beneficiaries. Housing can also be difficult for older same-sex couples. For example, public retirement housing often restricts "unrelated adults" from living together, and nursing homes and private retirement centers make the assumption that their residents are heterosexual and structure activities and social events based on this assumption.

Hospitalization. Hospitals often have a policy with seriously ill patients that only "immediate family members" are allowed to make decisions about care and only immediate family members are allowed to visit. *Immediate family* is usually defined by hospitals as a husband or wife, or a biological family member, a definition that excludes same-sex partners. For same-sex couples, the implications of these policies can be enormous. A same-sex partner with a hospitalized companion may be in the best position to understand the wishes and needs of the person hospitalized and yet be denied input into decisions regarding the companion's treatment. Both same-sex partners can be denied the emotional support that could be available from one another because they are separated, and this situation can lead to added feelings of stress, loneliness, and powerlessness.

Inheritance. Even when same-sex couples have well-planned strategies for ensuring inheritance, problems may arise. It is not uncommon for biological family members to contest a will that names a same-sex partner as the beneficiary and to win because there is no legally defined spousal relationship between same-sex partners. When properties are held in common, the biological family can force the sale of the property so that assets can be divided.

Social Bonds and Support Systems as Families of Choice. At the time when many older lesbians and gay men were becoming aware of their sexual orientation, social sanctions were much stronger and the risks of losing jobs and custody of children much greater. For this reason, many older lesbians and gay men developed close knit and hidden support networks, which have endured and serve family functions: for example, emotional and tangible support, nurturance, and acceptance. These guarded social networks may in part account for the age stratification and for the invisibility of older gays and lesbians within the gay and lesbian communities. An additional factor that probably adds to the exclusiveness of these support networks is a tendency among some gay men and lesbians to retain their ex-lovers as friends; these friendships are valued resources (see, for example, Becker, 1988). Although these support networks can provide a strong base of support for older lesbians and gay men, they also may serve to isolate the people within them. When these systems are closed to newcomers, isolation will increase as members of the network become ill or die. Another important concern is that age stratification and closed social networks deprive all age groups of a variety of role models for living, constructing families, and aging.

Although there may be a tendency for the support networks of older lesbians and gay men to be composed of people of the same gender (Lipman, 1986), many older lesbians and gay men do socialize and provide support for one another. In my own research with older lesbians and gay men, a number of respondents reported that not only had they maintained long-term friendships with opposite-sex homosexual friends but also that these friendships were sometimes used as a mutual cover to hide one's sexual orientation and to avoid stigmatization and discrimination. One respondent reported a friendship between herself and a gay man that had lasted more than 40 years. Both people were retired but had been professionals at conservative companies; in order to hide their sexual orientation they would attend business and social functions together, posing as a heterosexual couple.

The importance of a supportive social network or "chosen" family cannot be overemphasized. When people have been rejected by their biological families or when gay or lesbian identity is extremely hidden, support networks may be particularly crucial and can be made up of friends, selected family members, and companions. The important point is that the people who make up these networks are specifically selected, and the relationships are not mandated by social institutions or biology. These networks provide a source of support for and identification with the lesbian and gay subcultures and serve to sanction and validate relationships and life choices. Validation and support in a larger culture that condemns same-sex relationships may not be available from any other source beyond a person's family of choice (Clunis & Green, 1988).

BIOLOGICAL FAMILY

When biological families are supportive they can be an important resource for older lesbians and gay men; as Clunis and Green (1988) discuss, this may be particularly true for racial and ethnic minorities who have needed protection against a hostile mainstream society. Gays and lesbians must decide to whom in their biological families they will disclose their sexual orientation, and they must be prepared for negative reactions and rejection. As discussed earlier, many older gay men and lesbians may have made the choice not to disclose their sexual orientation to biological family members because of the potential risks, and they may alter their lives substantially in order to hide their sexual orientation from biological family members. For example, some lesbian and gay couples may live in separate residences in order to avoid suspicion and maintain relationships with biological family. Not disclosing to family also carries consequences because of the need to live a double identity. The stress involved in hiding one's sexual orientation may eventually lead to withdrawing from biological family members altogether.

Reactions of family members when gays and lesbians choose to disclose can vary from outright hostility or simply a lack of recognition or acknowledgment of sexual orientation to complete and open acceptance of a family member (Strommen, 1989). Parents and Friends of Lesbian and Gays (PFLAG) is a national organization designed as a support group and social action group; it is composed primarily of the biological family members of lesbians and gay men. Its purpose is to support families in the process of accepting a family member's sexual orientation and to combat discrimination against lesbians and gay men. Many PFLAG members are the parents, siblings, and children of older lesbians and gay men, who make an active effort to support gay and lesbian family members publicly and privately.

Kimmel (1992) also points out that gay men and lesbians may have a unique social position in their family of origin. As an "unmarried" member of the family, a person may be called upon to perform tasks such as taking on the role of caregiver for an aged parent or providing vocational, educational, financial, or counseling support to biological family members. Little attention has been paid by researchers to the roles that lesbians and gay men play, particularly as caregivers, but as mentioned earlier, the likelihood that the nature of these roles will differ between lesbians and gay men is probably great. Finally, another area in need of exploration is the role that families of origin and families of choice play in caregiving to elderly lesbians and gay men.

RELATIONSHIPS WITH CHILDREN

As noted by Hunt and Hunt (1977), many divorced men and women with children have entered the gay and lesbian communities rather than pursuing heterosexual relationships. In recent years, a number of studies have been made of the fathering practices of gay men. There are fewer studies of lesbian mothers, and these studies have focused primarily on younger, white, middle-class populations. For older lesbians and gay men, relationships with adult offspring are likely to be influenced by the social context and time period in which they reared their children. Some studies suggest, for example, that when children are told of their parent's homosexuality at an early age, they are more tolerant (Turner et al., 1985), and yet older lesbians and gay men raised their children at a time when disclosure was much more difficult and the consequences of disclosure potentially more devastating, a factor that likely inhibited disclosure to children at an early age.

In a review of the literature on gay fathers, Bozett (1989) compared studies of the parenting practices of lesbians and gay men and concluded that, in general, studies suggest that gay fathers have more difficulty than lesbian mothers in disclosing their gay identity to their children. Children's reactions to a disclosure of homosexuality are usually absent or positive, but negative reactions more often are reported by gay fathers than by lesbian mothers. Lesbian mothers are more likely than gay fathers to have custody of their children. Although gay fathers usually do not have physical custody of their children, gay fathers tend to maintain consistent contact with their children.

Studies of parent/offspring relationships among older gay men and lesbians are more limited. Kehoe (1989) studied 27 older lesbians who had married and had had children. Kehoe calls these women "late bloomers," because they recognized or acted on their same-sex sexual orientation later in life. Apparently those mothers who admitted their sexual orientation to their children "were often later ostracized by their own adult nongay children" (p. 30). An examination of the tables included in Kehoe's book indicates that 78% of the mothers never saw at least one son and 72% never saw at least one daughter. (Because these figures include deceased children, it is difficult to interpret the results.) About 63% of the mothers saw a daughter at least once a month, and 9% saw a son at least once a month. Kehoe noted that there were substantial offspring gender differences in frequency of contact with their lesbian mothers.

Berger (1982), in a study of older gay men, asked questions about biological family relationships, but he did not report his findings. In the interview section of the book, some of the men report on these relationships. For example, one man, Matthew, was in a heterosexual relationship but lived apart from his wife. Matthew reported that his older son had talked to him about gay friends and that his son had made derogatory remarks about gay people. The same subject also stated that his wife did not know of his homosexuality but suspected it and watched his behavior when he was around other men. William, another of Berger's respondents, recounted a more positive relationship with his son, who knew he was gay. He reported that his son seemed "genuinely pleased about the changes I was experiencing " (p. 54), changes related to leaving his wife and moving in with a man.

In all likelihood adult children's responses to and connectedness with their older lesbian or gay parents are probably dependent on a number of factors, including, for example, the relationship of the parent and adult child prior to disclosure and the gender of the offspring and parent (Bozett, 1989). It seems reasonable to suggest that gay men and lesbians may in some cases be less concerned with the exposure of their homosexuality as they age because their children are grown and family members such as parents may be deceased. However, the extent to which concealment of homosexuality increases or decreases with factors such as gender, age, and differences between age cohorts are issues still in need of exploration.

There may be benefits to psychological well-being when parents disclose their identity to their adult children and other significant people in their lives (Berger, 1982; Bozett, 1989; Kehoe, 1989) because they are released from the tension of living a dual identity. At the same time, there are also substantial risks, including the potential for alienation from children, grandchildren, and other family members at a time when these supports may be needed most.

Directions for Practice and Policy

One of the most important issues, regardless of the level of intervention, is the attitude of the professional. Negative stereotypes about older gay and lesbian people and their families are pervasive and when these stereotypes are internalized they affect self-esteem and family functioning as well as a person's ability to act on his or her own behalf. Negative stereotypes also work at larger systems levels to keep gay and lesbian people oppressed. In order for practitioners not to reinforce internalized or external negative beliefs, it is important that practitioners examine their own attitudes about homosexuality and work to eliminate biases where they exist. In this way, they can actively combat stereotypes rather than reinforce them.

LEGAL AND POLICY INTERVENTIONS
WITH OLDER LESBIANS AND GAY FAMILIES

One important role that professionals can play to assist lesbian and gay families is a facilitator for legal planning. Some older gays and lesbians may be unaware of the legal problems that they may face in retirement, housing, inheritance, and hospitalization. Although these problems cannot be completely eliminated under the current legal system, some precautions can be taken. For example, a living will that specifically states the wishes of the individuals should be in place, and some hospitals are more lenient than others with regard to visitation rights. These issues can be explored prior to a crisis situation so that some plan is in place for care, treatment, and preferred place of hospitalization.

In many areas competent attorneys are available who are familiar with the legal issues related to homosexual partnerships and inheritance. For example, joint tenancies may eliminate the need for a partner to sell a mutually owned home when his or her mate dies because the property will automatically go to a surviving partner. Practitioners should be aware of attorneys who can competently and compassionately deal with the legal issues faced by older gays and lesbians and should help clients to ensure that these plans are in place.

A second important role for professionals is as an advocate. In this role, practitioners work to eliminate the institutional bias and discrimination that fuels the problems at every other level. Unlike other minorities in the United States, lesbians and gay men can still be denied their civil rights. In the majority of states and municipalities, it is still legal to deny homosexuals resources such as housing and employment because of their sexual orientation. In fact, in many areas, homosexual acts between consenting adults are a criminal offense punishable by law. Furthermore, institutions such as marriage, which establish a legal relationship between partners and on which resources and services are based, are denied to same-sex couples.

The organizational policies of social service agencies, hospitals, insurance companies, educational institutions, and employers that discriminate against older same-sex couples must be changed to include these family forms. Pressure to change these policies can come from within the organization when practitioners take it on themselves to change discriminatory practices and educate fellow employees and administrators in their own organizations. Attitudinal changes can also occur if accurate information about older gays and lesbians is included as a regular part of both academic curricula and in-service training in agencies.

More globally, older lesbian and gay families must be included in local, state, and national policies as a protected minority group whose civil rights are constitutionally protected. Until the legal status of gays and lesbians is changed, little real equity in service provisions and other resources can be achieved, and older lesbian and gay families will continue to be denied the basic wherewithal to achieve psychological security, well-being, and the forming and nurturing of families.

COMMUNITY INTERVENTIONS

A third type of role that practitioners can play is as resource builders and linkers or as mediators. To be effective, practitioners must develop an understanding of the lesbian and gay communities and the resources that exist within them. These resources may vary from community to community, and professionals may need to be resourceful and to develop supports where none exist. Older people, like all of us, need others to survive, and these important interpersonal relationships include companions, friends, and relatives. However, older gays and lesbians may be estranged from biological families and not well connected to the gay and lesbian community. Therefore one of the most important interventions at this level is to build these natural support networks when they do not exist. In order to establish trust and communication, it is necessary for professionals to be empathetic and understanding in a nonjudgmental way and to be sensitive to the diversity that exists among the families of older lesbians and gay men. Few, if any, assumptions can be made about the nature, composition, or functioning of any single family, and each must be analyzed for its own strengths and dysfunctions. Older gay men and lesbians will display a variety of attitudes about using mainstream services, and they may or may not wish to have their sexual orientation revealed to service agencies.

Maguire (1983) identifies three stages of intervention in building on social supports: identification, analysis, and linking. Identification involves determining the size, relationships, and resources that are available in the existing network. The second stage is analyzing how well the client's emotional and physical needs are being met. The third stage involves expanding, strengthening, or creating linkages and social supports where they have not existed previously. For older lesbians and gay men, this third stage could, for example, involve connecting an older lesbian or gay person to an existing support group for older lesbians and gays or creating a support group of this kind. On the other hand, because there is some evidence to suggest that both intergenerational supports and heterogeneous supports may enhance the well-being of older lesbians and gay men (Adelman, 1980; Berger, 1982), special efforts may be needed to integrate older lesbians and gays into existing services for younger lesbians and gays and into traditional service networks. Resources for older homosexuals in many communities are very limited, and across the country only a handful of organizations exist specifically to meet the needs of older homosexuals. For this reason, professionals cannot rely on established supports. It may be necessary to sensitize administrators to the special needs and concerns of lesbian and gay clients and to the importance of addressing particular deficits in services and other resources.

FAMILY COUNSELING
AND THERAPY INTERVENTIONS

A fourth role that practitioners can play is that of family counselor or therapist. The families of older lesbians and gay men can and do experience difficulties that require counseling, but it is important to remember that dynamics in the families of older lesbians and gay men are influenced by the social pressures that they face. Certain aspects of these family systems may be an adaptive response to a hostile environment. For example, with regard to same-sex relationships, Decker (1985) notes the following:

> Too often clinicians automatically assume that problems around forming boundaries in same-sex couples indicate intrapsychic pathology resulting from homosexuality per se rather than taking into account how these difficulties may be related to normal adaptational mechanisms of all same-sex relationships. This does not necessarily mean that the clinician should engage in "blaming society" therapy or encourage politicizing of the issue of sexual preference when it is being used to avoid dealing with issues of intimacy and separation/individuation or the pain engendered by nonrecognition or total rejection by family, co-workers, or friends. (pp. 49-50)

One of the main points that Decker makes is that in order for therapists to be authentic and create a constructive helping relationship with older lesbian and gay families, they must have a basic belief in the worth of the family and a belief that a troubled lesbian or gay family can make changes for the better.

Decker also observes that the training and knowledge base of clinicians is very important. Clinicians must have a thorough grounding in psychodynamic and family systems principles, as well as an understanding of atypical socialization and stigmatization as they relate to identity problems and coming out of lesbian and gay people. Related to this idea, Stein (1988) observes: "The outcomes of psychotherapy for a gay person may be significantly affected by the failure of a therapist to have any knowledge about homosexuality or homosexual persons outside of a framework of pathology" (p. 83).

Systems theory is particularly useful both for working with the families of older gays and lesbians and for taking into account the environmental aspects that so heavily influence disenfranchised groups such as the families of older lesbians and gay men. Systems theory is also useful for organizing and using theories and research related to the families of older lesbians and gay men in a way that allows nonnormative models of relationships and family structures.

Therapy with the families of older gay men and lesbians involves general issues important to the practice of therapy, as well as issues specific to older gay men and lesbians, issues that directly affect the client-therapist relationship. For example, therapists should be aware that clients go through a sequence of stages related to discovering and accepting their same-sex sexual orientation, and they may enter therapy seeking help with this process. During this process they must be helped to explore their fears, to examine stereotypes and myths, and to acknowledge their same-sex identity not only to themselves but also to their social network (Cabaj, 1988). The stages of coming out can be applied at the individual, dyadic, or family level and are not necessarily sequential. Furthermore, each stage may be dealt with repeatedly, depending on an individual's particular circumstances. One model of the coming out process involves self-recognition, disclosure to others, socializing with other gay people, positive self-identification, and integration and acceptance (McWhirter & Mattison, 1984). As discussed earlier, older lesbians and gay men and members of their families may or may not have dealt with issues related to accepting their identity and, therefore, it cannot be assumed that these issues are resolved simply because of the age of the person involved.

Beyond these general clinical issues in dealing with the families of older lesbians and gay men, there are specific interventions related to the death of a companion, internalized negative stereotypes, and problems with boundaries that clinicians may encounter when dealing with the families of older lesbians and gay men.

Death of a Companion. Worden (1982) discusses three phases of the mourning process that are experienced by the mourning partner, including shock and denial, anger and depression, and moving on. Completion of the first phase, shock and denial, requires that the person accept the death of the companion. In the second phase, anger and depression, the task is to experience the grief and pain associated with the loss. In the third phase, moving on, the task is to be able to invest in other people and relationships. Recognizing these phases and helping survivors to move on can be an important and challenging issue. The last phase is particularly important for people who have become isolated in a closed support network that is slowly diminishing. Moving on may require the therapist to help clients learn social skills and acquire knowledge of the community that will enable them to reach out to others.

Internalizing Negative Stereotypes. It is not likely that people will seek therapy in order to deal with the internalization of negative stereotypes. Rather, it is more likely that they will seek help for other issues that are partly or fully a consequence of internalizing negative stereotypes. Therapists note a wide range of problems that are partially caused or are exacerbated through the internalization of negative stereotypes, including sexual dysfunction (Loulan, 1984) and isolation (Decker, 1985). The internalization process has been described in some of its permutations as a type of dysfunctional defense mechanism (Margolies, Becker, & Jackson-Brewer, 1987). In dealing with issues related to internalizing negative stereotypes, therapists can work to correct misconceptions about being lesbian or gay and can serve as a role model of someone who accepts, respects, and values the families of older lesbians and gay men.

Boundaries. Family boundaries can be problematic if they are too open and do not shield members from the environment or too closed and do not allow new resources into the system. Closed boundaries often occur as older lesbian and gay families try to insulate themselves from bias and negative reactions. On the other hand, families can become too open when roles and relationships within the family are not clearly defined because of a lack of sanctioning and the needs and wishes of people outside the family, such as unaccepting friends or family members, take precedence and obstruct the functioning of the family. In dealing with issues related to both the internalization of negative stereotypes and boundary issues, Decker (1985) suggests that:

> Same sex couples need to be helped to distinguish between exogenous and internalized homophobia and to see all the ways in which they may maintain a victim attitude or provoke and perpetuate their social isolation. However, in order to facilitate this process, the therapist must be fully aware and appreciative of the unique psychosocial pressures that same-sex couples face, while helping them to reframe the relationship as one that is inherently worthy of being valued

and capable of being maintained, and not one that is inherently sick and un-workable. (pp. 49-50)

Perhaps one of the most important issues in working with the families of older gay men and lesbians is that these individuals require respect and honesty. The families of older lesbians and gay men have had to develop considerable strengths and skills to deal with their environment and have been creative in forming relationships and families in an environment that provides few if any role models. Working with these families can provide an understanding of family functioning that expands the knowledge base in an era when a diversity of family forms is at its peak.

CASE EXAMPLES

The following case examples illustrate many of the key points made in this chapter.

MARGERY

The search for a family of choice came very late in life for Margery. She reached age 65, retired from a long career as an elementary school teacher, and went into therapy. Margery had spent her whole life hiding and trying to please others. She had married late and stayed married to avoid her mother's criticism of remaining single. She had two daughters, and her love for them kept her going when the rest of her life seemed hopeless. After the death of her mother and her husband, she was facing everything at once. All of her life, she had known that she was attracted to women, but she had not acted on these feelings except for a few very discreet and well-hidden affairs. All of her life, she had feared being found out, being labeled, and losing her job, her family, and her friends. For the last 10 years Margery had cared for her mother, who had died a few months earlier. Now, most of that was over and done, and Margery was left with facing herself.

She had tried to combat her feelings of loneliness by attending the local senior citizens center, but she didn't feel welcome there, didn't feel free to talk about the feelings and issues that were "really" important to her now, and didn't think she could ever find a woman with whom she could connect and grow old. "The women there were mostly interested in finding a man or were mourning for a man whom they had lost," she said. It was her therapist who sent her to a lesbian-owned bookstore and coffee shop.

Margery drove around the block four times before she parked her car, sat patiently for 40 minutes, and then went in. She entered, walked a few steps into the bookstore, and burst into sobs that lasted a very long time. The owner of the bookstore sat with her, served her tea, provided tissues, held her hands, and listened. Within a month, Margery was an enthusiastic volunteer, waiting on other women, spending long hours in talk, going to dinner with friends. She was a new woman, and she wasn't afraid anymore.

JAY

Jay had lost Gary, his partner of 40 years, after Gary suffered complications related to bypass surgery. Gary had been a high-level corporate executive and earned a substantial income; Jay had been self-employed as an artist, and his income was variable and unpredictable. Gary had made Jay the beneficiary of his corporate stock and life insurance, but when Gary died Jay was informed that he was not eligible to receive the stock or the insurance because only "spouses and biological relatives" were eligible. Gary's stock and insurance went to his brother, from whom he had been estranged since adolescence. Jay sold the house and moved in with his sister because he could no longer afford to live in a large house.

Jay and his sister, Martha, had always been close. Jay had supported Martha when her husband left her with a son to care for by herself. Jay had tried to be a role model for his nephew, and Gary had offered to pay tuition when Jay's nephew went to college. Still, even though he was close to his sister, Jay could not imagine life without Gary.

Jay and Gary met in the military. They had been stationed together in Korea. At that time, Gary was in the process of getting a divorce. Jay and Gary's attraction to one another was instant, and they had spent little time apart since their meeting. The beginning of their relationship had been difficult. Gary was from a religious family that looked negatively on divorce. Gary and Jay had spent many years trying to keep a low profile. Eventually, Gary's family did find out. He lost his visitation rights with his daughter, and few of his relatives would even speak to him. Gary and Jay had tried to live their lives unobtrusively and stayed to themselves except for their contact with Jay's sister, Martha. Now Jay felt very alone. Jay had tried to meet other people. He went to a local gay bar that his sister had told him about, but all of the people there seemed very young. He sat in a booth alone, feeling out of place. Jay did not know what to do next. How could he find others his own age who were like him and could understand his loss?

Discussion Questions

1. How do roles and relationships within the family of origin of older gay men differ from those of older lesbians?

2. Identify some techniques that gerontologists and family practitioners might use to examine their own stereotypes and biases regarding the family life of older gay men and lesbians.

3. What preventive intervention strategies could have been implemented by family practitioners and policymakers to avert the distress experienced by the subjects in the two case examples?

PART III

RECOGNIZING
SELECT FAMILY DYNAMICS

The four chapters in this section focus on a number of family dynamics that transcend the specific issues and concerns of aging families addressed in Parts I and II. Practitioners should be aware of such factors as family decision making, intimacy among family members, and the impact of ethnicity on family life. These issues are thematic to all families, and especially for those caring for a frail parent, confronting abuse of an elderly family member, or for older parents assisting their adult children with lifelong disabilities.

Power (Chapter 7) explores intergenerational functioning among families and affirms the belief that issues regarding aging family members overlap many different ages and life stages in families. The four-generation and even five-generation family has become an increasing phenomenon. Power shows that interventions responding to intergenerational issues include diverse kinds of family participants and range from providing information to intense working through of emotional difficulties. Major challenges for practitioners in this helping context are noted, including family cooperation, dealing with family resistance related to any involvement in counseling, attending to the needs of multiple generational family members, and creatively using for selected interventions the entire family setting. Balancing the individuation of each family member and concurrently promoting the interdependence of the individuals is frequently a daunting task for the practitioner.

Bata and Power (Chapter 8) focus on how to facilitate family decision making during the latter half of life. Although health care decision making occurs throughout the life course, this process can take on particular importance when families are caring for an elderly person. The presence of an older family member who has disabilities or is frail can change the quality of family interaction and family affect, such as the quality of affection, warmth, expectations, and support. These changes and complex factors interact to influence customary family decision making styles. In this chapter, Bata and Power identify two major periods in the decision process: (a) anticipation and (b) implementation and adjustment. The practitioner should help family members clarify alternatives and also be aware of any obstacles a family member might have during this process.

In Chapter 9, Whitbourne and Cassidy discuss the role of inti- macy in late-life marriages. The authors explain that when working with older couples, the practitioner might choose to incorporate one of the many techniques that have been found to facilitate intimacy in a close relationship. They emphasize both the practitioner's use of approaches that have been employed to address issues with earlier life stage couples and the importance of the life review technique that is often used with the elderly in situations that may involve the restoration of self-esteem. With the dynamic of intimacy, the process of life review can help the couple understand how their intimacy status has evolved and been affected by both external circumstances and intraindividual developmental processes.

Johnson (Chapter 10) highlights the importance of ethnosensitivity in interventions with families and the older person. In a theme similar to that identified in previous chapters, Johnson exhorts practitioners to eliminate their biases as much as possible and to appreciate, understand, and be sensitive to individuals and families that are unlike themselves. He also introduces the challenge to practitioners to resolve the frequent family conflicts around adherence to ethnic traditions within different family members or generations and to modify these traditions to suit the dominant cultural context without losing the family's basic ethnic integrity. With the other chapters in this book, Chapter 10 emphasizes the belief that older persons live their lives embedded within various relationships, among which the family is a major factor.

7

Understanding Intergenerational
Issues in Aging Families

PAUL W. POWER

One of the major demographic trends that has occurred since 1970 has been the increase in life expectancy (Bahr & Peterson, 1989). This increase is creating a dramatic change in family relationships, as extended three-, four-, and even five-generation family constellations become more common (Hargrave & Anderson, 1992). Intergenerational linkages and their consequences, such as frequency of interaction and conflictual issues between aging parents and their adult offspring, are receiving more attention by researchers and clinicians. This attention has stimulated the development of intergenerational intervention approaches to assist the elderly and their family members to resolve or remediate life adjustment problems. Different types of multigenerational therapies have been created that emphasize that aging usually occurs in an extended family context and that kinship network has a dynamic impact on other persons and the nuclear families (Duffy, 1986). The many problems associated with aging can be alleviated by viewing them in relation to the elder's interactional network.

This chapter will briefly identify the important problems when considering the intergenerational context of older persons and their kinship network; explain the types of existing interventions for families of the elderly, with a specific focus on multigenerational counseling approaches; and then discuss the contributions of selected traditional family counseling approaches and how these different strategies could be incorporated into an approach that responds to intergenerational issues. Special concerns that occur during intervention will also be identified and discussed, followed by the presentation of a case study that will illustrate an intervention approach for family members. An explanation of policy issues implied in family intervention strategies will conclude this chapter. To be noted is that each chapter in this book briefly explains an intervention approach relevant to the issues introduced in the particular chapter. This chapter discusses the generic issues of intervention in an intergenerational family context and highlights both the application of traditional family counseling approaches to families with an elderly person and the specific implications of the applications of these strategies.

Background

Aging is usually a long period of transition that affects the older person, immediate family members, and even the extended family. When viewing aging as an intrapersonal process, such problems and challenges emerge as loneliness; gradual deterioration of physical capacities; adjusting to retirement, widowhood, and perhaps its vague expectations; economic concerns; independence versus dependence difficulties; and possibly the re-experience of feelings of sadness, guilt, and mourning over past failings or the aging process itself (Bahr & Peterson, 1989; Hargrave & Anderson, 1992). When aging is seen in the perspective of an interpersonal process, then such issues arise as grandparenting, perhaps divorce and remarriage after retirement, a change in a long-standing marital relationship, dwindling social support, family relationships between elderly parents and their adult children, the possibility of alternative living arrangements, maintaining a healthy balance between one's own dependency needs and family demands, and changing roles within the family (Greene, 1989; Hargrave & Anderson, 1992; Herr & Weakland, 1979). All of these intra- and interpersonal factors not only affect the older person's immediate available family, but they can have a ripple effect on extended family members. Each factor can generate family conflict for the adult offspring and reverberate throughout much of the kinship network. For example, an elderly couple's economic concerns or increased dependency needs can affect many family members, who might have to become resources to alleviate these problems. When any of these aforementioned personal and family concerns does generate disruptive family conflict, then intervention can often be considered. Although the need for systematic, professional intervention with the elderly and their families has been well-established (Giordano & Beckman, 1985), counseling approaches for working with these populations have not been well-developed; approaches are usually based on the clinician's individual orientation in psychopathology (Rathbone-McCuan, 1991). Unfortunately there are not any established family counseling models that focus exclusively on the recognition of intergenerational family needs when caring for an elderly person and the alleviation of continued family problems that frequently emerge from these unmet needs (Gallagher, 1988; Rathbone-McCuan, 1991). Assisting families to satisfy these needs, as well as concerns that emerge from transitional events associated with aging, is an important target for intervention, necessitating counseling approaches that are not simply adaptations of intervention techniques that have been used with other groups. Traditionally the medical care model has been applied to services for the elderly and their families. But most families who are involved in managing living demands for their elderly parents are not seeking a cure for long-standing family dysfunction, but assistance both to relieve everyday burdens and to learn skills to manage their concerns (Ware & Carper, 1982). The kinds of problems and needs experienced by the aged and their intergenerational families are unique in terms of their time of onset, interpersonal amd material resources available, as well as how these problems experienced by the older person may exacerbate the emotional and family problems of other family members (Giordano & Beckman, 1985). When family members become at all involved with an elderly parent, they are usually engaged in two ongoing processes: (a) performing the tasks necessary to maintain the well-being of their own family members, such as cooking, cleaning, and providing support; and (b) maintaining a family environment necessary to provide assistance when needed for the older person. Performance of duties and maintenance of care are often undertaken amid the varied stressors that accompany meeting the needs of the elderly person. It may be very difficult for family members to take the appropriate responsibility for what they need to do for the older person. In responding to life cycle changes, necessary transitions, and interpersonal difficulties, it may also be quite difficult for the older person himself or herself. Interventions are needed, consequently, that respond both to the needs of the elderly person living in the intergenerational family system and to the family-based dilemmas associated with the aging process.

Elaboration of Family Issues

Although the intervention problems facing both the family and practitioner can originate from the lack of well-documented counseling approaches that focus on the elderly and their families, other issues relevant to family assistance emerge from larger systems or organizations. Obtaining assistance for an elderly person's emotional, financial, and even physical problems places other family members in short- or long-term interaction with specific health care providers or other community resources (Rathbone-McCuan, 1991). But because of the particular problem and its impact on the immediate family system, and possibly the intergenerational system, family needs emerge that may include requesting formal services from larger community agencies. Yet family members usually have little practice in articulating their needs to these organizations, and the organizations themselves may have little awareness of the many family concerns that arise from a significant life difficulty. These larger systems may not know how to deal with the family unit, and an intervention is only suggested when there is perceived severe family dysfunction. But family-oriented practice that is oriented to understanding and possibly remediating difficulties that affect all family members, including intergenerational families, should be increasing because to support family functioning and to resolve early, when possible, the difficulties that engender severe family conflicts, is cost-effective (Doherty & Baird 1983).

However, there are other issues that should also be recognized before an intervention approach is suggested. These include the importance of short-term, situation-oriented assistance, the counseling orientation of the practitioner, and the willingness of family members to participate in time-limited counseling. Families are usually more amenable to outside assistance when they realize that it will be brief and problem focused, in contrast to a long-term therapeutic involvement that targets changing the family as a system. Also the education of clinical practitioners has usually not included training in knowledge of specific family difficulties associated with the aging process and learning skills in how to handle these concerns. A further issue is the changing family needs that develop as there are continual life cycle changes for the older person. A counseling approach that may be appropriate at one point in time may be irrelevant at another time. Family stressors that emerge from financial difficulties and increased emotional burdens can be perceived differently at various stages of an older person's life cycle.

What further builds an understanding of a relevant intervention approach for the elderly living in a multigenerational context is the knowledge of current interventions for families with an elderly person and the understanding of how selected family therapy approaches can be modified to respond to the counseling needs of elderly persons. One way to organize these interventions is to focus on varied forms of assistance, namely, on family life education or providing counseling or psychotherapy for those family members who require it, on increasing social support for the family, or on some combination of these components (Gallagher, 1988). Aronson (1984) has identified some of the most common forms of interventions with elderly clients to be "categorical disease self-help groups, special short-term groups, family role maintenance services, respite service, home care services, financial planning, and public policy formulation. These intervention formats focus on specific issues that confront older families" (p. 57).

Family education includes teaching behavioral management strategies, sharing relevant information, and imparting stress reduction techniques. Educational interventions are especially appropriate for the elderly and their families because they use a wide variety of formats; are found in diverse settings, such as community agencies, churches, schools, and hospitals; and offer an approach to family problems conducted in an atmosphere that may be free from labeling or stigmatization (Giordano & Beckman, 1985). Family life education is the broadest category of educational intervention, providing information and addressing the cognitive domain of participants (L'Abate, 1978). Family life education has only more recently focused directly on the elderly, providing the older person and family members with such courses as myths and realities of aging, death and dying, managing financial resources, and home health and nutrition courses (Giordano & Beckman, 1985).

Emotional support for families is often an integral part of individual and family counseling, and it is also a substantial component of self-help groups developed to assist the elderly and their families. Support-oriented goals can be achieved through the communication of necessary information, the building of effective coping skills, and the expression of feelings, including guilt and shame, by family members (Rose, Finestone, & Bass, 1985). Many of the difficulties that families have with managing the concerns of their elderly family members, for example, can be dealt with in a support-group setting (Thornton, Plummer, & Seeman, 1981). Gartner and Riessman (1981) explain that an important factor operating in self-help groups is the satisfaction derived from helping others and the ease with which families can accept feedback from their peers. Because many family members have already experienced a specific family-related problem, most members have a general understanding of problems discussed within the self-help group. In working with this structure in a gerontologial practice context, the shorter-term groups have more flexibility and a greater likelihood of family member participation (Rathbone-McCuan, 1991).

Psychotherapeutic interventions also assist family members to function more effectively and efficiently in their roles. Such assistance can be provided on an individual family basis or in a discussion group format (Lazarus, Stafford, Cooper, Cohler, & Dysken, 1981; Steur & Clark, 1982; Ware & Carper, 1982). Cognitive and behavioral therapies may be used; if a more psychodynamic orientation is used, then introspection and increased personal understanding will be emphasized. Gallagher (1988) believes that psychodynamic therapy has been used with some success for treating the anticipatory grief reactions that some family members experience. All of these more psychotherapeutic-based interventions offer a blend of information, support, problem solving, and enhancement of positive coping to accomplish their goals (Gallagher, 1988).

Implicit in the knowledge of family psychotherapeutic approaches, and thematic to the contribution of assisting families undergoing a management experience with the elderly, is the belief that the family is a system, a unit of interacting parts, an interactional context (Watzlawick & Weakland, 1977). The family system consists of four subsystems: the marital (husband-wife interactions), the parental (parent-child interactions), the sibling (child-child interactions), and the extrafamilial system (nuclear family interactions with external systems and individals) (Office of Special Education, 1984). As outlined by Doherty and Baird (1983) and Herr and Weakland (1979), a family system's perspective establishes several core assumptions about families.

1. The family is more than a collection of individuals. Change or stress affecting one family member affects the whole family.
2. Families have repeating interaction patterns that regulate members' behavior. All families develop implicit rules for daily living, and how people interact with each other in the here and now very significantly influences how they function, for better or worse.
3. Individuals' symptoms may have a function within the family. A physical or psychosocial symptom, for example, may become incorporated into the

family interaction patterns in such a way that it seems essential for the family's harmony.

4. The ability to adapt to change is the hallmark of healthy family functioning. In the face of change, family flexibility or adaptability should be stressed.
5. Family members share joint responsibility for their problems.
6. When some behavior arises and persists that is seriously distressing either to the individual or to others concerned about the behavior, other behavior must be occurring within the system of interaction that provokes and maintains the problem behavior inadvertently and in spite of efforts to resolve it.

In addition to understanding the family as a system, there are other relevant concepts that are important when assisting families in an intergenerational perspective.

1. The family is held together by mutually reinforcing patterns, and its goal is the nurture, support, and direction of its members (Satir, 1967). Satir believes that the family is a system in which various physical and emotional needs are met at different levels, and that it is important both to work with families at the level of their day-to-day functioning and to teach family members congruent ways of communicating by helping them get in touch with and accept what they are feeling. She helped families to build a sense of self-worth and opened up the possibilities of making choices and bringing about changes in family life; she was more concerned with enhancing the quality of life of individuals within the family than with changing family system structures (Johnson, 1986). These beliefs are especially true in families attempting to respond to the elderly person's transitional needs. Situations that may create new needs for family members include the older member facing a changed body image, the impact of grief over multiple losses, the unwelcome expectations of grandparent-hood, the family's involvement in physical treatment demands, altered living arrangements, a new elderly parent because of divorce and remarriage, and other different limitations imposed on family members because of the frail elderly person. Satir (1967) emphasizes the necessity of attending to these needs, and she focuses on the identification of mutually reinforcing patterns within a family and how these patterns establish a family climate for successful coping. Unfortunately these patterns may be unknown to family members. The shared joys of the past, the perception that the older person is a unique individual with valuable resources, and the satisfaction gained from good listening and providing appropriate assistance

may be lost when the elderly person's problems are perceived as overwhelming. Yet intergenerational families need to maintain connections through love and nurturing (Hargrave & Anderson, 1992).

2. Family structure can be defined as a set of covert rules that regulate the ways in which family members interact with one another (Minuchin, 1974). Some rules that determine family organization are universal or generic (Rape, Bush, & Slavin, 1992). Many rules are idiosyncratic, and these involve mutual expectations and complementary roles that develop among particular family members. In accordance with this set of rules, family members divide into functional subsystems, some of which may be formed according to interests, roles, generation, or gender (Rape et al., 1992). Family structure also consists of tangible features that define the family and mold its interactions, including membership characteristics (family size, personal attributes of members), loyalties among family members, the nature of the extrafamilial system, cultural style (ethnicity, religion, socioeconomic status, and geographic location), and ideologic style (beliefs, values, and coping styles that give the family its sense of direction) (Office of Special Education, 1984).

Role definitions are an important aspect of family structure. Minuchin (1974) believes that family members will define themselves and their place in the family organization by their role interactions. During meetings with the family, the family therapist will watch these interactions, as they will indicate how family members accommodate to each other, the degree to which a family member is assimilated into the family, and whether the family operates as an open or closed system. Finally, integral to understanding this family theory is to be aware of the following transactional patterns that may occur in families: (a) enmeshment (poorly differentiated, weak, and easily crossed subsystem boundaries); (b) overprotectiveness of each other, not limited to one particular family member; (c) rigidity (retaining accustomed ways of interacting when no longer appropriate); and (d) lack of conflict resolution (leaving problems unresolved) (Minuchin, Rosman, & Baker, 1978).

3. Within most families there is a history antedating the current problems, and insights into and awareness of these difficulties are essential components of the intervention process (Johnson, 1986). Ackerman (1972) explains a conceptual model of "interlocking pathology" in family relationships, promoting family sessions in which such entanglements might be demonstrated to the family members as they occur, in order for them to begin working to eliminate them. Qualls (1992) summarizes these viewpoints by identifying the following tenets:

A. Interactional patterns are rooted in the specific developmental histories of each individual. Family conflicts are theorized to occur when individuals project onto each other the psychological needs and experiences drawn from their families of origin. In other words, psychological needs not met in childhood are unconsciously sought in other relationships (e.g., from one's children).

B. Ethical aspects of giving and receiving in families are reflected in common family values that constrain interaction. Invisible loyalties may be developed during a lifetime of perceived or real receiving that dictate obligation to give in return.

All three of the preceding viewpoints emphasize that for appropriate family intervention, the worker should attempt to gain access to the entire family system and evaluate the family system as a whole, rather than piecemeal through separate interviews with individual members (Doherty & Baird, 1983). In intergenerational family counseling the entire available family is treated as a client. When using this approach, interventions are designed consequently to modify those elements of the family relationship system that are interfering with the life tasks of the family and its members, as well as to focus on the impact of one family member's behavior on another (Greene, 1989). As many family members as possible are involved in problem resolution and in planning for the current level of function of the older relative.

Michael Duffy (1986) has made a compelling case for multigenerational therapy and has identified what professionals are doing in multigenerational therapy, with an emphasis on techniques and strategies. However, more attention needs to be given to creating other contextual arrangements when conducting intergenerational counseling, beyond those that are sporadically used, such as letters and audio-letters, phone calls, and the format for in-office sessions. Other factors needing added attention are the roles of the professional during intergenerational counseling and how time-limited intervention can be appropriately implemented for the older person, the adult children, and the kin network.

Although all of these intervention approaches employ a variety of techniques to assist family members, most families choose not to participate in long-term family counseling or therapy. There are many reasons for such a lack of participation, namely, financial costs, the stigma of being associated as a family with counseling or therapy, and the perceptions that any problem related to family management of the elderly is really not serious enough to warrant extended formal professional help. What is needed is the development of an intervention approach that considers these obstacles to family participation and at the same time helps family members manage the problems associated with aging in an intergenerational context.

Directions for Practice and Policy

Problems associated with managing elderly parents are complex, and, as Greene (1989) emphasizes, involve affective and instrumental components. Tasks of daily living, such as physical health or finances, may receive top priority in the minds of family members. Specific services for the older adult may be requested, which may be quite different than asking for counseling services. But Greene (1989) believes that "the therapist [should] look beyond concrete requests in order to understand how a particular service is perceived by the client's family as well as what need it fulfills" (p. 63). Needs associated with grandparenting, adjusting to different housing arrangements, independence versus dependence, mourning multiple losses, or, from the perspective of family members, those needs associated with parent care and adjusting to family role changes, may dominate in most families involved with elderly persons. To respond to these needs, the application of a broad-based, conceptual approach that focuses on time-limited and instrumental or affective problem-focused dimensions has not received much attention in the literature. For those family members who could benefit from some form of short-term assistance, an approach is now suggested. The recommended intervention has four steps: (a) engaging the family, (b) problem assessment, (c) specific strategies for assistance, and (d) follow-up.

ENGAGING THE FAMILY

Crucial for any family assistance is the cooperation of the appropriate family members. If the extended family is going to be involved in any intervention focusing primarily on the older person, then the first family contact will be crucial. Establishing a working relationship with the family is an important task; this relationship is often facilitated both by the location of the family meeting where an assessment of family dynamics is conducted and interventions are planned and the helping style of the family worker.

The initial family contact frequently takes place in a setting where family members are receiving medical services. Either someone who has identified a family concern makes a referral to a provider who specializes in family intervention, or a family member initiates some assistance because of a continued difficulty. Whatever the manner of the initial contact, it is important to offer the family the opportunity of a first meeting in their own home. This may be particularly appreciated when sickness or handicap prevents an older family member from coming to the office (Duffy, 1986). The home can provide a familiar atmosphere that may be more conducive to accepting an unknown service provider and less threatening for the discussion of topics that are difficult for family members (Power & Dell Orto, 1980). In the informal setting of the home families appear to relax more easily, and thus a more valid portrait of the family is often obtained (Power, 1988). A home visit puts the professional on consumer turf; provides insight, depth, and clarification to diagnostic impressions (Duffy, 1986); and gives the family an advantage in controlling a situation they may otherwise find out of control. But some families may find that a home visit produces stress in the form of unusual concern about a good appearance of the home and all family members (Crutcher, 1991). Visiting with the family in their own home, consequently, may not always be possible, but when it is, it gives the family worker the chance to observe first-hand different family dynamics that would not be revealed in a professional office; it often conveys the message to family members that the provider is genuinely interested in assisting them.

Integral to family cooperation is the manner in which the provider engages the family during the first meeting. Research indicates that certain traits and characteristics of helpers appear to affect the helping relationships positively (Okun, 1987). The more in touch professionals are with their own behaviors, feelings, and beliefs, and the more able they are to communicate this understanding genuinely, clearly, and empathically to family members, the more likely they are to be effective helpers. Sometimes communication with the elderly and their families is impeded by their rambling, lapses of continuity, and sudden topic shifts (O'Brien, Johnson, & Miller, 1979). Empathic patience becomes a crucial part of the helper's reply, and the helper needs to communicate the message that all family members are taken seriously, even when it is difficult to follow a train of thought or one is listening with obvious skepticism.

After the introductions, the worker should give each family member the opportunity to share his or her thoughts about the current situation, a sharing that can be prompted by such questions as "What do you believe are the concerns right now?" or "Are there any changes that you would like to see take place?" (Doherty & Baird, 1983). Family members seeking help usually express a sense of urgency, an urgency around a sudden change in the biopsychosocial status/needs of older family members (Greene, 1989). When possible, the older person should not be excluded from this first and subsequent family meetings. Involvement in the family meetings by all family members promotes a more accurate assessment of the presenting problem. Having this person present at the meeting may be a difficult issue for many family members due to feelings of anger, guilt, and even shame. Yet the elderly individual should feel involved, when appropriate, in the family contacts, and preexisting emotions among family members may have to be discussed separately with the provider before the family gathers for the initial meeting. This meeting may even create the opportunity for certain feelings to be revealed, and if appropriate, they may then be discussed during the family interaction. Yet there are no specific established guidelines on when to include the elderly person in the family meetings. This involvement and timing depend on family dynamics and communication styles, the mental ability of the older person, and the skills of the provider.

During the family discussion the counselor's listening ability and willingness to provide verbal reinforcement to family members at selected times can facilitate the family's willingness to identify the real problem underlying current difficulties. The goals of this first family meeting include this problem identification, as well as building rapport and the accompanying encouragement of family cooperation and understanding relevant family dynamics. Because this suggested intervention is time-limited, cooperation and understanding are important to develop at the first meeting. If the helper does not create an atmosphere that promotes the expression of family feelings and concerns, then family members can become resentful that more opportunity is not provided for the communication of their opinions or plans. Cooperation is encouraged, consequently, by the relationship the helper establishes with the family members. Greene (1989) explains that if a family systems perspective is held concerning family adaptation, then the family seeking assistance is experiencing a crisis that challenges its adaptive capacity. Accustomed patterns of emotional and social support are now being tested, and the family's ability to integrate losses and to reinvest its energy in the maintenance of family life is being stretched. The identified problem is then redefined in family terms, and family members are assisted to understand that the older person's problem is perhaps having a ripple effect throughout the entire family system. During the initial contact family members are made aware of this perspective.

However, many families may still be reluctant to share this viewpoint, to cooperate with the worker, and then to deal with the alleviation of the presenting problem. Qualls (1991) has identified many sources of resistance in older families, such as the distortion of the locus of problem, a distortion of the degree of the problem, and motivational issues. Families, for example, often focus the presenting problem on the behavior of the older person and tend to ignore the significant family issues that the problem generates among many family members. Or the family may deny or exaggerate the seriousness of a problem or distort the problem's impact on family life. Family members, moreover, may simply lack the motivation to engage in a change process, desiring not to get involved because, for example, hope for any remediation has been abandoned. Petersen (1990) explains that dependency and anger issues within the family also inhibit family involvement. The dependent family may believe they need someone to lean on, overlooking their own resources to get things done. Also, because of past conflicts the family may exhibit an anger pattern, refusing to cooperate because of past feelings toward the older person. During the initial family meeting, the worker should be prepared to assist the family member who is experiencing anxiety associated with unresolved conflicts and old regrets.

There are many developed strategies to deal with family resistance: sharing needed information, identifying and appropriately disclosing to family members the real reason for the reluctance, conveying to family members that they can learn problem solving skills to deal with the varied concerns, helping them to set limits for themselves and explaining those limits to family members, praising the family for their competence, reassuring them that as a helper you wish the family to be in charge, and encouraging family members to contribute to the decision making (Kemp, 1984; O'Brien et al., 1979; Petersen, 1990; Power & Dell Orto, 1980). The effectiveness of a particular technique to deal with family reluctance may depend on the cause of the reluctance (Ritchie, 1986). Reluctant families need a structure, specifically, one that is defined as a joint understanding between the worker and family members regarding the characteristics, conditions, procedures, and parameters of intervention (Day & Sparacio, 1980). Additional ways of managing this resistance may be to gently interpret to family members what their negative behavior is communicating and encouraging them to be part of the solution to the problem. Asking family members how they would like to change the current situation may also facilitate verbal feedback that eventually changes attitudes toward cooperation.

PROBLEM ASSESSMENT

As family members during the first family meeting discuss current difficulties, the worker is assessing the problem that should receive attention, and with a multigenerational perspective, what is the best way to deal with the specific concern. Understanding of problems usually emerges from the professional's theoretical orientation to family dynamics. Regardless of this theoretical perspective, an understanding of older families should comprise a knowledge of family needs, expectations, strengths, and previous family history (Power, Dell Orto, & Gibbons, 1988). Families have their own laws, in the form of unwritten shared expectations, and each family member is constantly subject to varying patterns of expectations to which he or she does or does not comply (Boszormenyi-Nagy & Spark, 1973). These areas have often been neglected in traditional family assessment approaches, but they are particularly appropriate to explore when using intergenerational family concepts and when identifying the source of difficulties for families living with the frail elderly. Other areas of assessment could be explored by using the following questions:

1. What activities do family members share together?
2. How much contact do family members have with each other and with past generations?
3. Do all family members express their opinions readily or is someone the spokesperson for the family?
4. What is the role of parents and other family members in the care of the older person: what is to be done, who is to do it, and who takes leadership in deciding on allocation of tasks?
5. What is the major source of stress for adult children?
6. What changes are needed in the family relationship in order to maintain the elderly person's life functioning?

Boszormenyi-Nagy and Spark (1973) introduced the concept of loyalty when attempting to understand family dynamics. Based on biological hereditary kinship, loyalty embraces the concepts of trust, reliability, commitment, and devotion to each other. A family assessment should then include identification of family loyalty, because the success of eventual intervention plans may depend on the extent of the family's investment, not only in the older person but also with other family members.

During a family meeting, moreover, the emotions of family members are usually quite apparent, but these feelings may suggest such needs as the desire to process information, to explore alternatives, to clarify frustrations, to be listened to empathically, and to receive support. Also, an exploration of a family history can reveal what the family has done so far to respond to the situation with the older person and what resources have been used in any past family crisis or severe illness.

An appraisal of selected areas of family functioning becomes the basis for the development of appropriate family helping strategies (Power, 1988). Without an understanding of the family situation and how other family members are affected by the problem, intervention approaches often go awry. Effective, timely intervention is based on the facts learned from a family assessment.

SPECIFIC INTERVENTION STRATEGIES

The goals for intervention should be identified soon after an initial assessment and should include mobilizing the family system on behalf of its members (Greene, 1989). Interventions will vary according to the nature of the identified problem and how family members can be used in problem remediation or resolution. An intervention may simply involve assisting family members to seek extended family therapy or to join a support group. The worker may not have the training or the opportunity to provide this specific assistance. The targets of intervention could also include communicating information, providing support as family members confront and deal with the problem, fostering clearer communication among family members concerning the nature of the problem and its resolution, and assisting adult children to come to terms with their own feelings. Communication with families often involves educating family members on available resources, such as peer support groups, respite care, and financial-aid opportunities, and assisting family members to learn behavior-management skills, coping skills, and how to modify family roles to accommodate the continued demands emerging from the needs of the elderly person. Support can include listening to family members, sitting quietly with the family, conveying acceptance, and offering reassurance and expressed concern to family members as they confront their feelings of anger, guilt, loss, and their own wishes for healing (Power, 1988).

Prevention entails offering advice to family members on the importance of being aware of escalating stressful situations and comprises any efforts to assist the family in their own mental health, assistance that could render family members less vulnerable to stress-induced illnesses or prolonged fatigue. Effective intervention with families and the elderly also involves early detection of possible problems.

Integral to effective intervention with multigenerational families is the creative use of the entire family context affected by the caring demands of the older person. As stated earlier in this chapter, this may entail the use of phone calls and letters for including the extended family in those situations when conjoint family sessions are not feasible (Duffy, 1986). This communication may include informing relatives about the counselor, the nature of the presenting problem, what others might be able to do to assist the adult children, and what their own expectations are for the care of the elderly person. Greene (1989) warns that the counselor should uphold the individuation of each family member but at the same time promote interdependence. In other words, family members should be encouraged to assume some responsibility for problem remediation, and this shared assumption could alleviate the burden, isolation, and even anger that adult children may feel. Even with this sharing there may still be unresolved loyalty conflicts and unsettled accounts between first and second-generation family members.

FOLLOW-UP

After the helper has assisted the family with a particular problem, family members usually need periodic contact that shows support for the recommended intervention. Many family members may have either forgotten or misunderstood the information that was communicated at the family meeting. Information or other intervention strategies may have to be repeated or encouragement from the helper reemphasized. The provision of support through a phone call or another form of brief contact should be an ever-present available resource for families as they learn to deal with responsibilities at home. But if family members have made necessary role changes, and there appears to be more cooperation among family members when responding to the elderly person's problem, then the intergenerational approach to intervention may be working (Greene, 1989).

POLICY

Interventions with families and their elderly members have many implications for existing policies and policy development. Whether policies are formal or informal, and consist of either goals, procedures, or general guidelines for action, current enactments have not encouraged the family systems orientation as a basis for assistance (Flynn, 1993). Yet the intervention suggested in this chapter implies the engagement of both younger and older family members, family role flexibility, and the coordination of services. However, social policies are targeted to individuals with certain age and problem characteristics, are lacking in a holistic approach to family role adaptation, tend to discourage "intergenerational transfers of mutual assistance" (Flynn, 1993, p. 162) and limit intervention options because they are restricted as to the legal nature of the relationship, geographic boundaries, and age (Flynn, 1993). Funding has promoted fragmented and individualized services, with family meetings that are clinic-based.

With the increasing importance of providing assistance to family members for maintaining the elderly as long as possible in the home, there is accelerating pressure at both the state and federal levels for the provision of family support. Most of this pressure has focused on helping parents of children with a handicapping condition, with assistance emphasizing the family's social, psychological, educational, or health needs (Roberts, Wasik, Casto, & Ramey, 1991). Concerns for the elderly have yet to stimulate policy development on such issues as home visiting, multigenerational use in family intervention, and coordination of services by a wide range of professionals and paraprofessionals. Moreover, any beginning policy formulation appears to be more reactive, namely, exploring forms of assistance after the problem has become very serious and disruptive to family functioning. Preventive, more proactive services are needed if costs are going to be reduced for family care and the elderly person.

Serious thought needs to be given to these policy shortcomings in terms of fundamental understandings of the nature of the family's role with the care of the elderly and how interventions can become more effective when multigenerations are included in a helping approach. Rathbone-McCuan (1991) believes that "even traditional nuclear family work with the older or younger generations of family members can maintain ongoing concern for how public policies impact on family functioning" (p. 60). Innovative approaches and services are needed, consequently, to meet the counseling needs of older persons and their families.

CASE EXAMPLE

The following case illustrates a problem-focused, time-limited intervention in a family with an older member and emphasizes the suggested counseling steps identified in this chapter.

During her father's scheduled medical check-up, Lorraine told the physician that he seldom took his prescribed medicine. This apparent negligence was causing sores to appear on his legs, hampering circulation and mobility. Lorraine's 74-year-old father lives in an apartment five blocks away from his daughter and her husband of 32 years. Lorraine has a sister 5 years older who lives a 30-minute drive away, two daughters who are both married and visit their mother frequently during the week, and a married brother who lives in a neighboring state. Lorraine's daughters and their husbands are close to their grandfather, accompany him to a restaurant at least once a month, and visit often with him at other times. Lorraine's sister has many personal problems and usually contacts her father only when she has a financial need. The father is able to manage many personal care activities, and prepares several of his own meals each week, but relies on his daughter for shopping, social, and banking needs. The daughter would prefer that her father live with her family in their large home, but the father constantly maintains that he wants to be as independent as possible. The daughter's husband appears quite ambivalent about this proposed move.

Because of the perceived seriousness of the recurring skin lesions and the father's reluctance to follow a treatment regimen, the doctor recommends that the daughter, her husband, and father make an appointment with a counselor who has worked with families referred by the physician. The daughter agrees because she is very worried about her father's behavior and its consequences on his health. Although the involved parties explain that they are not accustomed to such mental health intervention in their lives, the father and husband agree to an initial family visit because the father does not want to displease his daughter, to whom he is very devoted, and the husband wishes to support his wife in her efforts.

The counselor schedules a visit with the family in the father's apartment. After the introductions, the counselor inquires about the makeup of the extended family and members' roles in the father's life and asks the daughter and her husband to explain their viewpoint on the apparent problem. The counselor then asks permission to invite Lorraine's two daughters and their husbands to the next session, to be scheduled very soon after the introductory meeting, and requests that the sister and brother also be contacted in order to explain the current situation. Lorraine agrees. Toward the end of this first session the counselor also asks them, "How could this situation be different?" The father explains his distrust of doctors and drugs, claiming that he has lived all these years without prolonged serious medical problems, and, "I am going to die anyway, that is nature's way, so why should I be uncomfortable with this medicine because it makes me go to the bathroom too often." The daughter becomes very distressed with that statement, stating that "it was important for her to keep her father alive as long as possible."

After calling the sister and brother and exploring their viewpoints about the problem and how they could contribute to its resolution, the counselor conducts a second session during which all family members share their expectations for the grandfather's lifestyle. Through empathic listening, summarizing statements made by each person, asking for clarification on specific issues raised during the verbal interaction, and identifying current family needs, the counselor realizes that independence is a primary life concern for the father, the daughter needs her father's medical compliance for her own mental health, and the husband wants the father-in-law to remain as long as possible in the apartment. The counselor also observes that the daughter enjoys watching over the father but allows her father little freedom in how to manage his day, in choice of foods, and in when to socialize with other family members. Lorraine's daughters, sister, and brother concur in this judgment; her sister feels resentful that more decisions affecting the father are not shared.

From this assessment, the counselor communicates these observations, identifies the conflict, and then asks each family member how he or she would resolve it. Fortunately, the father says that he is aware of the noncompliance problem, does not want to see his daughter unhappy, and will listen to some remedial suggestions, but he still wants his daughter to be less intrusive in his own life. The daughter agrees to this if her father will take his medicine regularly. The counselor establishes a plan for the family members that involves the father taking his medicine at established times during the day and informing his daughter each evening about this behavior. In turn, the daughter promises not to interfere as much with her father's daily schedule and meal choices, and the specifics of this noninterference are identified. The noninterference becomes, consequently, a source of reinforcement of the father's medicine-taking behavior. Lorraine also agrees that her sister and daughters should assume some of the duties associated with her father, such as taking her father to the bank, the grocery store, and the occasional physician's appointments. Lorraine realizes that this "letting-go" will be a slow, difficult process but is willing to make the initial attempt.

One week after the family visit the counselor calls both the father and daughter to assess the curent situation and does so again 3 weeks later and then 4 weeks afterward. Satisfied that the father is following the medicine schedule, she told the daughter that she would be available again if there was a recurring problem.

Although other dynamics could be addressed with this family, the counselor chose to focus on the current problem and offered suggestions for remediation. Other families, of course, may need more counseling attention and perhaps long-term therapy. But the intervention that is promoted in this chapter is time limited, broad based, problem focused, and developed more from the current needs and expectations of family members.

Discussion Questions

1. From reading the case study, what further suggestions could be made to improve the father's quality of life?

2. What does the case study indicate about how this family's "repeating interaction patterns" have affected the father's behavior?

3. Do you believe that the family depicted in the case study should be initially seen in the father's apartment or in the case worker's office? Why?

8

Facilitating Health Care
Decisions Within Aging Families

EVELYN J. BATA

PAUL W. POWER

This chapter focuses on various issues relevant to family decision making for health care of elderly people. It specifies the problem domain when facilitating health care decisions; identifies special needs, obstacles, and contextual variables that emerge from the topic; and clarifies some of the issues that the helping professional needs to know when confronted with assisting families or significant others in decision making. A case example is presented, illustrating a decision-making process and highlighting the difficulties a family may encounter in the process. Although the chapter addresses the most salient issues in aging families, many of the principles encompassed could generalize to other issues as well, be they retirement, relocation, financial, or legal matters that can affect the existing family system.

The aging process affects not only the individual who may be experiencing a change in mental and bodily functions, but it also affects the family and significant others. Lives are embedded in relationships, and the context of interpersonal dynamics often determines how both elderly persons and family members adapt to daily living and health care demands.

Positive adaptation to changing health care demands of the aged person requires thoughtful and informed decision making by the individual and significant others. Even so, family processing is not always an easy task for any of those concerned.

Background

Family decision making is a continuous process extending over a long period of time triggered by new crises, changes in personnel and community resources, or unexpected changes in the elderly person's health. Decision making involves exploring values and alternatives, identifying a choice, developing a plan, and then acting on a judgment. The decision itself can be made by an individual, or the process can be a shared one. Within the family of an elderly person, decisions are often precipitated by daily living tasks and demands and by expected and unexpected transitions, such as the planned entry to a nursing home or a sudden illness requiring skilled nursing care. For an elderly person confronted with many changes, family decision making is an especially complex process, and important decisions are made by a variety of people such as family members, close friends, or health professionals. Yet little is known about the process by which family members or other involved persons decide on what should be done for the elderly individual and who should do it (Cicirelli, 1992a).

There are various decision styles that characterize families with an elderly person. Some families make decisions on the basis of feeling or impulse, whereas others base their decisions on exploration, analyses, and qualification of alternatives. Some weigh the advice of health care professionals and then make decisions through a rational evaluation of options and consideration of values and feelings. Families using a more self-directed approach in decision making often experience confidence and satisfaction.

When decision making occurs for the older person, it frequently involves difficulties related to intrafamily dynamics resulting from unfairly shared caregiving, failure to respect the ideas or wishes of the elderly person, or inability or reluctance to initiate or respond to issues emanating from the formal health care community. Intrafamily dynamics is a key issue in collective decision making. When family members, in responding to daily care demands, have adopted a style of decision making that meets the needs of the elderly person without compromising the individual's autonomy and integrity, this style may continue to be facilitative when interacting with health care professionals or when the family is confronted with life-threatening health decisions.

Decision making generates special problems when focusing on aged persons and health care. These concerns include (a) identifying the issues, (b) decision making within the family system, and (c) clarifying the issues of autonomy and paternalism within the system. The concerns are evident in all of the decision-making processes for the older person.

Elaboration of Family Issues

IDENTIFYING THE ISSUES

McCullough, Wilson, Teasdale, Kolpakchi, and Skelly (1993) state that "acute care typically involves well-defined problems that make it possible to identify clearly any conflicts between competing perspectives on what is in the patient's interest" while "long-term care, in contrast, is undramatic and routine, an arena in which matters are more difficult to clarify" (p. 324). Long-term care embraces a wide range of services, and the related decisions usually occur in a series that concerns nearly all aspects of a person's daily life for a long time (Kane & Kane, 1982; Pelaez & David, 1991). Long-term care, in fact, and the associated issues of guardianship and power of attorney are the most frequently encountered problems to be addressed by families (Brashler & Hartke, 1991; Kapp, 1991). In this chapter, health care decisions for the elderly are understood in both acute and long-term care situations.

When considering the family decision-making process, many problems arise from daily, caregiving functions and responsibilities, such as the allocation of tasks among family members or what community resources should be used. Other problems may be generated by the elderly person's rapidly deteriorating condition, including such concerns as who will provide the health care within the home, who within the family will be the spokesperson to the health community, how much decision-making responsibility should be turned over to sources outside of the family? But decision making for the older person is truly a family concern. Typically many family members, including adult children, the spouse, older siblings, adult grandchildren, and even in-laws may become involved in and are affected by health care decisions made. The financial impact itself may affect various family members. Also the possible lack of cognitive competence of the elderly person may require ongoing decision making by various capable relatives.

DECISION MAKING
WITHIN THE FAMILY SYSTEM

To develop appropriate decisions in the areas mentioned requires positive communication among family members, professional and legal consultation, and family awareness of its value system. Values form the bedrock of these decisions and contribute to their complexities. For example, family members may perceive differently the need for institutionalization. The daughter of an elderly person may believe that it is her duty and the honorable thing to do to care for her parent in the home, regardless of the emotional cost. However, her spouse may strongly believe that only outside caregiving would relieve the perceived constant stress and its negative effects on the spousal relationship.

In many families, the problem that initially needs decision making is who will provide health care for the elderly person. There may be an implicit understanding of where responsibilities lie when an older person becomes impaired. Yet some family members or significant others may feel inadequate to or resent taking this primary responsibility. Instead of simply assuming that a certain person will take over the main caregiving functions, and to reduce family conflict, the family needs to generate better communication with each other and the elderly person about this important issue and to go through a decision-making process. Each caregiver experience is unique and complex, requiring varied and situation-appropriate decisions.

Who within the family will be the spokesperson to the health community is another problem that initially surfaces. The primary caregiver may be quite willing and capable to manage daily health care tasks but very reluctant to speak out and articulate the needs of the elderly person, or the caregiver may feel intimidated by or not understand information that is imparted by health care professionals. To handle the communication process between the family and the professional entails the skills of assertiveness and the ability to comprehend treatment directions.

Should family members depend on outside sources when making important health care decisions? The answer has provoked different viewpoints. Historically, physicians, often backed by the courts, have played a prominent role in facilitating decisions (Heifetz, 1978). Yet many family caregivers harbor concern and resentment about the poor responsiveness of doctors to psychosocial concerns of the elderly that are relevant to decision making (Ashworth, Williamson, & Montano, 1984; Greene, Hoffman, Charon, & Adelman, 1987). There even appears to be a continued movement away from physicians as final arbiters of life-and-death decisions. Many states are now recognizing legal guidelines such as a living will that allow individuals, and family members acting for them, to decide whether to accept or continue heroic life-sustaining measures in the case of severe disability or terminal illness (Henderson, 1990; Hooyman & Kiyak, 1993). It can be a weighty matter, considering the responsible party's values, available choices, and emotional involvement with the older ill person.

AUTONOMY VERSUS PATERNALISM

Although caregivers assume important functions when fulfilling their responsibilities, the primary decision maker may still be the elderly person. A well-functioning family may be quite careful to respect the rights and wishes of the capable older individual so that this person alone may determine a care plan or placement in a long-term care facility. Yet there are instances when neither the older person nor the family member want to be empowered as the sole decision maker (Kapp, 1991). Responsibility for health care decisions may be perceived as too stressful for the older person, the spouse, or other family members. In such instances, shared decision making may lessen the perceived responsibility for all concerned, while preserving the autonomy and dignity of the aged individual.

There are many dilemmas in the exercise of personal autonomy relevant to decision making: for example, when unassisted independence is no longer a feasible alternative for an elderly person, when serious communication problems exist between the elderly individual and health care providers because of sensory or cognitive impairments, and when decisions are made of necessity that override the older person's wishes (Kapp, 1991). These dilemmas often trigger conflict and guilt among family members. It appears that preserving autonomy in health care decisions presents a major challenge.

Cicirelli (1992a) has identified the family's health belief system, their expectations of each other, and their attitudes toward professional health care providers as factors that influence both the elderly person's autonomy and the family's autonomy in the decision-making process. Although autonomy for the older person is the ideal or goal, to make a decision for the welfare of an individual who is incapable of reasonable judgment may imply paternalism. In this situation, the decision does not imply an increasing attempt to control, manipulate, or manage that person. It may be considered justifiable paternalism of family members and health care professionals in the older person's best interest (Brashler & Hartke, 1991; Cicirelli, 1992a).

However, there are instances when health care professionals choose to influence the health care decision based on their own values rather than on the wishes of the individual or family. In such an instance, the health care professional may be considered guilty of the worst sort of paternalism. Family members need to be alert to their own value system and the older person's wishes to guard against hasty or ill-advised paternalistic decision making (Nuland, 1994). It is only when the older person, family members, and health care professionals work together as a team or unit for the well-being of the individual that there can be a blend of autonomy and beneficence that complements and supports each concept. It illustrates that autonomy and paternalism are not necessarily opposites (Moody, 1988).

There are other obstacles to family decision making that may include dysfunctional family communication patterns, lack of knowledge and competence, serious communication problems with health care providers, lack of trust, moral conflicts, attitudes, and few available resources. Accurate and effective decisions are frequently hard to achieve, but the identification of obstacles can lead to the development of workable decision-making approaches.

DYSFUNCTIONAL COMMUNICATION PATTERNS

A family may have a history of not discussing important issues concerning an individual's welfare, leaving it to one family member to make significant decisions. Family communication may also be characterized by anger, an anger that emerges from unresolved conflicts or the frustration from attempting to cope with many stressors. Blaming, scapegoating, continued unwarranted silence, and intentional nonlistening may be the usual behaviors of family members when interacting with each other (Power & Dell Orto, 1980). Consequently when confronted with an important health decision, the family is not accustomed to exploring and discussing different options and choices.

LACK OF KNOWLEDGE AND COMPETENCE

Lack of knowledge and lack of competence are two separate issues. Lack of competence may refer to an inadequacy to make important, even necessary decisions. This inadequacy may be caused by fear, by anxiety about risk taking or facing the unknown, or by a cognitive and emotional inability to understand the relevant facts that are the basis for appropriate decisions. Lack of knowledge implies that family members are not acquainted with vital information. Many health care decisions are complex, and such issues as guardianship or the best resources for health care may involve an understanding of technical information. Family members are usually not accustomed to having such knowledge, and they need to inquire about relevant facts and explore options before health care decisions are made. A lack of knowledge or competence can shape the nature and number of these options, as well as the way in which the family member responds to them (Krumboltz, 1983).

COMMUNICATION PROBLEMS
WITH HEALTH PROVIDERS

To most elderly persons and their families, a health provider is a formidable person. Often better educated and more knowledgeable about the problem at hand, the health professional may unknowingly be patronizing or not explain carefully the necessary facts relevant to a specific situation (Greene, Adelman, Charon, & Hoffman, 1986; Haug & Ory, 1986). Also, many individuals outside of the health care community hesitate to be assertive or ask questions about available options. This lack of comprehensive information may compromise the decision-making process.

In addition, particular dynamics come into play in a geriatric triad when an elderly person is accompanied to the medical encounter by a family caregiver (Coe & Prendergast, 1985; Rosow, 1981). The caregiver and the professional may form a coalition and ignore or discount the patient during discussion of care options in their attempt to make a decision for the elderly person. Coalitions that affect the communication process and decision making may also be formed between the family member and older person or between the older person and the health professional. If health care decisions are to be made during the visit, then several questions can be raised such as: What is the caregiver's contribution to the encounter? Does the caregiver have a personal agenda not in harmony with that of the patient? How will decision making differ when the caregiver is present? Is the elderly person inhibited in communicating personal choice of care options by the presence of the third party? (Adelman, Greene, & Charon, 1987).

The health professional needs to have a clear understanding that the client is, in fact, the elderly person. To communicate clearly and directly with that individual is the appropriate ethical action. However, if there appear to be questions of patient competency or other salient issues, then family members may be requested to be present, at the option of either the family member or the health professional.

RESOURCES

Decision making takes into account various resources, which may include financial assets, the availability of a wide selection of health care providers, family members who are genuinely interested in shared decision making, and a variety of community agencies that offer effective services. Resources are a key issue when family members and the elderly person explore choices. Limitations or unavailability of certain resources because of geographic location or limited financial assets present obstacles for both autonomous or shared family decision making. When choices become very limited, the decision-making process may become less complex, but the outcome may not be the most productive for the elderly person and the family. What works then is compromise based on available choices and options that can be agreed on by all concerned and in the best interest of the elderly person.

LACK OF TRUST

Trust is an integral issue in shared decision making. A lack of trust is reflected not only in family verbal communication behaviors, but also in the willingness of family members to listen to the viewpoints of others, including those who provide services. An unfortunate experience in health care services may dominate the memory of a family member who is deciding on the most appropriate use of health resources for an aging frail parent or spouse. Also, an elderly person with a history of behavioral problems emanating from alcoholism may have destroyed the trust of family members who wish to include that person in important decisions.

MORAL CONFLICTS, VALUES,
AND ETHICAL CONSIDERATIONS

Values and ethical considerations play an integral role in shared decision making. Kapp (1991) believes that communal moral reasoning entails "a continuous dialogue with others whose views and interests are a dialectical part of one's own values" (p. 620). Jecker (1990) explains that values are sharpened by being tried out on family members and getting their feedback.

Decisions related to guardianship, nursing home care, and death and dying are both complex and challenging to a family member's values and moral beliefs, and the consequences of such decisions assume paramount importance. For instance, family members and the professional health provider may view the consequences from different perspectives. A physician may believe that nursing home care is in the best interest of the older person, but the spouse recalls the vows of "in sickness and in health, until death do us part" and may believe it would be morally wrong for her not to provide care at home.

Family concerns with death and dying can create conflictual issues also. Because of religious orientation or cultural values, families may be at odds when having to decide on such procedures as life-sustaining intervention or regressive intervention. Their religious beliefs and moral reasoning affect the weighty responsibility of life and death decision making for the frail, ill older person.

Guardianship and conservatorship of the older person's body and finances are often made as a last resort when the individual is judged unable to care for self or estate (Keith & Wacker, 1991). Family members, depending on their moral or ethical persuasions, may see such action as dramatically intrusive of the individual's autonomy or personal freedom and find decision making for acceptance or assignment of this responsibility to be stressful and guilt producing.

It would seem that the time to undertake ethical considerations for health care decisions is when the older person is still cognitively intact to be able to make a decision and when open and honest discussion regarding values and preferences takes place between the individual and the family. Overall the major ethical concern should be whether or not the family is acting in the best interest of its elderly member.

Information presented in this chapter indicates that family decisions are difficult and often highly emotionally charged. They are as much a consequence of the people who make them as the objective facts on which they are made.

Directions for Practice and Policy

Much of the stress emanating from the decision-making process can be alleviated by accurate information, empathic communication, and family member accommodation. This section addresses these criteria and presents a case example in family decision making.

INTERVENTIONS

To facilitate effective decision making in aging families, interventions can be developed to include a complement of family education and family counseling.

Education. Family education can take place considerably earlier than when heavy caregiving demands are imminent, and it can be incorporated into a workshop that addresses such concerns as: understanding health care needs; information on a particular relevant disease, such as Parkinson's or Alzheimer's; behavioral and management strategies; community resources such as respite services, home health aides, and transportation services; Medicaid, Medicare, and other insurance benefits; financial and legal assistance; how to choose a long-term care facility; and end of life arrangements. A family education approach creates an opportunity for members to identify and learn more about alternatives and options in caregiving that may be best suited to their particular needs. The decision-making process itself considers the ever-increasing amount of knowledge and skills that family members acquire (Hazler & Roberts, 1984).

Two major periods in the process have been identified: (a) anticipation and (b) implementation and adjustment (Tiedeman, 1961). In the anticipation period, the family first explores a random variety of alternatives. During this period, the helping professional can assist family members or potential caregivers to obtain adequate information, identify values, and then compare the probable implications and consequences of each alternative. In addition, family members can learn and practice skills and strategies to locate relevant facts, to better understand identified necessary information, to improve communication with health care professionals, to be appropriately assertive, and to use time management techniques.

In the implementation and adjustment phase, family members act on their choices and then alter them based on how satisfactorily the choices respond to the realities of the environment (Hazler & Roberts, 1984). For

Health Care Decisions 153

example, a decision may be made concerning in-home treatment or a community resource to use, such as a respite day care center. However, the decision may have to be modified when caregiving becomes more demanding or the day care center is not meeting expectations. Modification and reevaluation of past decisions will take place for family members throughout the life of the older person. As new issues are presented, relevant skills and strategies learned earlier can be put into place at any time during the decision-making process.

Counseling. The helping professional addresses many issues to enable aging families to successfully cope with their roles and make effective decisions. Providing family members with a sense of competency to deal with caregiving issues can alleviate feelings of helplessness and assist them in regaining control of their lives. They also need to see themselves making choices, solving problems, and having a sense of control for the well-being of their significant elderly relative (Rodin, 1980). Developing an awareness of the individual's strengths and competencies as reflected in their caregiving role, in their role within the family context, and in past decisions made can enable them to draw on previous successful coping and decision-making strategies used.

Enabling an individual to identify role expectations perceived by self, the older person, or other family members, helps that individual to identify motives in decision making. Moreover, identification of one's own values, needs, and expectations can lead to an understanding of resistance or undecidedness in the decision-making process.

Many family members experience guilt when having to consider outside care for a significant older person. Empathic understanding and communication can help relieve the perceived stressors of loss and guilt that often influence decisions based on emotions rather than on sound values and knowledgeable assessments.

In assisting family members of an elderly dependent relative, it is important to recognize that an overburdened family caregiver, struggling to maintain an emotional balance, will have difficulty in making sound decisions that affect the family system. One's well-being need not be sacrificed for the caregiving role. Spouses or adult children "in the middle" can be counseled about caregiver burnout they may experience. They can be encouraged to decide on respite care or support services so that they do not have to spend as much time in caregiving. Getting rid of the guilt and using time management techniques may enable them to have much needed time for their own self-care and leisure, more time for other family members, and quality time for the older relative. Also, individuals who attend to positive health habits, recreational routines, and social events are less prone to negative emotional affect and may practice more problem-focused decision making.

The helping professional can be especially alert to the psychosocial needs of the family member who is also an elderly spouse and who is responsible for health care decision making. Nursing home placement of a mate of many years can trigger overwhelming grief and sadness. The counselor can provide grief counseling, and when appropriate, introduce a life review for reaffirmation of the older person's life and successes. Arranging for the family member to eat a nourishing meal daily with the spouse in the nursing home will enable both of them to have some aspect of a continuing relationship and is important not only as a ritual, but to the physical well-being of the visiting spouse as well.

Family dynamics, hidden agendas, and unfinished business can pose multiple stressors for family members who have the responsibility for health care decisions and these issues need to be addressed in interventions. Yet whatever issues may be involved, the decision-making process itself allows for the possibility of compromise. The family has to learn that an important decision made for a frail older relative cannot satisfy the personal needs and values of all concerned. The final compromise agreed on should be for the well-being of the relative.

Decision making within the family system is unique to each situation. A caregiver, whether it be a spouse, adult child, sibling, or significant other, is not always taxed beyond endurance. Yet when a dramatic change or crisis occurs in an older person's physical or mental health, those individuals may be called on to respond to immediate needs and relevant issues affecting the person's welfare. Responses to needs and issues through decision making are illustrated in the following case example.

CASE EXAMPLE

Marian, a 69-year-old retired government economist, has severe osteoporosis as a result of an early hysterectomy she experienced years ago when no replacement estrogen was prescribed. A widow with no children, she is bright, articulate, an avid crossword puzzle enthusiast, and a voracious reader.

Her only family members are two brothers, one of whom, an accountant, has been especially supportive of her, but whose own wife has advanced diabetes. Her younger brother, an unemployed widower and recovering alcoholic, has called his sister only occasionally.

Marian had 11 bone fractures in 3 years resulting in hospitalizations followed by admissions to nursing and rehabilitation centers. She was always highly motivated to return to her home and did so after each discharge from the nursing centers. Her most recent hospitalization resulted from a stroke and shoulder fracture she suffered while alone in her home. There was some brain damage resulting in aphasia.

Decisions to Be Made

Marian's physician stated that she should no longer return to her home to live. Her older brother realized that his wife's medical condition and his work responsibilities prevented him from caring for Marian. Moreover, he had helped arrange for his sister's care in her own home previously, and it was not always consistent and dependable. He concluded that long-term professional placement was in her best interest.

However, the younger brother wanted Marian to live with him because he was alone since his wife died. He wanted Marian's house sold and the funds entrusted to him to provide care for the rest of her life.

The older brother realized that guardianship was crucial to making decisions for Marian's welfare. He consulted her family lawyer for legal clarification and direction. The younger brother's input was also invited. The court awarded guardianship and conservatorship to the older brother and the lawyer. They decided on placement in a long-term care center for Marian.

Although decisions had to be made in Marian's behalf because of the immediacy of the situation, her older brother wanted to respect her right of autonomy regarding disposal of her home and prized possessions. A review of Marian's financial assets indicated that the house did not have to be sold immediately. Her guardians decided to wait for 6 months to see if her condition would allow her to participate in the decision and in the disposal of her belongings.

Exploration of Alternatives

Marian had stayed at several nursing care centers previously; however, she was not able to express clear judgment or preference about placement this time, so her brother explained to her that he would arrange placement considering her past comments on preferences, quality of service, and convenience of the center's location for visiting. He visited three facilities and compared them based on a resource guide obtained from the county office on aging, as well as on the administrators' recollections and comments on Marian's previous stays at their facilities. He also talked to some family members who were visiting relatives to get their assessments. The younger brother was invited to visit the facilities and participate in the decision but refused.

Once the long-term care center was selected, the older brother explained to Marian that after she got settled in, had therapy, and progressed, she would continue to participate in decisions affecting her living arrangements and the issue of her home.

Implementing the Decision and Reevaluation

As Marian's guardian, her brother admitted her to the center and arranged for her care. The attorney provided monthly statements of the cost and of her financial status to both brothers.

Although Marian's osteoporosis continues to be debilitating, her improvement from the stroke was remarkable. Speech therapy was quite successful and enabled Marian to make her wishes known. Reevaluation of her placement resulted in her decision to move to an alternate nursing center that was one of the three early choices. She preferred the ecological design of the alternate center with a one-floor plan, the dining room arrangement, and the center outdoor courtyard.

Marian recovered from her stroke substantially, but she realized that she could never again manage to be in her own home. Although it was painful for her, she made the decision to sell the property and directed her brother as to how to dispose of her personal possessions. She had autonomy in this decision. Her brother was supportive and helped carry out her wishes.

This case illustrates family factors and dynamics that play a part in decision making in aging families, and it illustrates the reality that though autonomous decision making by the older person is the ideal, it may be difficult to achieve in actuality. Although a paternalistic or beneficent approach was taken for Marian's welfare initially by the physician, lawyer, and her brother, a sincere effort was made to have her share, as much as possible, in the decision making. However, autonomy was achieved with her own decision to remain in the long-term care center and sell her home.

Discussion Questions

1. How are the anticipation and implementation/adjustment phases of decision making applied to the case study?

2. What do you believe is the dominant problem, among the many discussed in this chapter, that impedes effective decision making for the elderly person and family members?

3. Concerning family decision-making, the chapter discusses the issues of lack of knowledge and lack of competence. Do you believe that they are separate issues, and why?

4. Identify the decision making resources within the family presented as a case study that will aid family members when caring for the elderly person.

9

Achieving Intimacy
in Late-Life Marriages

SUSAN KRAUSS WHITBOURNE

ERIN L. CASSIDY

Challenges in late-life marriages can be understood from a life span perspective, in which constructs relevant to intimacy across the adult years are applied to the specific concerns of older couples. In this chapter, we will describe a framework that has proved useful in the study of intimacy in young and middle-aged adults and show how this framework can be adapted to understand and treat the marital concerns of late-life couples.

Background

The term *intimacy* is used in the psychological literature to refer to the individual's capacity to enter into relationships characterized by mutuality, open communication, constructive conflict resolution, and enduring emotional commitments. From a developmental perspective, the individual's potential for intimacy can be seen as fluctuating throughout the adult years as a function of changes within the individual and changes within the couple.

THE CONCEPT OF INTIMACY
IN ADULT RELATIONSHIPS

Erikson's (1963) life span psychosocial development theory postulates that issues relevant to intimacy reach ascendancy in the early years of adulthood. The intimacy versus isolation crisis, as described by Erikson, is a transition point in the life course when the individual seeks to establish a close and enduring relationship with a partner. Two opposing forces face the individual during this transition. One is the pull toward intimacy, which draws the individual to share a significant part of his or her identity with a long-term partner. Countering this force is the fear that one's identity will be lost within the intensity of the intimate relationship. Favorable resolution of this crisis and the achievement of an intimate relationship depend in part on the individual's positive resolution of past psychosocial crises and in part on the individual's response to the unique demands of a close relationship. Those who are unable to resolve the crisis in a favorable way, according to Erikson, become isolates, unable to establish a close lasting tie with another. Although Erikson proposed that the intimacy versus isolation crisis reaches its peak in young adulthood, he maintained that the crisis could arise at younger ages or at any point later in the life course.

Following from Erikson's original theoretical statement, investigators interested in psychosocial development in college students developed the construct of *intimacy statuses,* or alternate modes of resolving the intimacy versus isolation crisis (Orlofsky, Marcia, & Lesser, 1973). Intimacy status is measured by administering a structured interview that assesses the individual's level of involvement in close relationships. Although it was originally developed as a means of describing intimacy in male college students, the intimacy status construct was successfully applied to a sample of male and female young adults, all of whom were in their early to mid-20s (Tesch & Whitbourne, 1982). In subsequent studies, the intimacy status construct gained explanatory power as a characteristic of individuals (Whitbourne & Tesch, 1985) and adult married couples (Whitbourne & Ebmeyer, 1990). It is important to point out that intimacy status, as it is most commonly used, applies to the individual's potential for intimacy rather than the actual dynamics of a long-term relationship. A person with a high potential for intimacy may be involved in a relationship with a partner whose ability to share is constricted. This type of relationship may create severe communication difficulties when the highly intimate individual comes to the realization that the partner will never change. On the other hand, the intimate partner may "educate" the other to reach new levels of communication and closeness.

The intimacy statuses incorporate the positive and negative resolutions described by Erikson (1963), but they go beyond Erikson's initial formulation by postulating two additional positions along the intimacy-isolation continuum. *Mutual intimacy* represents the positive outcome described by Erikson's theory in which the individual is capable of establishing a relationship characterized by commitment, open communication, and an equal division of power. At the other extreme, people in the *isolate* status lack the ability to establish a close and lasting relationship. In between these two polarities are people who are committed to a partner in a long-term relationship, but this relationship lacks either true communication or equality. Individuals in the *pseudointimate* status are unable to communicate at a deep personal level. The partners in this status value the relationship not for its emotional quality but for the practical purposes that it serves. Finally, people in the *merger* status are in relationships characterized by inequality in the distribution of power and interdependence.

Although these intimacy statuses have not yet been applied empirically to marital and long-term relationships in the elderly, the intimacy status construct appears to provide a useful heuristic for identifying potential stresses in late-life marriages. This construct incorporates the dimensions of communication, conflict resolution, and degree of commitment, components of intimacy identified throughout the marital and close relationship literature (Kelley et al., 1983; Levinger, 1980; Whitbourne, 1986). The concept of statuses implies that couples can be evaluated on these dimensions in a way that does not place them into types or categories but allows for the possibility of shifts in any of the components of intimacy throughout the adult years. Differing trajectories for individuals in each of these statuses can be projected, as can their responses to common themes of later life. In this chapter, we will attempt to provide these applications in the hopes that they can be helpful to clinicians and family life educators in understanding this component of late-life families. We will limit our discussion to traditional heterosexual late-life couples who have been married to each other over the years of adulthood. It would be expected that many of the processes described here would apply to variants on this relationship, and we have chosen to focus only on traditional couples to simplify the presentation.

INTIMACY STATUSES
DURING THE ADULT YEARS

The intimacy statuses, as ratings applied to individuals, provide only a partial basis for predicting the future development of that individual over the course of adulthood. A mutually intimate person paired with a pseudo-intimate partner would be expected to experience strains not found if that person were paired with a mutually intimate partner (Whitbourne & Ebmeyer, 1990). However, for the purpose of discussion, we will describe the intimacy statuses as if they applied to couples with the same individual intimacy statuses.

Mutually Intimate Couples. As is implied by Erikson's theory, the mutually intimate couple should show the most favorable path of development through adulthood. There is a vitality to this type of relationship that comes from the openness and willingness of each partner to take an honest look at themselves as individuals and as a couple. Their flexibility and adaptability to change keeps them from becoming bored with life or each other, constantly seeking out new challenges and rewards. These individuals should be able to adapt to changes in the external demands on the couple caused by the entry and exit of children through the stages of the family life cycle. It is well-established in the family life cycle literature that the movement of children into and out of the home influences the parents' communication patterns, modes of conflict resolution, and delegation of power (Whitbourne, 1986). Because the partners in a mutually intimate relationship are constantly talking about their feelings, verifying the reactions of their partners, and participating in equitable conflict resolution and because they remain deeply committed to the relationship, the vicissitudes of family life with young or teenage children should not erode their relationship. Similarly this couple should be able to withstand the external pressures caused by time commitments away from the home to job and career. Their sexual relationship should deepen and become more satisfying as they work toward finding new ways of expanding their level of involvement and physical intimacy. With the passing of the years, these couples should be able to take advantage of the benefits of decades of shared experiences, becoming more closely bonded to each other, both emotionally and physically (Sternberg, 1986).

Pseudointimate Couples. In the pseudointimate relationship, the picture is very different. These individuals retain their sense of commitment to each other during the course of adulthood, but their relationship lacks the energy and openness of the mutually intimate couple. In many ways, the pseudointimate couple may adapt very well to the demands of family life and work obligations, having arrived at an efficient and pragmatic solution to the need to juggle various time commitments. In middle adulthood, when these demands are at their peak, the partners in this type of relationship divide up equally and without argument the weekend car pooling, laundry, grocery shopping, and various household chores. However, they perform these tasks with little interaction or sharing of experiences, more as members of a team than a couple. Rather than confront conflict, these couples prefer to stay away from challenging situations in which they might oppose each other. Although this avoidance may carry with it the benefit of maintaining a quieter and more peaceful home existence, the partners fail to benefit from the compromises exacted through open sharing of ideas, feelings, and perspectives. Their sexual relationship, although perhaps satisfactory, lacks variety and over the years may become nothing more than a mechanical physical act.

Merger Couples. Looking at the merger relationship, the pattern during adulthood may take very different turns depending on the relative positions and developmental paths of the dominant and submissive partners. It is possible that within this relationship the dominant partner's control erodes as the submissive partner gains strength and autonomy over the early years of adulthood. Such gains for the submissive partner may occur as the result of feelings of heightened confidence and self-esteem through outside achievements, or as the result of exposure to friends or external influences pointing to the need for this individual to seek greater power within the relationship. For example, women who were married in the 1950s or early 1960s within a traditional relationship may, through exposure to the feminist movement of the 1970s, have discovered their need for greater independence. It is also possible that the dominant partner may lose power as the result of job loss or demotion, or as the balance within the family changes with the birth and growth of children.

Along with changes in relative positions of dominant and submissive partners may be emotional changes within the partners in a stable relationship. Thus the submissive partner may not take on more overt power but may become increasingly resentful of the hold that the dominant partner has in the relationship. This resentment may lead to covert attempts to control the outcome of events within the family. Conversely, the dominant partner may feel an increased need to maintain power in the face of real or imagined threats to the status quo. Some of these emotional conflicts around issues of control may be expected to be played out in the sexual arena. The submissive partner who resents the control of the dominant partner may use this one facet of the relationship to express this resentment, further adding to the dominant partner's desire to determine the nature and outcome of sexual interactions. It is within the merger relationship that the traditional "battle of the sexes" would be expected to reach its peak, with both partners complaining that the other one is manipulative and unsympathetic.

Elaboration of Family Issues

Against this backdrop of the couple's experiences during the adult years, the changes associated with the aging process can now be focused on in greater depth. Although the aging experience is highly variable from individual to individual, there are several common themes faced by many late-life couples. These themes pertain to physical aging changes, health problems, cognitive changes, family changes, and retirement. We will briefly discuss these issues, particularly as they have evolved to affect recent cohorts of elders and then examine them in the context of variations by intimacy status. As in the previous discussion, we will approach this discussion with the assumption that both partners in the relationship are of the same intimacy status as they enter the later adult years.

COMMON THEMES
IN AGING COUPLES

Changes in physical functioning associated with the aging process and declines of physical health are significant threats to the later-life relationship. From the standpoint of the individual, changes in physical health status can have a great influence on psychological well-being (Deimling & Harel, 1984) and challenge the individual's own adaptive capacity (Whitbourne, 1987). The task of caring for a married elder who becomes infirm due to physical changes or Alzheimer's disease typically falls on the spouse, and this can be a source of unending stress and burden (Soldo & Agree, 1988; Wright, 1991).

Another set of challenges pertains to the area of sexuality. There are many common stereotypes and misconceptions regarding the potential for enjoyment in the later years. Older couples can sometimes be affected by these negative, and usually inaccurate, beliefs. For example, some individuals might think that it is abnormal, or even morally wrong, to maintain an active sexual life into their later years. But for most couples, sexual intimacy does continue over the years of marriage. Even if this intimacy does not consist of sexual intercourse, the expression of affection and loyalty can become very important in the later years (Reedy, Birren, & Schaie, 1981). In this regard, it is worth noting that although older couples still view sexual intimacy as important, they also place a greater value on aspects that develop over time, such as security and level of commitment to each other. This is true particularly for women, who at all ages report greater satisfaction in the area of sexual intimacy than their male counterparts (Rhyne, 1981).

The exit and reentry of grown children has become a common occurrence with the economic downturns of the late 1980s. Changes caused by the movement of children into and out of the home not only affect the physical space and privacy of the older couple, but their intimate relationship as well. The return of adult children can require the older couple to reestablish interaction patterns within the household more characteristic of their middle adult years, leading to an exacerbation of potential stresses existing at that time (Brubaker & Roberto, 1993).

Traditionally households have one person that retires, but here again patterns are changing so that there are increasing numbers of households in which both the husband and wife are employed. In this case, the couple may choose to retire at different times or plan their retirement together. Choosing to retire in a dissynchronized fashion (Brubaker, 1985) can have a major impact on intimacy due to the fact that each partner in the relationship faces role changes at different times, making the adjustment to a new life style as a couple potentially more challenging. After retirement, the daily lives of both members in the relationship change drastically. Time once occupied by the requirements of work no longer presents restrictions, and other activities must be found to take their place. As a result of this transition, couples find that they are able to spend a considerably greater amount of time on the growth of their relationship, perhaps narrowing their interactions increasingly to each other and a few close friends (Carstensen, 1992). This increased time together may have favorable effects. Couples who remain together can become more accepting, tolerant, and respectful of their partners, behaving in ways that are more affectionate and loving (Weishaus & Field, 1988). The increase in free time may lead some couples to spend some of that time interacting with friends, an activity that can bolster marital satisfaction through strengthening the partners' identity as a couple (Lee, 1988).

There can be benefits, then, as well as challenges, as the married couple ages. Personal differences, which for many years may have been held in abeyance due to the competing demands of children and work, often come back into focus at this time. In learning to interact as a dyad once again, the couple is often faced with developing new ways to communicate and make decisions (Brubaker & Roberto, 1993). By identifying and working out solutions to marital difficulties, the couple can often maintain a satisfying relationship, as well as developing an even greater level of enjoyment from the partnership. This is an especially challenging task in the postretirement years, because the couple will not only be working on their relationship together, but learning to restructure their own personal time as well.

CHALLENGES TO INTIMACY
IN LATE-LIFE COUPLES

We have just described some of the more salient challenges and potential sources of growth for late-life couples. In this section, we will discuss how these issues unfold among aging partners in the intimacy statuses.

Mutually Intimate Couples. For the couple in mutual intimacy status, the changes brought about by the aging process represent another one of many demands for adaptations encountered by the couple throughout adulthood. Although each partner in the relationship has a history of making flexible adaptations to developmental changes in the other, the changes associated with the aging process may place an unusual degree of strain on each. Mutually intimate partners have become so close to each other during the years that the prospect of either one becoming incapacitated or dying may be seen as overwhelming. Life without the partner, with whom one has shared every experience during a 40- to 50-year period, may seem too painful to bear. Apart from these personal fears and the toll that they take, the partners would nevertheless be expected to support each other, both emotionally and practically, as each spouse experiences changes in physical functioning and health associated with the aging process. Assuming that the couple maintains its pattern of open communication and a constructive approach to conflict resolution, they should be able to adapt steadily and gradually to these changes and the impact of these changes on the relationship.

However, physical changes brought about by the normal aging process or by disease in later life can lead to a new balance of power in the relationship. The partner who suffers from problems in mobility or who has become cognitively infirm becomes less able to carry out the role of equal partner in the relationship. This individual may become unable to participate in the physical activities to which the couple had become accustomed, or as the result of memory loss and other cognitive changes, may be unable to participate in the emotional interchange within the relationship. By virtue of these changes, the other partner assumes a more dominant role, a role to which he or she may be unaccustomed. Problems in communication and conflict resolution might develop as the healthy partner feels reluctant to burden the infirm partner with his or her feelings of discomfort in this new role. At the same time, the infirm partner may resent being in a position of dependency and unable to share in the lifestyle the couple enjoyed when they were younger. A rift may develop between the partners as each either retreats to private ruminations or turns to others for support and comfort. Yet another challenge may develop when the need for institutionalization becomes unavoidable, and the infirm partner must be physically sent away from home. Needless to say, the area of sexuality is another possible source of difficulty as the weaker partner becomes too impaired, either physically or cognitively, to participate in ongoing sexual relations.

The high degree of closeness and sharing to which the mutually intimate couple have become accustomed, then, may be precisely the factor that leads them to experience even greater difficulties in later life than couples without such a history. Nevertheless, given the couple's past patterns of resolving adaptive challenges by confronting them and seeking mutually rewarding solutions, they may be able to overcome the multiple threats to their relationship associated with the physical and cognitive aspects of aging and disease. Other potential late-life challenges in the areas of family changes and retirement represent a higher degree of continuity with previous adult challenges and should cause less of a disruption in the mutually intimate couple. With their past patterns of resolving difficulties with children, other relatives, and work commitments, the later-life changes in these areas should be accommodated to with a similar degree of success.

Pseudointimate Couples. The pseudointimate couple can in later life function like a well-oiled machine that has been running for decades to maintain an efficient household, find ways for the partners to spend their leisure time, and resolve any difficulties that arise from grown children or extended family members. Although they do not share their experiences at a deep level, they nevertheless maintain a compatibility that comes from years of living together and knowing each other's habits. In fact, after so many years as a couple, these individuals may develop a newly emerging deeper affection. One is reminded of Goldie and Tevye in *Fiddler on the Roof,* who acknowledge that after 25 years they probably do, in fact, love each other. There is empirical evidence to support the position that during the course of a marriage, if the partners remain committed to the relationship, there can be a decrease in the number of marital problems (Swensen, Eskew, & Kohlhepp, 1981; Swensen & Trauhaug, 1985).

Challenges to the relationship associated with the aging process or disease can disrupt the smooth functioning of the pseudointimate couple, but presumably more at a practical cost rather than in terms of emotional turmoil. Because the pseudointimate couple has not tended to focus on the emotional significance of their relationship, changes in physical or cognitive capacity are viewed in terms of how they affect the household's everyday routine rather than the psychological underpinnings of the relationship. When one partner is unable to participate in the couple's usual schedule, this is seen as an annoyance or inconvenience, but not as a powerful threat to the other partner's emotional well-being. However, this is not to say that there is no sadness involved in the recognition that one's partner is ailing. Furthermore, experiences of either partner involving a brush with death may remind the couple of how interdependent they have become over the years. We might be reminded, in this sense, of another fictitious example, the couple in the movie *On Golden Pond.* This couple did not have a highly intimate relationship, but in the final moments of the movie, the husband's near-death attack brought out both sadness in the wife and, it appeared, a greater sense of closeness in the couple as they looked for the first time together at the prospect of the relationship's ending.

Merger Couples. Individuals in the merger intimacy status might well be expected to face the most difficult set of challenges associated with the aging process. The inequality of power and control in these relationships has depended for many years on the willingness of both partners to assume dominant and submissive roles. In contrast to the other intimacy statuses, which are based on a more stable balance of equal sharing, the merger status is highly vulnerable to a tipping of the scales in either direction. Such alterations add a new source of challenge to the adaptational demands already presented by age-related or disease-related changes in each individual. Physical changes that weaken the dominant partner leave the submissive partner in a totally unfamiliar role as caregiver or supporter. Conversely, if the submissive partner becomes unable to function within the relationship, the dominant partner, who is used to wielding power over an actively submissive mate, now faces the prospect of maintaining this power in what is no longer an "even playing field." Controlling a physically or cognitively weak partner lacks the same emotional satisfaction that the power-seeking partner has derived from years of domination. Furthermore, if the dominant partner is the man and he now faces caring for his infirm spouse, he may be uncomfortable with the role of having to take on the domestic responsibilities of a caregiver (Schulz & Williamson, 1991).

In the area of family relationships, partners in the merger couple would be expected to maintain the years of an imbalance of power and control. However, the addition of new members to the family, both through in-laws and grandchildren, might tip this imbalance the other way to favor the submissive partner. If the submissive partner is able to muster the support of these extended kin, he or she may be able to prevail over the wishes of the dominant partner by virtue of sheer numbers. It is also possible that members of these younger generations may give the elder family member support and encouragement to try to gain more power. This might be expected to occur in families in which the elder female, socialized during more traditional times to take on a submissive role, is educated by her children and grandchildren to become more "liberated."

Retirement is another major change that can upset the imbalance of the merger relationship. If it is the dominant partner who is retiring, whatever loss of status there is associated with transition out of the career role may translate into threats to the established basis of power at home. To make up for loss of control at work, the dominant partner may seek ways to broaden control at home, perhaps by suggesting that the submissive partner find new ways of handling household routines. The intrusion of the retired partner, when it is the husband, is suggested by the long-standing humorous comment made by wives that "I married him for better or worse, but not for lunch!" Conversely a reduction in the paycheck of the submissive partner may downgrade even further whatever control he or she maintained in the relationship. In either case, the increase in time together as a couple that occurs after retirement may lead to an increase in conflict between the partners as they attempt to adjust to new schedules and routines.

The more dependent partner may look forward to having more time to spend with the dominant partner who, in turn, resents having to account for his or her whereabouts now that the daytime hours are no longer spent at work. However, equally plausible is anger on the part of the dominant partner at not being able to control the comings and goings of the submissive partner, who is expected to remain at home.

As mentioned earlier, the imbalance in the merger relationship might lead to greater volatility and instability over time. Years of resentment by the submissive partner over being dominated may be transformed into passive but destructive anger that expresses itself in the emotional and physical aspects of the relationship. An example from Yalom's fascinating first-person account of psychotherapy case studies provides just such a case. *Phyllis* was dominated by her husband *Marvin* for many years, and in their mid-60s they were struggling with sexual problems. In responding to the therapist's inquiries about her attempts to control their sexual relationship, Phyllis observed that "I guess I had to have something that Marvin wanted. . . . Often I feel I don't have much else to offer. . . . I have no talents or skills" (Yalom, 1989, p. 265). The crisis brought about by the husband's need to seek therapy eventually led to an opening of routes of communication between the partners, growth in each as individuals, and a renegotiating of their power distribution.

Directions for Practice and Policy

APPLYING THE INTIMACY STATUS MODEL

There are many challenges faced by the practitioner in assisting late-life couples with issues related to intimacy. Given the potential areas of physical, cognitive, and social changes in later adulthood, the task may sometimes appear ominous. Application of the intimacy status model to late-life couples can prove useful, both in assessing the nature and extent of their difficulties and in charting a course for treatment.

The intimacy status, as it is employed for research purposes on adults, involves the assessment of three domains of the relationship along three relational dimensions (Whitbourne & Ebmeyer, 1990). These three relationship domains are the practical, the psychological, and the physical. The practical domain of the relationship includes the everyday household management tasks, such as grocery shopping, taking out garbage, and running errands. The psychological domain includes the emotional relationship between the partners and the intimacy potential that each has to share significant parts of the self with another person. The physical domain includes the expression of affection and sexual relations. Each of these areas is assessed along the dimensions of communication, conflict resolution, and control. The communication dimension refers to how openly and frequently partners share feelings. Conflict resolution refers to the characteristic way the individuals handle disputes: through avoidance, constructive conflict resolution, or destructive conflict resolution. The dimension of control incorporates the balance of power and whether one partner holds emotional dominance over the other, who in turn is higher in dependency.

To use this framework in an assessment format, questions should be asked within each area or block of the matrix formed by crossing the three domains of the relationship by the three relational dimensions. For example, in the practical-communication block of the matrix, the individual would be asked whether the couple discusses who does household chores. A psychological-communication question would address whether the partners discuss their feelings about each other. In the physical-control area, the individual would be asked who initiates sexual activity and determines what activities the couple engage in. An assessment of intimacy status can follow from a 20- to 30-minute interview covering these blocks of the domain-dimension matrix. Partners in the mutual intimacy status indicate that they communicate openly and often in all three relationship domains, that they try to approach conflict constructively, and that they have an equal balance of power. Partners in the pseudointimate status lack communication, avoid conflict, and share equally in decision making. The distinguishing feature of merger relationships is the unequal balance of power. They may or may not communicate openly, and they rely either on avoidance or destructive engagement when faced with conflict.

Given the many complicating factors that can alter the course of intimacy in later life, a full evaluation of both individuals in the areas of physical, cognitive, and social functioning is another important preliminary step to beginning work with the couple. For example, seeming inattentiveness on the part of one partner to the other may be a function of hearing problems or cognitive changes that have caused the partner unintentionally to ignore the other. By diagnosing and treating these difficulties, the marital relationship might show improvements without any need to intervene at the level of the couple's interactional patterns.

In moving from assessment to intervention, the differentiation should be made between the intimacy of the individual under treatment, the intimacy of the partner, and the intimacy of the relationship itself. Once this differentiation has been made, the clinician needs to target the intervention to the nature of the intimacy statuses represented by each individual separately and by the couple as a unit. The clinician, perhaps in collaboration with the couple, must weigh whether to try to move the couple to a different intimacy status, one that will allow each partner to experience greater individual satisfaction and enhanced functioning as a dyad.

Interventions made on the basis of this assessment and consideration of goals should also take into account the couple's history. If the partners have grown apart after years attending to the demands of children and work, new communication skills can be taught so the couple regains this route to a more intimate relationship. Issues relating to power imbalance in merger relationships can be addressed by encouraging the partners to define their individual needs and expectations of each other. The couple can set goals, both individually and together, that they would like to achieve in their lives. New methods of conflict resolution in which partners respect each other's needs as individuals can help to reset the power dynamics to a more equitable level.

Clinicians working with older couples might choose to incorporate one of the many techniques that have been found to facilitate intimacy in a close relationship. The tools that can assist couples in the pursuit of higher levels of intimate involvement depend greatly on the individual situation in terms of personal styles as well as the environment, such as relations with other family members. Because of this variation, couples and professionals need to select those methods that appear to be the most applicable to their personal life situations.

Specific treatment methods that can be used involve attempts to move couples along the dimensions of intimacy represented by the intimacy statuses. Couples can be assisted in establishing new ways of communicating with each other, to replace modes previously used that may have worked in the past but have now become dysfunctional or dissatisfying. In addition to communication methods, couples can also be encouraged to plan special time that they can spend together enjoying mutually satisfying activities. Also, due to the tendency for both the satisfying and dissatisfying aspects of the marital relationship to become more prominent in the later years (Brubaker, 1985), couples may find it helpful to identify those qualities that they would like to strengthen in their relationship. By identifying the negative and positive elements of their relationship, a couple can be assisted in further developing and emphasizing the positive qualities. They can also learn to cope more effectively with those areas that are more difficult and perhaps harder to change, such as physical illness or economic hardships. The sexual relationship can be explored to target areas that could potentially heighten enjoyment for both partners. The effects of disease, drugs, and psychosocial factors can be discussed in terms of sexual involvement, using a psychoeducational approach to alert couples to factors that are likely to remain stable as well as those they can change (Brubaker & Roberto, 1993).

Finally, clinicians may want to take advantage of a technique that has proven effective in helping many older adults cope with individual difficulties pertaining to depression and despair. Life review techniques can be used in the context of the couple or family to help partners develop an understanding of their present relationship in terms of the development of the marriage during the course of their adult lives (Hargrave & Anderson, 1992). The process of life review can help the couple understand how their intimacy status has evolved and been affected by both external circumstances and intraindividual developmental processes. By understanding these past influences, couples can achieve a new intimacy based on a shared realistic perspective on the factors leading to their present status and examine their goals and desires for change.

The intimacy status model is one that can easily be explained to elder clients, perhaps with the aid of a chart illustrating the dimensions and domains of intimacy. Assuming that the individual client or couple are truly interested in seeking a change, the clinician can share the intimacy status model as a basis for assessment and goals for areas of growth. A psychoeducational approach can also be useful in alerting clients to the normal changes involved in the aging process and the types of health problems that are likely to create difficulties in late-life relationships. Finally, a willingness to maintain an optimistic attitude about the lifelong potential for psychological growth and change can help the clinician maintain a perspective that will truly facilitate the couple's ability to overcome the challenges faced in their later years.

CASE EXAMPLE

The following case example comes from the clinical work of the first author, who saw a 68-year-old woman in individual treatment for undifferentiated feelings of depression and anxiety. Mrs. T complained of anxiety following a minor incident in which she accidentally collided, while walking on the sidewalk, with a neighbor's child. Following this incident, Mrs. T was unable to sleep and experienced periods of depression, low self-esteem, and an unwillingness to leave the house. Mrs. T was also under medical treatment for a cancer that was in remission. Ten years earlier, Mrs. T's oldest daughter was killed in an automobile accident. In describing her marriage to Mr. T, a formal army officer, it was apparent that the couple's relationship could be characterized by the merger status, as Mr. T was very domineering and tended to paternalize Mrs. T. He, rather than she, recommended that she seek therapy. Mrs. T herself was uncomfortable about being in therapy and during the course of the 6 months of treatment never fully relaxed in sessions.

After it became apparent that Mrs. T was the submissive partner in a merger type of relationship, her feelings of depression and low self-esteem were consistent with a picture of a woman raised in a traditional era and context who could not overtly express her longings for greater decision-making power. Attempts were made in individual therapy to bolster her self-esteem through cognitive interventions, such as helping her understand her negative views of self and how they influenced her interactions with others. Mrs. T also was encouraged to talk about her previously unexpressed grief over the loss of her daughter and her fears about her illness. Throughout the course of therapy, Mrs. T eventually became more assertive with others, including her husband, and her feelings of depression lifted. By the end of the therapy, she felt confident that her "spell" of anxiety and depression was past and follow-up one year later confirmed that she was free of further symptoms.

This example illustrates that by framing Mrs. T's symptoms in terms of relationship difficulties, as well as the other relevant physical health and family issues in her life, it was possible to alleviate her psychological distress. Her increased assertiveness and willingness to examine painful areas of her past life seemed to give her greater strength in relation to her husband and to help her achieve some relief from her dysphoric feelings. Couples therapy would undoubtedly have been beneficial, particularly if it allowed Mr. T to see the need to give Mrs. T more opportunities to express her autonomous feelings within the relationship.

Discussion Questions

1. How can the intimacy status model proposed by the authors be used to understand the relationship of Mr. and Mrs. T, as described in the case example?

2. Besides the special treatment methods that the authors suggest "to move couples along the dimensions of intimacy," can you suggest any other methods that would help couples establish new ways of communicating with each other?

3. The authors explain that a couple's past patterns of resolving adaptive challenges by confronting them and seeking mutually rewarding solutions facilitate the coping with multiple threats in the relationship brought on by the physical and cognitive aspects of aging and disease. What are other ways for an elderly couple to handle current challenges in their relationship besides learning how one manages past difficulties?

10

Utilizing Culture in
Work With Aging Families

THOMAS W. JOHNSON

Ethnicity is an important component of personal and familial identity, regardless of whether it emerges in actual behavior, attitudes, or feelings. Particularly in the aging phase of a family's life cycle, ethnicity exerts a powerful effect on expectations, decision making, and the development of shared meanings. It is so fundamental a variable in family life that it colors all of the important issues of aging families—issues also covered in this book, such as later-life couple and sibling relationships, elder care, and elder abuse. This chapter will offer a picture of how ethnicity wields its influence in the key dimensions of the family life of aging members. However, it is important to note at the outset that the review of ethnic variables offered here is not an exhaustive one: Not all ethnic groups are mentioned, and not all potential cultural influences are described.

Background

For many years, the dominant ethnic perspective of the United States—this "nation of immigrants"—was that cultural differences eventually dissipate through the assimilationist forces of the American melting pot.

However, this view has been challenged during the past 2 to 3 decades as some authors (Greeley, 1969; McGoldrick, 1982) maintained that ethnic and cultural characteristics may persist across many decades of family life. The impact of ethnicity is often dramatically apparent in the manner in which a family addresses the aging and loss of its members. An excerpt from the opening scene of Kushner's (1992) play, *Angels in America,* illustrates some of the ways ethnicity wields its influence through multiple generations of an Eastern European Jewish family. The passage is taken from the eulogy delivered by a rabbi at the passing of an elderly grandmother.

> Descendants of this immigrant woman, you do not grow up in America, you and your children and their children with the goyische names. You do not live in America. No such place exists. Your clay is the clay of some Litvak shtetl, your air the air of the steppes—because she carried the old world on her back across the ocean, in a boat, and she put it down on Grand Concourse Avenue, or in Flatbush, and she worked that earth into your bones, and you pass it to your children, this ancient, ancient culture and home. (p. 10)

The passage dramatically depicts the deeply held cultural identification that persists across generations despite the pressure to assimilate: For even the grandchildren with the *goyische* names carry the ancient traditions in their bones and breathe the air of the steppes. This identification and the worldview that emanates from it can serve as a resource for a family adjusting to the aging of its members, or it can offer unwelcome complexity if there is a poor fit between the cultural values and the family's contemporary life. For example, ethnic traditions often supply a sense of continuity and meaning for older adults who are bombarded with one demand for adaptation after another. However, their adult children and grandchildren may need to alter the traditions to varying degrees to suit the demands of their life stages and social context. Conflict then emerges.

The passage also poignantly describes the pain and conflict that assimilation can engender in a family. This is especially the case for older adults who witness modifications of their cultural traditions from one descendant to the next. They are often left with a sense of loss and alienation, whereas their children struggle with guilt and shame at the perceived abandonment of the family's traditions. A related issue embedded in the passage, and a very potent issue, is the legacy of loyalty and debt that passes through the family around duty and obligation to protect familial and cultural traditions. Clinicians working with aging-focused families spend considerable time addressing this issue of intergenerational loyalty at all levels of the family system.

It is only a relatively recent phenomenon that clinicians and researchers have begun to account for ethnic and cultural factors in their work (Boyd-Franklin, 1988; Gelfand & Kutzik, 1979; McAdoo, 1993; McGoldrick, Pearce, & Giordano, 1982; Mindel, 1983; Riess, 1993). Out of a belief that people are more alike than they are different in their basic humanness, and out of a belief in the objectivity of the scientific method, researchers have often ignored ethnocentrism—both their own and that of their subjects. As Boyd-Franklin (1993) suggests, the ethnic or cultural perspective is "often dismissed as totally irrelevant to general research design or clinical practice or, at best, as interesting yet peripheral digressions" (p. 39).

Unfortunately, clinical practice and policy decisions have been made based on "objective" research findings that derive from a mistaken belief that fundamentally "we are all the same." Service delivery systems, particularly ones targeted for the elderly, are often not culturally informed or sensitive. For example, "fictive kin," who are nonblood intimates counted as family by certain groups, are often omitted in research about family response to chronic illness and are often omitted from institutional family policies—such as hospital visitation policies (Boyd-Franklin, 1993). This can create cultural alienation for families who rely on this sort of relative for support and care, as is the case for some African American families. Family researcher David Riess (1993) noted the importance of using culturally relevant definitions of family, particularly in terms of fictive kin, to ensure the validity of his research on family support of non-White inner-city patients with chronic renal failure.

Part of the problem with the inclusion of ethnic factors in aging research may have to do with the methodological complexity that occurs with respect to this variable, as described by Rosenthal (1986). The first issue is a fundamental one: What is the operating definition of ethnicity? The definition used in this chapter is basically the one employed by McGoldrick (1989) in her work:

Ethnicity as used here refers to a concept of a group's "peoplehood" based on a combination of race, religion, and cultural history, whether or not members realize their commonalities with each other. It describes a commonality transmitted by the family over generations and reinforced by the surrounding community. . . . It unites those who conceive of themselves as alike by virtue of their common ancestry, real or fictitious, and who are so regarded by others. (p. 69)

However, even if a more scientifically precise definition is used, as Rosenthal (1986) notes, there are many confounding methodological questions. Primarily, how do researchers or practitioners operationalize their definition of ethnicity? Is ethnicity indicated by national origin, measures of identification and affiliation, measures of assimilation, or by all of these indicators taken simultaneously? What is the most valid measure of ethnicity—attitudes and beliefs, behaviors, or all of these dimensions? How is the inconsistency between cognitive and behavioral indicators of ethnic identification understood? What is the effect of interaction between ethnicity and class, or between ethnicity and stigma?

Rosenthal (1986) also contends that the general model of ethnicity employed by the researcher, practitioner, or policymaker is important to identify and that the model has significant implications for the findings or recommendations that are disseminated and for addressing the questions listed above. From her review of the literature on ethnicity and aging, she notes the frequent appearance of the following three models: (a) ethnicity as an expression of culture; (b) ethnicity as a determinant of social equality or minority status; and (c) ethnicity as an indicator of traditional ways of thinking and behaving (as opposed to the modern ways of the nonethnic Anglo families at the modern end of a traditional/modern continuum).

The specific model employed by the researcher or practitioner influences interpretations of family behavior and process. For example, the situation of a Chinese American son who struggles with a decision about whether or not to bring his demented mother to a day care program could be understood differently by each of the three models. His ambivalence might reflect a culturally determined preference for familial caregiving and a reluctance to open his family problems to the influence of outsiders. This interpretation is consistent with the ethnicity as culture model. However, his ambivalence could also be understood as "healthy cultural paranoia," a characteristic of Black Americans noted by Grier and Cobbs (1968), in which the Chinese American son's feelings possibly reflect mistrust and low expectations for effective help from White-dominant cultural institutions. This would reflect the ethnicity as social inequality model. The third interpretation is that the son views his family as a traditional one and that the use of community supports is a modern intervention inconsistent with his family's more insular and family-centered traditions in approaching problems. This is the ethnicity as adherence to traditional ways of thinking and behaving model. All three imply different approaches to understanding and intervening with this son's dilemma.

Elaboration of Family Issues

Among the many ways of understanding the influence of family ethnicity and culture, there are five dimensions of family life that powerfully illustrate the impact of ethnicity on how a family deals with the aging of its members. The first is the way the construct of "family" is understood and experienced. This dimension refers to the ethnic variations in how families draw boundaries regarding who is considered a family member and who is not. This issue, as described earlier, is very important in the context of aging families. For example, if a family incorporates fictive kin into its circle, there may be a cultural clash with health care organizations regarding which people are seen as the key resources and the family executives in caring for an impaired older family member. The second dimension is the way family roles and responsibilities are defined and distributed (particularly in terms of intergenerational relationships). This dimension refers to the cultural differences that exist around the recursive normative expectations between older relatives and their descendants. The third dimension is intergenerational strain. This refers to the tension created when there is an uneasy fit between the culturally normative roles and responsibilities set down for each generation in a family. The fourth dimension is the conceptualization of illness. Ethnic differences abound on what constitutes illness and disability for older adults. In this regard there is fertile ground for cultural misunderstandings between culturally mainstream health care organizations and older adults operating out of orthodox ethnic criteria for what constitutes illness. The fifth and last dimension is attitudes about help seeking. This dimension refers to the cultural differences that exist around what constitutes an illness worthy of treatment and what effective treatment might entail for that illness. Older adults differ in their endorsement of medical solutions for physical problems. Each of these dimensions will be examined in turn, with examples of case composites supplied by the author's practice in a geropsychiatric outpatient service of a community mental health center, which serves both an urban and suburban region of central New Jersey.

ETHNICITY AND THE CONSTRUCT OF FAMILY

As noted by McGoldrick (1982, 1989), the basic definition of family and the parameters of family membership can vary from culture to culture. She offers as one example the Italian family, in which "there is no such thing as the 'nuclear' family" (1982, p. 10). Family includes a closely tied three- or four-generation unit that might also include godparents and intimate friends (Rotunno & McGoldrick, 1982). This stands in contrast to the traditional "American" notion of family, which divides the system into the nuclear and the extended subsystems, with the nuclear system typically privileged as the more important or significant. McGoldrick also mentions the alternative family construct of Chinese families, who include as family all their ancestors from the beginning of time to their descendants in the infinite future. Shon and Ja (1982) note that because of this sense of the continuity of family over time,

> the individual's behavior has a different importance and consequence. Personal actions reflect not only on the individual and the nuclear and extended families, but also on all of the preceding generations of the family since the beginning of time. And individual actions will impact upon all future generations as well. Therefore, there is a burden of responsibility that transcends the individual's personal concerns. (p. 211)

Boyd-Franklin and Hines (1982) also note this pattern of prioritization of family and community identity over individual identity in African American families, which derives in large part from an African cultural heritage. Given these more expanded notions of family, it becomes clear how much more complex it can be for an Italian, African American, or Chinese older adult or family member to make decisions about handling an aging-related issue than it might be for a culturally mainstream American family: Decisions have reverberations for the family, perhaps across multiple generations, and are not just an individual affair. However, from another vantage point the situation might be less complex because of clear cultural scripts or because of norms that supply a built-in symbolic support network.

Another crucial issue in terms of the cultural variations in the conceptualization of family is a construct noted earlier—fictive kin. In many cultures, nonblood intimates are added to the family's membership list and are counted on for support and care. Rotunno and McGoldrick (1982) indicate that this surfaces in the Italian notion of *gumbares* and godparents, who assume important supportive roles in Italian families. Boyd-Franklin (1988, 1993) describes the importance of fictive aunts, uncles, and godparents in African American families and indicates that only rarely do family researchers integrate this variable in their understanding of African American family process. She also maintains that many clinicians might neglect to inquire about and include highly important fictive kin in their treatment of these families because of a cultural blind spot about what constitutes a family. Fictive kin may play a key role in the provision of support to an aged family member, or in some families an older adult may be a fictive relative who plays an influential part in the functioning of the family. An example of a cross-cultural breakdown that could emerge around this issue in a geriatric context might be if a dementia evaluation clinic neglects to include an important fictive relative in the evaluation process or neglects to accord this kind of family member the familial respect it might offer a blood relative. A potential for geriatric cross-cultural breakdown also appears in the Intensive Care Unit (ICU) visitation policies that are commonly reinforced by hospitals (Boyd-Franklin, 1993). These rules are typically discriminatory against fictive relatives, who may in fact be more crucial supports than immediate blood family.

McGoldrick (1982, 1989) notes that ethnicity and culture create variations in another important component of what constitutes family—the family life cycle. This concept refers to the family's developmental movement through time as a discrete family unit. The cultural variations in the life cycle process are critical points for family clinicians to grasp so that they do not apply contextually inappropriate expectations to families with strong ethnic values and norms. For example, Falicov and Karrer (1980) note that Mexican American families lengthen the phase their members spend in childhood, shorten the adolescent phase, and expand the midlife phase well into what traditional American families would consider older adulthood. The Irish, as reported by McGoldrick (1982, 1990), are the ethnic group with the lowest rate of marriage and the oldest age at the time of first marriage. This pattern often leaves Irish sons and daughters (particularly daughters) in an extended, unattached young-adult position and makes them prime candidates for the role of caregiver to an aged parent. Hines (1989) contends that, in practice, there is no "empty nest" experience for older, midlife low-income Black parents, as they are typically intensely involved in providing care, particularly child care, throughout their extended family systems, and they are often active providers of practical assistance and key members of expanded households.

Migration also has a profound effect on the family life cycle. McGoldrick (1982, 1989) claims that it is such a destabilizing experience for extended family systems that it may add another stage to the family life cycle. The extra stage entails regrouping, adjusting to the new context, recasting expectations to conform to the new context, and possibly reenumerating who is the primary family and who is not. The movement into older adulthood for late-midlife family members may be delayed because of the need for financial and pragmatic contributions to the survival of the immigrant family unit. The immigration may also create confusion for the older adult, who may not have familial age counterparts or an even older generation to turn to for advice, support, and identification. In this way a reidentification of self as an older adult may be delayed, which in turn may create role confusion and chaos about intergenerational expectations for the younger generation. McGoldrick (1982, 1989) implies that all of this complexity may freeze the family's movement through the life cycle for the length of time it takes to readjust.

Cultural relativism is clearly an important standpoint to take in understanding the variability in definitions of family. The implications of this position for research, policy, and practice in terms of aging families are twofold:

1. Professionals need to be careful about the assumptions they make about who is in the family and who is a key relative.
2. Professionals need to be careful about their developmental expectations regarding normative family process given the impact of culture, the sociocultural surround of the dominant culture, and migration.

ETHNICITY AND FAMILY
ROLES AND RESPONSIBILITIES

Ethnicity places intergenerational roles and responsibilities in an important context that redefines normalcy and recasts "normative" expectations in culture-fair terms. As McGoldrick notes (1982, 1989), ethnic traits are apparent even three and four generations beyond the arrival of the immigrant generation in the United States. Yet many Americans would dismiss this influence, given their endorsement of the myth of the American melting pot. Assimilation certainly plays a part in the American way of life; however, it may not be as complete a process as we assume.

A number of writers have charted cultural differences in terms of the intergenerational roles and responsibilities germane to aging. Understanding these differences is key to performing valid research, policy making, and treatment. For example, McGill and Pearce (1982) claim that White Anglo Saxon Protestant (WASP) families operate with a tradition of self-sufficiency and "hyperindividualism" that extends into older adulthood. They suggest that WASP families greet aging with an anxiety about incapacity and dependence and that older adults are expected to function self-sufficiently and independently in relation to their adult children. There is a great deal of dread about becoming a burden to one's family. The WASP family stands in stark contrast to the Italian family. According to some authors (McGoldrick, 1989; Michaud, 1990; Rotunno & McGoldrick, 1982), there is a strong tradition of daughters and daughters-in-law ministering to the needs of elderly parents in Italian families. This is consistent with the preference for use of extended family resources to deal with problems documented by the above clinicians. According to 1970s data, Italians have a low rate of nursing home placement of relatives compared to other ethnic groups (Fandetti & Gelfand, 1976). Keeping in mind the issue of acculturation and assimilation, this kind of data needs to be collected with a more contemporary sample, not only with Italian families but with other groups as well, to see if the pattern still holds.

In addition to the Italian family, the WASP family also stands in dramatic contrast to the Mexican American family, as described by Falicov and Karrer (1980). These authors contend that independence

> is not expected from a sick person and therefore the expectation is that the young will take care of the old until the end and not place parents in nursing homes. . . . Sometimes nervousness, illnesses, and ailment are called upon to remind adult children about their obligations to their parents. (p. 419)

A mainstream American therapist might be horrified by such a display of distress by a Mexican parent and work with the son or daughter at facing up to "this manipulation." The authors also report that "spoiling" and "overprotecting" are seen as competent and sensitive nurture. However, simultaneously, Mexican older adults participate actively in the life of the family and offer such practical assistance as child care. Mindel (1983) reports that 1980 U.S. Census data reveal that more Latino elderly live with relatives and that fewer Latino elderly live as heads of households in comparison to Anglo elderly. However, Mindel's review of empirical studies of Latino families also establishes that the exchange of assistance and support between the Latino elderly and their families is higher than in Anglo families. In summary, then, in Mexican and perhaps in other Latino families, older adults are protected and given care as needed; however, they also continue to contribute to the pragmatic survival of the family. It is also important to keep in mind the question that Mindel asks: Is this pattern a reflection of adherence to the norms of "the old country," or rather, an adaptation to life in the United States as a disenfranchised minority group? Diminished access to privilege is always a factor to be considered in understanding nondominant culture in the United States.

African American families evidence some similarities to Mexican families in intergenerational norms relevant to aging. As noted by many clinicians and researchers (Baker, 1994; Boyd-Franklin, 1988, 1993; Boyd-Franklin & Aleman, 1990; Boyd-Franklin & Hines, 1982; Hines, 1989, 1990; McGoldrick, 1989; Mindel, 1983; Riess, 1993; Walls & Zarit, 1991), African American families prefer to make use of extended family resources in handling problems, which can include such concerns as provision of care to an impaired older relative. However, the elderly in African American families are often at the top of the family's power hierarchy and continue to take an active role in the survival and management of the family. African American grandparents are more often the heads of multigenerational households than are their White counterparts (Mindel, 1983), and they are often integrally involved in child care and important family decision making. As Boyd-Franklin and Aleman (1990) note, African American grandmothers are often the "switchboards" of their extended systems. Given this family function, the impairment or death of an elder in an African American family might constitute a different kind of crisis for the family than in other cultural groups: The loss might entail a call for hierarchical readjustment. However, as Boyd-Franklin and Hines (1982) assert, role flexibility and adaptation are the hallmarks of African American family strengths.

The above descriptions of ethnic variation in terms of intergenerational roles and responsibilities are just a glimpse of the broad array of patterns in that only a few ethnic groups were mentioned. Clearly there is considerably more variation. All of this points out the complexity that can ensue when the clinician or researcher from one ethnic tradition encounters a family from another, with the dominant mainstream American culture also serving as an influential backdrop. A case example illustrates the ethnic variations about intergenerational roles and responsibilities in greater detail.

Maria is a 74-year-old Italian immigrant who had migrated to the United States after World War II with her husband and two young children. Her husband died 2 years previous to admission, after a 3-year illness with cancer. Shortly after his death Maria began to show signs of severe depression and cognitive impairment. The depression improved with antidepressant medication, but the cognitive impairment persisted and eventually worsened. Her oldest child, Nina, a divorced mental health professional, lived a few towns away from Maria. She refused to take on primary caregiver responsibilities for her mother and quickly received stern censure from the rest of her family. The younger child, Paul, assumed leadership of the family following his father's death and was the loudest voice in the chorus who criticized Nina for "abandoning" her mother. Nina became quite depressed and a break ensued with her brother. Paul's wife, Patricia, became the primary caregiver when Maria moved into their home. Patricia halfheartedly assumed the responsibility and indicated that in her Irish family, home health care and day care were the options used for impaired elderly. She also was depressed given the recent death of her father, and she felt over-whelmed by also having to care for her three young children.

Culturally mainstream therapists might make certain invalid assumptions about this case. For example, they might dismiss Paul as demanding, insensitive, and authoritarian. Or they might see the level of responsibility taken on by Paul and Patricia as "overresponsibility" or as a manifestation of dysfunctional enmeshment. Or they might see Nina's guilt and shame as a neurotic process indicating her fusion with her mother. And related to this, they might minimize Paul's sense of betrayal by Nina as a sexist stance of male entitlement. Or Maria might be considered the "villain of the piece," and the conflict, guilt, and burden experienced by her children might be seen as the legacy of her guilt-inducement and inability to tolerate her children's autonomy.

None of these positions would have been helpful to this family because they would have missed the family's ethnic phenomenology. Paul felt that he was "doing the right thing" as a son in an Italian family, and Nina's depression and reactivity related to her guilt and shame at having "abandoned" her family's traditions in favor of an assimilated "American way of life." She even partially agreed, at some level, that Paul's points were valid. This family needed what McGoldrick (1982) refers to as a "cultural broker"—a therapist who validates their ethnic traditions, helps them make sense of the differences in assimilation level between each of the members, validates the anxiety created by reconciling ethnic traditions with the cultural mainstream, and helps them sort through what traditions they can productively maintain and which ones need modification. In order to help Paul successfully negotiate his differences with his wife and sister, the first order of business needed to be validation of his position in terms of ethnic identification. However, his wife's position needed to be validated as well, given her ethnic values and the recent circumstances of her life. The couple needed to see their differences as akin to linguistic dissimilarity. Moreover, Nina needed to see her assimilation in terms of her family history rather than as solely attributable to her unique personality.

She was the first family member to learn English after migration to the United States, and her role had always been cultural broker for the family. In this way, she learned more about mainstream culture and was more exposed to its influence. The family had also banked a great deal of its hopes for her, and in this way she was "set up" to become career- and achievement-oriented. Couple and family sessions focused on these issues. In addition, solutions consistent with the culture were constructed. Paul became more amenable to the use of day care, but, in addition, a family-wide "tag-team" schedule of respite for Patricia and Paul also made sense to him to decrease Patricia's burden, reinvolve Nina, and shore up the family's sense of shared involvement in the crisis of Maria's illness.

ETHNICITY AND INTERGENERATIONAL STRAIN

As mentioned earlier, assimilation can create intergenerational strain and confusion at all levels of a family system. Ethnically traditional or immigrant parents may feel poised to experience loss and alienation as they watch their children navigate the assimilation process. The sons and daughters may feel that they have a foot in two worlds: the old world of family cultural traditions and the mainstream world of the dominant culture. Often the demands of both worlds are incompatible, and conflicts arise about loyalty, responsibility, autonomy, values, and upward mobility. Amy Tan's (1989) novel, *The Joy Luck Club*, articulates this strain effectively in its portrayal of the struggle related to attachment, loyalty, and autonomy between four Chinese mothers and their Americanized daughters. The words of one daughter give a good example of the strain:

> Over the years, I learned to choose from the best opinions. Chinese people had Chinese opinions. American people had American opinions. And in almost every case, the American version was much better. . . . It was only later that I discovered that there was a serious flaw with the American version. There were too many choices, so it was easy to get confused and pick the wrong one. (p. 214)

It is crucial for family service providers to be familiar with this sort of strain and to address it in their interventions, whether they are clinical or otherwise. It is also important for policymakers to consider the potential for adding to intergenerational strain in the service recommendations they make.

Migration creates great potential for intergenerational strain (McGoldrick, 1982, 1989). For example, given that children often pick up new languages more quickly than their elders, a potential for confusion in family hierarchy and generational boundaries exists. If the child is used as the family's broker with the outside world because of the child's competence with the host country's language, he or she may be moved into a very powerful and responsible position in the family. This role may serve as fertile ground for that child to enter into a position of overresponsibility for the parents and the family. This key position may become burdensome over time, especially as greater and greater demands for acculturation are required in the personal life of the child. In addition, the family's chances for achieving some cross-cultural competence may be diminished by long-term overreliance on the child. The demands of mainstream life, combined with the press of such a level of family responsibility, may place an adult son or daughter in an untenable position.

Migration may also either consciously or inadvertently result in breaks with the extended family left behind in "the old country" (McGoldrick, 1982, 1989). This loss may lead to greater emotional dependence on children and grandchildren and to a tightening of the family boundaries to avert any further loss. This kind of intense affiliation may make the acculturation process even more fraught with complexity and anxiety for the first- or second-generation descendants. Conflicts may erupt around a first-generation child's "upward mobility," in that there may be a concern by the family about that child losing ethnic identity as he or she negotiates the demands of mainstream American culture. However, at the same time the adult child may feel pressure to become successful in order to improve the family's lot or to reclaim their sense of competence and achievement. This bind can be overwhelming. The child may also experience stigmatization related to his or her ethnic affiliation and feel inclined to make this part of identity less visible. Ambivalence and shame about ethnic heritage may surface, creating internal loyalty and identity conflicts as well as painful conflicts with the family. Herein lies the potential for another break in the family, for chronic conflict and strain, or for superficial and detached pseudorelationships between the child and the family.

The generation that "carries" the culture, as opposed to the generation that becomes more acculturated, does not necessarily have to be an immigrant generation. It can consist of the generation that has remained ensconced in ethnic communities even one or two generations beyond the immigration. Many families who live in New York's Little Italy or San Francisco's Chinatown are examples of such families. The carriers of the

family culture can also simply be those members who remain totally im-
mersed in the family's traditions and norms regardless of how many generations have elapsed since the original migration. However, for those family
members who begin to step outside of the traditions and risk significant
assimilation, there is the great risk of "role overload." This situation is
typically seen in the case of assimilated adult sons and daughters caring
for elderly relatives who live fully within an orthodox cultural tradition.
The child strives to meet the demands of mainstream American life in
terms of work, success, and nuclear family demands (such as helping with
the children's homework, working 50 hours a week, coaching a Little
League team, or taking one's turn in a neighborhood car pool), while being
responsive to elderly relatives in ways that are ethnically sensitive but
perhaps incompatible with the rest of the son or daughter's life.

Karen is a 39-year-old single African American woman with a 5-year-old son.
Karen presented for help with depression. Her father died 2 years ago from
cancer after 1 year of illness during which time Karen cared for him in her home.
Following her father's death, his brother was removed from the brother's apartment because of nonpayment of rent and health violations. Karen brought her
uncle into her home, and it quickly became apparent that he was suffering from
Alzheimer's disease. She was experiencing difficulty making ends meet financially because her salary at her bookkeeping job was not paying enough and
her son's father was chronically negligent in sending child support. Her son
was experiencing academic difficulties, and this, combined with her difficulty
handling her uncle's agitation and paranoia, was overwhelming. She reported
feeling like a failure and experiencing significant guilt at entertaining the
idea of placing her uncle in a nursing home: "We just don't do that in Black
families—particularly my family. Why am I such a failure?" Her depression was
significant enough to require medication.

Karen's "role overload" situation is in part explainable by what Hines
(1990) refers to as "the myth of the Black superwoman," in which "stories
about the strength of their forebearers serve to increase the pressure that
African American women put upon themselves to handle everything" (p. 28).

Karen realized that she was contending with an enormous amount of
strain but felt deficient in her inability to manage it all when she compared
herself to the strong women in her family network, past and present. She
was adamant that it was her responsibility to find a way to meet the demands
of her life and simultaneously respond to extended family needs within
the traditions of her culture and family. Of course many of these traditions
were easier to handle in the historical past. Clinical approaches involving

confrontation about her overresponsibility without exploring the cultural context would make no sense to her. For example, when confronted sympathetically in the early stages of treatment about her perfectionistic standards, her response was: "You don't understand the way our families work. You can get away with being a sloppy housekeeper or a lazy son because no one is looking at you to see if you're a credit to your race." Moreover, an approach that would disqualify her family's demands as unrealistic would be alienating.

Karen was able to achieve some flexibility in her assumption of responsibilities after a series of interventions in which she was asked to talk to trusted female members of her family network and her friendship network about her situation and about the question of how much responsibility is too much. She received culturally sanctioned permission from her natural support system to relax her standards and to take care of her own needs in addition to those of her family. Her family role was also further discussed in therapy from a perspective of role confusion and role overload rather than from an individual or familial pathology perspective.

It is also important to keep in mind that role overload for African American women does not just occur in the younger generations. Boyd-Franklin and Aleman (1990) report that in the inner-city Black community, a significant amount of the caregiving burden related to AIDS has been placed on the shoulders of already greatly-taxed older women. The authors describe the frequent occurrence of grandmothers caring for HIV-infected grandchildren left behind following the deaths of their parents from AIDS. Thus these grandmothers are struggling with the premature deaths of their own children and the likely deaths of the ill grandchildren for whom they are caring. This overload creates significant health risks for these older women.

ETHNICITY AND
CONCEPTUALIZATION OF ILLNESS

McGoldrick (1982) maintains that there are also ethnic variations in what is categorized as a problem. Specifically, in terms of the kinds of problems that would bring a family in for family therapy, she claims:

WASPs may be concerned about dependency or emotionality, the Irish about "making a scene," Italians about disloyalty to the family, Greeks about any insult to their pride, or *filotimo*, Jews about their children not being successful, or Puerto Ricans about their children not showing respect. (p. 11)

There are also ethnic variations in what is defined as a medical problem and what symptoms are deserving of treatment. For example, among African American older adults, one's ability to handle basic activities of daily living in an autonomous fashion often constitutes the criterion for deciding whether one has a health problem worthy of pursuing medical attention (Baker, 1994). This sort of definition may result in what the mainstream medical system claims is a "delay" in seeking medical attention. A common example might be an older African American woman who, at a friend's persuasion, stops by a health fair, has her blood pressure taken, and finds out that she has moderate hypertension. She reports that she has been having headaches, fatigue, and spells of dizziness for almost a year and has not pursued medical treatment even though a brother has recently suffered a stroke, and her mother died from a stroke. She states that she has not worried about her health because she has been able to perform her daily routine and has "just been so busy" with family obligations.

There is considerable cultural variation in how illness is experienced, and empirical evidence for this was provided by a landmark study done in 1969 by Zborowski. The author compared differences in the phenomenology of physical symptoms and pain in Jewish, Italian, Irish, and WASP patients. His results showed that Irish and WASP patients were typically inclined not to complain about their pain, as compared to Jewish and Italian patients, whose complaints were at a much higher frequency. In addition, Jewish and WASP patients were reportedly more "accurate" in describing their pain sensations, whereas the Italian and Irish patients were not. Zborowski maintained that the Irish underestimated their pain and seemed to try to block its effects, maintaining a stoic and fatalistic stance about their illness, whereas the Italian patients reportedly overestimated their pain sensations. Moreover, Zborowski also reported that the culturally mainstream "American" medical staff saw the reactions of Italian and Jewish patients as excessive. This issue of a cultural "clash" of meaning and perception was also revealed in another study. Zola (1966) found that physicians more often attributed the dramatic behavior of their Italian patients to mental illness, even in the absence of clear criteria data. Unfortunately this kind of culture-bound perspective may lead to problems in developing a good working alliance with patients and their families, at best, or to misdiagnosis and inappropriate treatment, at worst.

Differences in spirituality and in attitudes toward death may also create problems in mental health and health care of patients, particularly in the case of treating the elderly. For example, McGoldrick (1989) reports that the Irish and African Americans often take a standpoint that death is an important transition in the life cycle that is not unwelcome—death may represent a release from the burdens and cares of the world and an opportunity to go "home" to one's final reward in heaven. Falicov and Karrer (1980) report that Mexicans take an almost "counterphobic" approach to death as revealed in the Day of the Dead festival held yearly in Mexico. Aphorisms and jokes about mastery over and outwitting of death, as well as the candy and paper skulls and skeletons seen in Day of the Dead celebrations, reveal a more open and less anxious and helpless position about death. Therefore a Mexican patient might have much less anxiety about the consequences of noncompliance with a treatment recommended by an American doctor. Similarly, an Irish or African American patient might have less of a sense of urgency about defeating mortality with regular checkups and proper adherence to treatment recommendations. Moreover, the Irish patient might not even use pain management as a motivator to pursue and comply with treatment, given the cultural norms relating to suffering and pain perception.

Mary is a 72-year-old Irish American woman in the intermediate stages of Alzheimer's disease. During a routine examination, her physician found a significant-sized lump in her breast, which was eventually determined to be malignant. She had a complete mastectomy. Four days after the surgery her husband brought her back to the day care program she attended, without any sense that she might need more time to recover. Mary was cognizant of her diagnosis, the operation, and of her recovery process; however, she offered no complaints of physical distress. Both Mary and her husband took the position that she was "fine" and was ready to resume her life, much to the consternation of the day care staff.

This ethnic variability in what is defined as an illness or even as a problem has clear implications for the validity of research assumptions in terms of needs assessments and outcome studies. The implications are also clear for service providers and policymakers in terms of taking a culturally aware position about what constitutes effective service and understanding what will enhance compliance.

ETHNICITY AND ATTITUDES ABOUT HELP SEEKING

Ethnic variations also exist concerning whether to seek help outside the familial network and what kind of help to seek. For example, clinicians have observed that Italians are loath to go outside the extended family for help (Michaud, 1990; Rotunno & McGoldrick, 1982). A preference for obtaining assistance from natural supports is a norm in many ethnic groups. For African Americans at all stages of the life cycle, extended family and the church are important sources of support. Among African American elderly, the presence of extended family and church support are significant predictors of perceived well-being (Walls & Zarit, 1991). This is consistent with clinical literature, which indicates that African Americans turn more often to family and to the church for assistance (Adebimpe, 1994; Boyd-Franklin, 1988; Boyd-Franklin & Hines, 1982). As in the African American community, spirituality is an important source of meaning in the Puerto Rican community, and these families may also turn to spiritual resources before other sorts of professional institutions (Garcia-Preto, 1982). In addition, compliance with treatment offered by dominant culture institutions may be affected by other sorts of social system variables. For ethnic minority families who have experienced stigma and exclusion, a "healthy cultural paranoia" may exist vis-à-vis the dominant culture (Grier & Cobbs, 1968), which produces caution and tentativeness in using the help offered by dominant culture institutions (Boyd-Franklin, 1988).

All of these above factors create fertile ground for a mismatch between mental health and health care institutions, the elderly, and their families, thereby creating a context in which problems in service access emerge. Herein lies the urgency for the development of cross-cultural competence in institutions serving the elderly.

The case of Alice, which dramatically illustrates the problem of a mismatch between service providers and families of the elderly in terms of what constitutes help, will be discussed later in the chapter. This case will serve as a "grand case example" in that it demonstrates the potential for cross-cultural misunderstanding not only in apprehending the family's attitudes about help seeking but also in apprehending almost all of the other dimensions of family life previously discussed.

Directions for Practice and Policy

Mismatch of expectations is often a key theme in addressing ethnic variables in family treatment, research, and policy pertaining to the elderly. There is the mismatch between the family's cultural expectations and those of the surrounding culture, as embodied in the clinician, the researcher, or the policymaker. However, there is also intrafamilial mismatch, which consists of conflicts concerning adherence to ethnic traditions within different family members or generations, which can also be an important variable in understanding family adaptations to the aging of its members. This theme of mismatch needs to be fully appreciated and not marginalized in the professional literature because the price of ignoring the issue is ineffective service delivery for older adults and their families. What follows is a description of how ethnic mismatch and misapprehension is addressed in clinical service, nonclinical service, research, and policy contexts.

CLINICAL TREATMENT

In terms of how a family clinician can be helpful with the problem of mismatch or cross-cultural understanding, there are three basic clinical considerations to make that are specific to cross-cultural work. Of course, these considerations are applied in addition to the routine skills involved in providing good clinical treatment to any family. The first consideration for the clinician is to ensure that they are fully informed regarding the ethnic norms of families they are treating. When clinicians are basically unfamiliar with the culture of a family they are treating, this may involve obtaining supervision from colleagues with more experience with the family's ethnicity. This might seem to be an obvious recommendation, but many practitioners may assume that their theoretical grounding and training may apply to all families across the board. The second consideration is to pay careful attention to the engagement component of treatment. This is particularly crucial if the family's experience in the dominant culture is one of disempowerment and alienation. It is usually useful to take a deferential perspective with the family about the need to be informed and advised about their ethnic perspective on presenting problems and concerns.

The third consideration is McGoldrick's (1982) notion of taking the role of cultural broker when working with nondominant culture elderly and their families. In working this way, the therapist goes back and forth between the ethnic loyalty position and the assimilated/assimilating position, establishing the validity of each standpoint. The therapist uses a "both/ and" approach, in which he or she helps the family to struggle with integration of both perspectives into the system, rather than struggling to pick one position over the other. Using a more specific example, this might involve helping a family to affirm its identity as an Indian family with its rituals and traditions, while at the same time figuring out how to modify the traditions to suit the dominant culture context without losing their basic ethnic integrity. The other function of the cultural broker is to serve as a translator between the dominant culture and the family.

The case of Alice illustrates these three important considerations in working cross-culturally with older adults and their families. The case also demonstrates the ethnic variations in how families handle the aging of its members in terms of the basic dimensions of family life discussed earlier. The variations in this case provided multiple opportunities for cross-cultural misunderstanding in the relationship between the service providers and the family.

CASE STUDY

Alice is a 50-year-old African American woman whose family was referred for community support services involved in providing care for her 78-year-old mother. Alice is a divorced mother of three young-adult children. At the time of the referral, Alice, her mother, her father, and Alice's three children were living in the elderly parents' home. Her mother was bedridden with multiple disabling orthopedic, cardiac, and pulmonary problems. Her father had symptoms suggestive of dementia, but given his capacity for self-care and mobility within the inner-city community where they lived, he was not defined as impaired by this family. A referral was made for home health care by the elderly mother's medical team, who were concerned that she needed more care than her daughter could provide. Alice, who had been employed as a nurse, had been her mother's primary caregiver, but she had become increasingly impaired by rheumatoid arthritis. She was in chronic pain and had pursued treatment after treatment with no success. However, physicians she had worked with reported that she was often noncompliant with their recommended plan.

Alice fired one home health aide after another and was often embroiled in heated conflicts with elder care agencies. The agencies became so frustrated that they referred Alice and the family to the geriatric service of the local community health center. During family and individual interviews Alice revealed that she felt frustrated, guilty, and ashamed about her inability "to care for a mother who never denied me." She began to put pressure on her 25-year-old daughter to help.

The daughter tried halfheartedly to assist, but she began to stay out all night drinking with friends.

Alice frequently rebuffed the White therapist assigned to work with her and her family: "What could you possibly know about my life, and how on earth could you ever help me?" The therapist persisted. Outreach calls and home visits over about a year's time finally engaged her. Family sessions were used to discuss Alice's guilt regarding her limited ability to care for her mother. Efforts were made to use both agency resources and family resources in the caregiving. Alice eventually became a bit more cooperative with the outside care, but only after regular empathic validation of the value conflict entailed in having outsiders take care of her mother. Alice frequently made use of the resources of the Baptist church her family belonged to, and she often saw prayer as a valuable solution. In fact, she had successfully overcome an addiction to pain medications with, by her reports, the help of prayer, Bible reading, and church attendance: "AA wasn't going to do anything for me—it's the Lord's help I needed." She often asked her therapist about his spiritual beliefs and felt relieved that she could use a spiritual framework for understanding her problems during therapy sessions. The therapist also often advocated for her with her medical team and frequently intervened systemically in the relationship between Alice and her physicians. After a considerable amount of work, a successful alliance was established between Alice and her therapist, and she made use of his support when her mother died. Her summary of their relationship was: "You're alright! You hung in there when I needed to be convinced that you really wanted to help me and that you really had something to offer. I tested you and you passed!"

This case illustrates the importance of careful attention paid to engagement and cross-cultural competence in terms of familiarity with ethnic variations in norms and belief systems. The treatment would have surely failed if these issues were given short shrift and if more attention was paid to the standard techniques of family therapy. The clinician also had to function as a cultural broker by helping Alice and her family move into a both/and position about their values and the services offered to them. Another cultural broker function was translating the standpoints of the service provider system and the family to each other in order to reduce the level of conflict.

The case also reveals the difference in perception, between the service provider system and the family in terms of the family dimensions described earlier. Alice felt strongly that it was her responsibility to care for her mother directly, and she rejected the notion of home care assistance regardless of her disabilities. The outside system saw her as unrealistic and overly responsible. Intergenerational strain also surfaced between Alice and her daughter about expectations for filial duty and obligation. The system of service providers at times was not helpful in this area, when they would take a position defending the appropriateness of the daughter's feelings. In addition, the differences in conceptualization of illness were striking in this case. Alice's ideas about her capabilities in light of her rheumatoid arthritis, and her family's sense of her father's capabilities in light of his dementia, were often contradictory to the standpoints of the various health professionals involved in this case. In summary, this case presented opportunity after opportunity for cross-cultural clash.

However, the most instructive aspect of this case is how the impact of ethnicity on help-seeking attitudes can create a cross-cultural gulf between families of older adults and the system of service-providers involved in their lives and how one addresses this in treatment. Alice amply displayed the "healthy cultural paranoia" that was discussed previously. Her caution in seeking help outside her family needed to be tolerated, and the therapist had to log significant amounts of time establishing his consistency and concern. Alice and her family also talked openly about their expectation that a White professional would not understand them and might approach them with racist bias, and open examination of the therapeutic relationship in terms of these variables helped to engage Alice's trust.

Along these lines, this case illustrates the importance of an emotionally engaged, genuine, and less professionally formal and distant relationship with an African American family (Boyd-Franklin, 1988; Boyd-Franklin & Hines, 1982). In addition, openness to the spiritual dimension of the family's life seemed to be a crucial variable in engaging the family. Many of these factors that made engagement of Alice successful may be inconsistent with the role supported by dominant culture institutions, which prioritizes efficient, cost-effective, professional services delivered to as many as possible in as brief a time as possible.

It is in this regard that policymakers need to balance the realistic demands of their funding structure with the demands of cultural competence if they are going to work with nondominant culture groups. In addition there was a gap in terms of the perceived urgency of Alice and her mother's situation. The home-health care agency and her mother's medical team saw a compelling need for immediate care. Alice felt she needed time to sort out what she was capable of doing and what she thought others might do for her mother. She felt that both she and her mother could survive the time she needed to think through her options. Taking the time needed to sort out these concerns ended up being cost-effective in the long run, given time saved in angry phone calls and hiring and rehiring home-care staff. This time lag may create great anxiety for a medical team accustomed to answering urgent medical needs as fast as possible. In this situation a medical staff may need support from the therapist involved in the case to wait patiently for the family to make the necessary adjustments and decisions.

Boyd-Franklin and Hines (1982) indicate that African American families typically prefer a treatment that emphasizes the importance of family and that offers pragmatic problem solving. The pragmatism of the therapist's interventions with Alice and her family seemed to be a crucial ingredient for success. Alice also needed a cultural broker, and in this regard she needed the therapist's help to advocate with the health care professionals taking care of both her and her mother in order to ensure they understood her family's values and needs. However, at times, Alice also needed the therapist to interpret the needs and values of the institutions so that she could operate effectively with them herself. Sharing this information with her helped to empower her when she interacted with the multiple medical and social service systems involved with her family. This case illustrates the need to tailor and retool expectations and approaches with ethnically nonmainstream older adults and their families. Service flexibility based on cultural awareness was a crucial element for successful service delivery in all the service systems involved with Alice and her family. This case is also useful in terms of its application to outcome research. Alice and her family had very clear ideas about what constituted effective service to their elderly relatives. And their ideas might be fairly consistent with those of other African American families. It would probably be useful to employ valid and reliable operationalizations of the ideas of the ethnic group as outcome measures when considering outcome assessment with these families.

NONCLINICAL SERVICES

Community services such as social/recreational opportunities, housing, social service entitlement, family life education, and community outreach programs are no less compelled to develop cross-cultural competence in delivering services to ethnic minority communities. Families may be as disinclined to accept seemingly nonthreatening support services to assist in the care of an aging relative as they are to accept medical and mental health services. Again the underlying issue is often ethnic values and beliefs about using nonfamily resources to adapt to family problems, or the issue might be institutional mistrust given long-standing feelings of marginalization and alienation in relationship to the larger dominant culture.

The solutions to this dilemma are similar to the recommendations made about engaging ethnic minority older adults and their families to accept mental health interventions. Nonclinical service staff need to pay close attention to their fund of knowledge about the ethnic groups whom they serve, to their engagement skills in working with ethnic minority families, and to their ability to work as cultural brokers, in which they try to help ethnic minority families find both/and solutions to their separatist/assimilationist dilemma regarding services to their elderly relatives.

There are also some programmatic recommendations that might help to engage ethnic minority older adults in receiving community services. First, the use of grassroots, indigenous staff conveys to the community serious commitment to engaging the community and respecting its values. Second, an outreach component that involves engagement of potential clients on their own turf also demonstrates serious commitment to the community. In this regard it might also be useful to work with the natural supports of ethnic minority older adults. For example, for many minority communities, religious institutions serve as a primary resource, which is typically the case for African American older adults and their families (Boyd-Franklin, 1988; Walls & Zarit, 1991). A social service program seeking to improve its effectiveness and to increase its number of contacts with the African American elderly population would be well-advised to develop an effective liaison relationship with the local African American churches and conceivably to offer services on-site at the church or to recruit the church to function as an intermediary in engaging potential clients. A third recommendation involves recruiting minority elders in the community to function as advisers and consultants in program development and evaluation. This also demonstrates respect and appreciation of diverse cultural perspectives, but an advisory council of this sort also serves as an informational resource about the culture and about the program's progress in becoming more culturally competent.

RESEARCH AND POLICY

The most fundamental recommendation in terms of ensuring that research is ethnically informed is a simple one: Maintain awareness of ethnicity, race, and culture as crucial independent variables, and do not dismiss them as tangential to scientific research. It is always important for the researcher to maintain a position of cultural relativism about each of the five dimensions of family life discussed earlier, and for variables related to these dimensions not only to be scientifically precise in their operationalization but also to be culturally valid. Outcome research also needs to include dependent variables that are culturally appropriate. For example, an African American family's satisfaction with services might be dramatically different from an institution's perspective. In this regard, an African American family might not assume that medical compliance is as desirable an outcome of treatment as, for example, improvement in functional abilities of an elderly relative.

With regard to policy, on a microlevel, institutions need to assess their procedures with an eye toward their ethnic sensitivity and bias. From a service delivery standpoint, Hernandez (1991) maintains that inattention to culture leads to misapprehension of service needs relevant to ethnic minority elderly and to utility problems with the services that are constructed by various policy decisions. She notes that home health care policies can be particularly vulnerable to this problem of cultural invalidity. For example, a Cambodian family might be in desperate need of home care for an elderly parent with advanced dementia. However, they might be adamantly against hiring a nonfamily member or a non-Cambodian person to provide the care. Hiring an extended family member or a Cambodian neighbor to offer the service would represent an ideal solution, but the policies of the local social service agency might refuse to reimburse anyone other than a licensed, agency-affiliated person. In addition, the local home care agency might not have prioritized recruitment of indigenous home care staff, and therefore they would not have an ethnically acceptable person to offer the family. In this regard, microlevel agency policies recapitulate the family's experience of marginalization and alienation. In response, the agency might claim that they do not have the funds to recruit and train indigenous workers, even though their agency serves a region with a sizable number of Cambodian families with elderly members. Both parties are left feeling misunderstood and alienated.

Macrolevel policy decisions on a municipal or state level that prioritize the needs of the major ethnic minority groups in the region would establish the support necessary for smaller service agencies to function in a more ethnically sensitive manner. So assessment of cross-cultural competence needs to take place at both the micro- and macrolevels.

CONCLUSION

In all probability, only a very small majority would argue against the importance of considering ethnicity in research, practice, and policy making regarding the elderly and their families. However, differences ensue in the level of attention paid to these factors when the pressure of limited resources in time, money, and person power are faced. Researchers might argue that ethnicity is a less critical independent variable when decisions and priorities are made. The director of an outpatient mental health clinic might argue that she is unable to spare the staff time and cost to allow too many home visits to an unengaged ethnic community. And with the pressure to offer cost-effective services, a medical or mental health treatment team may not feel they have the "luxury" of adapting to a family's traditional ethnic framework about chronic and severe illnesses like cancer or dementia: Professionals may feel the need to assert their diagnosis and recommendations and achieve compliance from the patient and the family as rapidly as possible. In essence, developing a culturally sensitive and informed perspective takes time and conscious commitment. Even if the time and commitment are available, the work of maintaining cross-cultural competence is difficult. As McGoldrick (1982) notes, "most Americans probably come to understand well only three or four groups in the course of a lifetime" (p. 27). The crucial component of this endeavor is in the attempt, and in the metaposition of cultural relativism, which keeps a person open to the idea that truth is a matter of cultural vantage point. Holding this perspective of perceptual openness is more valuable than knowing the cultural norms of 3 or 4 or 20 different ethnic groups. Hopefully, this openness will come to be seen as cost-effective in that it may eventually spare communities of service providers and prospective clients mutual disappointment and frustration.

Discussion Questions

1. When working with a family that represents a different ethnic culture than that of the practitioner, how can the practitioner establish rapport with such a family, laying the foundation for an effective helping relationship?

2. Do you believe, as the author says, that ethnicity refers not only to race and cultural history, but also to religion? Why or why not?

3. The author identifies five dimensions of family life that illustrate the impact of ethnicity. How do these dimensions apply to the case study identified as the family life of Alice?

PART IV

A SYNTHESIS
OF INTERVENTIONS
FOR AGING FAMILIES

This final section contains three chapters that encompass interventions that have been discussed in the previous 10 chapters. Whereas in each of these previous chapters a range of interventions was introduced that could benefit the specific needs of one kind of aging family, here we pull together—or, if you will, synthesize—interventions across the several kinds of aging families.

In Chapter 11, Tobin and Power discuss the diversity of direct practice. Then, in Chapter 12, Smith broadens our purview by addressing many prevention approaches that build competencies in aging families. Brubaker and Brubaker (Chapter 13) focus on policies that enhance family functioning, particularly when caring for one of its members. In each of these three concluding chapters, the authors return to the contents of the earlier chapters to illustrate and discuss ways to strengthen aging families. However, each of the first 10 chapters provides such a richness of interventions that every intervention discussed earlier is not included in this final section. For example, readers will have to return to specialized chapters, such as Kosberg and Garcia's (Chapter 4) discussion of maltreatment of elders and to Fullmer's (Chapter 6) discussion of gay and lesbian families, for more specifics on direct treatment, on prevention that builds competencies, or on policies that enhance family functioning. Still, it will become readily apparent that within each chapter the variety of interventions is organized in a systematic, logical, and comprehensible manner.

11

The Diversity of Direct Practice

SHELDON S. TOBIN

PAUL W. POWER

The diversity of practice with aging families has been well documented in the previous 10 chapters. Whereas practice in its generic sense refers to the myriad of interventions to enhance functioning, in the context of this chapter on direct practice, its meaning is more specific. Here practice refers to face-to-face direct contact with members of aging families to enable functioning by advice giving, counseling, and psychotherapy. Because distinctions among advice giving, counseling, and psychotherapy are blurred in direct practice, this trichotomy is used for heuristic purposes, that is, to sort out levels of intensity of direct practice with aging families. Advice giving, which is sometimes referred to as consulting and is the lowest level of intensity in therapeutic encounters, consists of providing information about, and discussing, alternative courses of actions that can be followed. Counseling of families goes further by helping clients to understand their current behaviors, where behaviors encompass thoughts, feelings, and actions, particularly regarding interactions with family members. In turn, psychotherapy seeks this understanding, often referred to as insight, by assisting clients to explore in-depth relationships between current behaviors and their causes in early socialization; it includes the uncovering of less conscious feelings and motives. As shown in Table 11.1, the three practice approaches are prevalent throughout the family life cycle and for the variety of clients in family treatment noted throughout this volume. Moreover, clinicians may employ one or more of the three levels of practice with a targeted individual or set of family clients when focusing, for example, on supporting families in caregiving (Toseland, Smith, and McCallion, Chapter 1) or being a "culture broker" who is sensitive to ethnic and racial issues in practice with families (Johnson, Chapter 10) or when working with gay and lesbian clients (Fullmer, Chapter 6). Yet one level may dominate when practicing with a specific kind of aging family. Advice giving is the norm when fostering family involvement in institutional care that will benefit an elderly member who is a resident in a long-term care facility (Tobin, Chapter 2) or when urging an older mother to consider making permanent residential plans for an offspring with mental retardation for the future time when she can no longer provide care at home consequent to her illness or death (Smith, Tobin, and Fullmer, Chapter 5). Counseling is typical when assisting families in making here-and-now health care decisions for an eldest member (Bata and Power, Chapter 8). In turn, whereas counseling is also most prevalent for helping families to work out intergenerational conflicts, psychotherapy may be essential to ameliorate dysfunction (Power, Chapter 7), as is also the case when assisting individuals or couples who are having problems in their late-life marriages (Whitbourne and Cassidy, Chapter 9) or when attempting to reduce elder abuse by a family member (Kosberg and Garcia, Chapter 4).

Feelings of Practitioners

Clinicians who enable aging families by any of these three kinds of interventions may be different than practitioners who choose to work with other groups of clients. Those who practice with aging families must confront, and hopefully have resolved, personal feelings that are evoked when working with or for aging persons. If practitioners are too uncomfortable with issues of disability, dependency, and death, they cannot practice effectively with aging families because these feelings will interfere with their advice giving, counseling, and psychotherapy.

Fears of dependency arise in practitioners not only from their awareness that adverse events, such as sudden illness or accident, can cause them to be overly dependent on others but also that their parents are likely to be dependent on them for care or may even now be dependent on them.

TABLE 11.1 An Overview of Practice With Families

	Life Cycle Stages	Clients	Practices
Chapter 1			
Supporting the Family in Elder Care	Older-old years	Primary care-givers, adult daughter	Advice giving, counseling, and psychotherapy and also support and counseling groups, to decrease care burden
Chapter 2			
Fostering Family Involvement in Institutional Care	Nursing Homes	Family members, usually adult children, who may themselves be over 65	Advice giving, individually or in support groups, to reduce apprehension and increase involvement; counseling to reduce conflict with parents in homes
Chapter 3			
Strengthening Sibling Relationships in the Later Years	Latter half of life	Siblings together	Including siblings in counseling; using reminiscence in counseling or psychotherapy where conflicts can be resolved.
	(Parents early in life)	(Individuals or a whole family)	(Counseling or psychotherapy can make a healthier family, resulting in stronger bonds later in life.)
Chapter 4			
Confronting Maltreatment of Elders by Their Family	Latter half of life when care is needed	Family caregivers	Assessment and screening to detect abuse; advice, counseling and psychotherapy with individual, dyads, and whole families to reduce stress that causes abuse
	(Child early in life)	(Individual or whole family)	(Psychotherapy to reduce psychopathology that can cause parent abuse later in life)
Chapter 5			
Assisting Older Families of Adults With Lifelong Disabilities	Latter half of life	Parents, but also adult children who are siblings	Advice giving and counseling. Families particularly regarding permanency planning for offspring
		(Counselors)	(Educating practitioners)
Chapter 6			
Challenging Biases Against Families of Older Gays and Lesbians	Latter half of life	Individual and couples	Empathic, nonjudgmental advice giving, counseling, and psychotherapy

(continued)

TABLE 11.1 Continued

	Life Cycle Stages	Clients	Practices
Chapter 7			
Understanding Intergenera- tional Issues in Aging Families	Latter half of life	Whole family system; spouses, children, and even at times grandchildren	Family counseling and psychotherapy counseling and psychotherapy to enhance intergenerational family functioning
Chapter 8			
Facilitating Health Care Decisions Within Aging Families	Latter half of life	Family members of whole families	Counseling about making health care decisions
Chapter 9			
Achieving Inti- macy in Late- Life Marriages	Latter half of life	The couple	Counseling, including life review to enhance intimacy
Chapter 10			
Utilizing Culture in Work With Aging Families	Latter half of life	Individual or whole families (Practitioners)	Ethnosensitive advice giving, counseling, and psychotherapy that includes being a "cultural broker"
			(Education to be ethnosensitive)

Although interdependency in families is natural throughout the life course, independence and self-sufficiency, characteristics that are inculcated early in life, are as American as apple pie. Thoughts of losing independence and self-sufficiency are upsetting and frightening; the formerly vigorous father who becomes frail, burdened with disabilities, and only a shell of his previous self is himself a reminder of our vulnerability, but his condition also provokes thoughts of appropriateness of responses to his dependency. Will I do, or am I doing, what is best for him? Or will I be guided, or am I being guided, too much by my own self-interest? How will I, or can I, balance my responsibility to him with responsibilities to my spouse?

Fears arising from dependency cause even the most skilled of clinicians who have not previously practiced with elderly clients to want to do too much for them, because they are perceived as frail people who are not unlike dependent parents (see, for example, Poggi & Berland, 1985, on child psychoanalysts who reported on an initial experience working with elderly people). Then, too, there are practitioners who completely avoid any work with elderly clients from fears of dependency. They can rightly be called gerontophobic.

Fears of death may also cause a purposeful avoidance of elderly clients and their families. Noteworthy is that middle-aged clinicians are likely to fear death, and not older people at the end of their life courses. The oldest people fear nonbeing less and fear more the process of dying—not wishing to die alone, in intractable pain, immobile, and (increasingly because of the prevalence of Alzheimer's disease) irreversibly confused.

Fears of disability, dependency, and death can be considered unavoidable concerns evoked in clinicians who practice with aging families, concerns that necessitate maturity to handle effectively. If handled effectively, some gratifications ensue. Assistance provided in any form becomes useful to families so that coping is improved, and helping younger family members facilitates their providing more help to their older generations, an indirect effect often accrued in practice. In turn, curiosity (or if you wish, voyeurism) is always satisfying, as clients tell their stories; satisfaction is especially enhanced when listening to an older person's history, a historical review often dating back many, many decades that includes a complexity of family dynamics and how they have been manifest during a lifetime. And not to be underestimated is how helpful it is to practitioners for understanding their own aging, their caring for their own oldest dependent members, and their acceptance of death.

The Scope of Practice

This volume does not limit itself to practice in which the eldest member is frail, dependent, and near death. These kinds of aging families are the primary focus in Chapter 1 (Toseland et al.) on supporting families in caregiving and in Chapter 2 (Tobin) on the increasing involvement of families when a member lives in a long-term care setting; they are also considered in cases in other chapters, including Chapter 4 (Kosberg and Garcia) on maltreatment in the family, Chapter 8 (Bata and Power) on health care decisions, and Chapter 10 (Johnson) on ethnosensitive practice. Elsewhere other kinds of families are included. Family practice in the latter half of life does not always focus on oldest impaired family members but includes, for example, strengthening sibling bonds in later life (Cicirelli, Chapter 3), assisting older parents who are not yet frail to make future plans for adult daughters and sons with mental retardation (Smith et al., Chapter 5), counseling gays and lesbians in their young old years (Fullmer, Chapter 6), counseling multigenerational families (Power, Chapter 7), and facilitating intimacy in late-life marriages (Whitbourne and Cassidy, Chapter 9).

The scope of practice with aging families includes a great variety of clients and many stages of the life course, and all will be covered in the sections that follow. First, there is a discussion of stages in the life cycle that are encompassed in practice with aging families, ranging from families early in their formation and development to the death of the oldest family member at the end of the life course. Discussed next is the variety of clients, as well as the distinction between clients seen in direct face-to-face practice and clients not seen, such as the confused elderly family member with Alzheimer's disease for whom advice or counseling is sought. Both family caregivers who are seen by the practitioner and the unseen Alzheimer's disease victim can be considered as the clients in direct practice. The third section, on practice, includes discussions of assessment, choice of treatment, and a comment on relationships between process and outcome in direct practice. The fourth and final section, on doing differently, begins a discourse on how practice should be modified when working with or for aging families.

Stages in the Family Life Cycle

Stages in the family life cycle that are encompassed in this volume on strengthening aging families range from an earliest stage when offspring are birthed through death of a family member at the end of the life cycle.

Birthing an offspring with mental retardation and then choosing to provide care at home has profound effects on parents in their later years, including the time when permanent residential plans should be made (Smith et al., Chapter 5). These families are decidedly different from normative families because their expectations for a daughter or son with developmental disability must be tempered by their offspring's functional impairments. The burden is even greater for parents of adult children with mental illness because the disability is likely not to have become manifest until adolescence or young adulthood. These latter parents, therefore, expected their children to live normal adult lives, only to have their expectations thwarted.

Families with children in their formative years have obvious effects on their behaviors in their later years. Conflicts among siblings can be traced back to family dynamics in childhood (Cicirelli, Chapter 3), which may be exacerbated when one sibling assumes responsibility as the primary caregiver for an ill elderly parent (Toseland et al., Chapter 1) or when one adult child assumes decision making for an elderly parent without consulting her siblings because of her own needs for attachment (Power, Chapter 7) or when health decisions must be made for a severely impaired oldest family member (Bata and Power, Chapter 8). Childhood experiences, and especially family dysfunction, may be causes for maltreatment later in life by family members (Kosberg and Garcia, Chapter 4), and certainly the psychodynamics of individuals that are developed early in life must be considered in intergenerational counseling of normative older families (Power, Chapter 7), as well as with lesbian and gay families (Fullmer, Chapter 6), late-life marriages (Whitbourne and Cassidy, Chapter 9), and in ethnosensitive practice (Johnson, Chapter 10).

Concurrent with the persistence of individual psychodynamics, family members age together. From being parents of a young child to launching a last child and experiencing an empty nest, for example, usually takes about 20 years. Grandparents are aging, too, during this time, typically from middle age to their young-old years, from their 40s or 50s through their 60s and 70s. They too may have parents who are the oldest of a four-generation family, in which members of the oldest generation are in their 80s and 90s or are even centenarians who are more than 100 years of age. A counterpart to the increase in generations within families that must be considered when intergenerational counseling (Power, Chapter 7) and assisting in health care decisions (Bata and Power, Chapter 8) is the later ages at which frailty occurs. Whereas a few generations ago, for example, the couple in a late-life marriage was likely to be in their 50s, the couple may now be in their 60s (Whitbourne and Cassidy, Chapter 9) and, correspondingly, adult children who are caregivers may themselves be "old," above 65, whether caring at home without any signs of abuse (Toseland et al., Chapter 1) or where there is elder abuse (Kosberg and Garcia, Chapter 4) or when their parents are in nursing homes (Tobin, Chapter 2). Thus the generation referred to as the "sandwich generation" or the "generation caught in the middle" was previously caught between caring at home for children and parent care; now it is more likely to be caught between parents who need care and husbands who wish to enjoy their retirement years, with children having been launched several years earlier. Alice, the African American mother discussed in Chapter 10 (Johnson) on ethnosensitive counseling, is caught between caring for her failing mother and her 25-year-old son.

Although the post-empty nest years through the young-old years before parent care are usually good years for the current cohort, there may be problems resulting from the freeing up of time and energies that have been devoted to parental imperatives and to work. Couples, for example, may now need to confront their pseudointimacy (Whitbourne and Cassidy, Chapter 9). Still, for most couples, there are some "golden years" following the empty nest, the menopause of women, and, increasingly, retirement of both husband and wife, who now often leave the labor force together before 65. Couples can relax and enjoy life as children now relate to parents as adults, and intergeneration solidarity, including relationships with siblings, is renewed and enhanced.

However, the golden years become tarnished when illness, disability, and frailty necessitate care. Now the aging individual must preserve the self against age-associated assaults by maintaining or reestablishing control over activities of everyday life, by being sufficiently assertive so as not to give into passivity, and by using reminiscence to affirm the continuity of identity. In turn, family members who become caregivers, first spouses and then adult children, must cope with their care burden, especially with feelings that the situation is out of control or can rapidly become beyond their control (see cases in Chapters 1, 4, 7, 8, and 10).

They also must deal with their anger, anger at themselves for inadequacies in caring and anger toward the care recipient who placed them in a situation where they feel inadequate. Paradoxically, processes that help the older-old care recipient to preserve the self, such as exerting control and assertiveness, can be aggravating to caregivers, especially when beliefs in control that enhance a sense of autonomy place the older person in jeopardy from accidents or other negative effects and when assertiveness takes the form of nastiness (see Tobin, 1991, who provides a case of a family he counseled and then discusses this paradox).

Although at any one time only 5% of persons 65 and older reside in long-term care facilities, to live beyond 65 carries nearly a one in two chance of spending some later years in a facility, usually when beyond 80 years of age (Tobin, Chapter 2). Aging persons in facilities use the same psychological mechanisms that older persons cared for at home use to preserve their sense of self. If they cannot, their deaths will be hastened. Passivity, for example, is lethally life shortening for older persons who are relocated to nursing homes. Family members, in turn, must cope with guilt from feelings of having abandoned a loved one (Tobin, 1991).

Older people at the end of the life cycle can generally accept their deaths, but for those who cannot, counseling can be helpful. Although placement in a nursing home often begins the process of anticipatory grief for family members, some family members may not be able to resolve their mourning following the death of their aged member. Counseling can also be helpful for these persons, because anger and guilt may linger long after someone's death and inhibit the family member's later adjustment to other eventual family changes.

Whether families are nonnormative, such as families caring for younger members with disabilities (Chapter 5) and gay and lesbian families (Chapter 6), or normative (as is the case in most of the other chapters), age-associated stresses can cause strain and anguish that can be ameliorated by direct practice. All families, in turn, can be helped when under the stress of making health care decisions (Chapter 8), when spousal and parent caregiving (Chapter 1), and when oldest family members are in nursing homes (Chapter 2).

The Clients of Aging Families

Clients in direct practice can be individuals; dyads as in counseling of couples or in intergenerational counseling, when the older person and a responsible adult child are facing a health decision; and also larger family sets of family members, when, for example, siblings and grandchildren are included in whole family counseling. Yet this is a simplification because a distinction can be made between the client or clients being counseled and a client targeted for assistance. Family members, for example, who are given advice on ways to be involved in nursing home care may be clients only because assistance to them will be helpful to their institutionalized family member. Provoking an elderly mother into making permanent residential plans for her adult daughter with mental retardation may be in the daughter's best interest rather than the mother's best interest, to the extent that she is gaining much gratification from caring for her daughter and successfully suppressing any painful thoughts associated with the future. An abusing family member may be assisted by restructuring caregiving, such as by using in-home respite care, that lessens abuse, but this does not provide the kind of counseling for her that can decrease the internal conflicts that in part precipitated the abuse.

These kinds of distinctions, unfortunately, can lead to trading off what is best for both clients. The daughter whose mother resides in a nursing home can be encouraged to share in caring while also being counseled to relieve her anxieties, as well as her guilt from spending less time with her now-retired husband. The elderly mother who should, or must, make permanency plans for her daughter with disabilities can be helped to make these plans while also being helped to feel relieved from the making of plans. Intervention with a son who is abusing his mother should lessen her abuse, while helping him to relieve the pressures that led to his abuse, both his internal pressures and the external pressures on him from the stressful situation.

Practice

Levels of practice were discussed earlier. Advice giving occurs when the practitioner limits treatment to offering a single course of action or one or more alternatives that can be followed. Counseling goes further and assists clients in sorting out alternatives by helping them understand their feelings and interactions with others and by helping them to consider in new ways their thoughts, feelings, and actions, as well as alternatives. Psychotherapy, in turn, refers to gaining this restructuring of perceptions of oneself, others, and situations by a greater and more explicit focus on less conscious motives and how these motives were developed in childhood socialization. In doing so, it is assumed that greater insight into intrapsychic conflicts is achieved that eventually leads to enhanced functioning.

Assessment. As discussed throughout all 10 preceding chapters, all interventions must be based on assessment. In Chapter 1, "Supporting the Family in Elder Care," the case vignette illustrates how the practitioner's appraisal of the situation, described in the client's words and feelings, leads to an opening up of the issue of control and anger toward a sibling. To go in this direction is a decision of the practitioner based on assessment of needs of the client when overburdened by the caregiving situation. Yet the practitioner could have pursued the earliest target of anger that was mentioned—the client's parent, for whom she was providing care. In choosing not to open a discussion of the daughter's anger toward her parent at this early point in treatment, the practitioner could have deferred this discussion until a later session but chose not to follow this lead. If the practitioner had done so, it might have led to a psychotherapeutic encounter containing content from early in life that led to the current psychodynamics in her relationship with parents.

In Chapter 7 on intergenerational counseling, assessment during the first family meeting was discussed. The practitioner must decide "on the problem that should receive attention" and "what is the best way to deal with the specific concern." Other areas that also must be assessed are delineated, including activities shared by family members, the extent of contact among them, whether all members express their opinions or only the family spokesperson, roles and allocation of tasks among family members, major sources of stress, and changes needed to maintain and enhance functioning.

The practitioner must decide on the problem that should be addressed. Sometimes the problem is very evident, as in the Chapter 9 discussion of intimacy in late-life marriages, where the focus is on relieving Mrs. T's "spell" of anxiety and depression. Cognitive counseling was used to bolster her self-esteem by "helping her understand her negative views of self and how they influence her interaction with others." It would have been more helpful to her if Mr. T was included in the sessions in couple therapy, which could allow "Mr. T to see the need to give Mrs. T more opportunities to express her autonomous feelings within the relationship." Without Mr. T's participation, this was not possible. Although it might have been possible, and even beneficial, to probe and uncover the causes in Mrs. T's early socialization for her becoming "the submissive partner in a merger type of relationship," the practitioner apparently made a conscious decision not to do so at this time.

As stated in previous chapters, consequently, the focus of assessment depends not only on the practitioner's orientation, but it also can include an exploration of the information families might or might not have about available community resources or the differences between normal aging and disease. The expectations family members have for the everyday functioning of the older person, the health of family members, the level of family stress, and the recognition of "old family business" should also be target areas for assessment. If old resentments or unresolved anger are not recognized, they can represent obstacles to intervention.

Choice of Intervention. Assessment leads to choice of how to treat—and sometimes even not to treat—in direct practice. A situation of elder abuse may be assessed as so severe and unamenable to remediation that immediate separation of the abused elder from the abusing family member is essential. When intervention is indicated, a choice must be made whether to stay at the level of advice giving, to initiate counseling, or to consider psychotherapy. Some family problems necessitate only advice giving, such as fostering involvement in nursing home care. Others suggest the need for intensive psychotherapy, such as when the client's presenting problem of a conflict with a sibling masks an intrapsychic problem that can only be resolved with in-depth therapy.

Influencing the choice of intervention is the predilection and training of the practitioner. Some practitioners are trained in counseling, and although they understand psychodynamics, many do not have expertise in in-depth psychotherapy. However, having this expertise does not necessarily mean that it will be used with all clients. Some clients do not have the capacity for insight therapy or, if they do, cannot tolerate the anxiety generated by looking at their intrapsychic conflicts. For many of these latter clients, the anxiety that cannot be tolerated when seeing a practitioner for an acute crisis may be tolerated at a later time after the acute crisis has been resolved.

Although difficulties are both diverse and unique to each family, there are certain commonalities to the identification of intervention goals for the elderly and family members. These include a redefinition of the role the elderly person has in the family and the assistance the family can provide to maintain the self-esteem and dignity of the older individual. Yet a main target for intervention with this population, including family members, is on the teaching of coping skills. Elderly persons are dealing with personal and environmental changes, and coping abilities may have to be strengthened or new ones learned to deal with perhaps a drastically changed lifestyle. Family members, of course, are also attempting to manage considerable changes, many of which have been identified in different chapters of this book. All of these chapters highlight various issues and illustrate that interventions within the normative and nonnormative aging context demand a wide variety of helping approaches.

Short-term counseling is a pivotal and often essential intervention to help families use appropriate resources or achieve most of the stated objectives for assistance identified in earlier chapters. As distinct from advice giving, within the counseling process there are specific techniques that can be used to alleviate particular problems. These include reframing, the appropriate expression of feelings, individual and peer group support, and such behavioral strategies as stress reduction approaches, role reversal, and reinforcement planning. Each of these techniques can help family members become a partner in the elderly person's own goal of life satisfaction. The techniques of cognitive restructuring and reframing, for example, are effective coping strategies for many everyday, difficult problems faced by the elderly person and family members; they can bring a new perspective on current limitations created by old age or caretaking responsibilities. Another coping behavior, reminiscence, can be encouraged by family members when assisting their elderly family member to deal with perceived losses and physical deterioration.

All the intervention approaches build on the thematic understanding that family functioning is understood in a systems perspective. In other words, individual problems with the elderly are embedded in the family's interactive social system. The behavior of one family member influences another member, and family difficulties with elder care should be understood within a family context. In maintaining this viewpoint, many interventions are suggested in this book that primarily focus on assisting family members to help the elderly person toward a more satisfactory life adjustment. This unique orientation emphasizes the importance of more short-term, family-related assistance when helping the elderly. Of course, the role that the family plays in collaborating with any assistance depends on the family structure, the quality of the family relationships, economic resources, and the competing demands on the family's energy and time. When family interventions are directed toward using family members for the adjustment and life functioning of the elderly, the practitioner should understand the specific family situation and what helping approach will best work in those circumstances.

One intervention goal that is implicit with much of the family assistance suggested in the different chapters is to facilitate the family's use of formal services. Family members are frequently reluctant to use community resources for a variety of reasons. Problems in the service systems, attitudes held by caregivers and practitioners toward the elderly and their families, the dilemmas created by the complexity and difficulty of caregiving tasks, and the amount of initial time and emotional investment in obtaining and trying services are important reasons for this reluctance. For elderly people to use a new service involves change, and change is difficult for older people whose behavioral patterns and attitudes may have remained constant for 80 or more years. The obstacles encountered when negotiating change become all the greater when identified services may be inaccessible, fragmented, or of known poor quality. Many services may also not be affordable to those who are poor. Among family members a feeling of pessimism or skepticism can then prevail, accompanied by the covert message that assistance may actually be quite hopeless. If families are eventually to use any needed community services, a relationship of trust, empathy, and reflective caring is essential between the family members and the practitioner. When this relationship is established, then the family could be receptive to advice giving and the communication of information about the opportunities that specific agencies offer for the family and older person. A helping relationship, information sharing, and advocacy functions are all intertwined when assisting families to use services.

Yet there are limits to what a practitioner can accomplish during intervention. The many case studies presented in this book accentuate the difficulties for effective interventions. A particular approach may only offer a very short-term solution for a long-term problem. Specific assistance may only begin to touch on issues that need long-term resolution. Assessment, guided by theory, leads to decisions on outcomes to be achieved and also the process used to achieve outcomes. Whether to stay at the level of advice giving or to counsel or to uncover less conscious motives in in-depth psychotherapy is a decision of the practitioner, but the initial ground plan may change as the therapeutic encounter proceeds. The practitioner may decide that counseling to change attitudes, perceptions, and behaviors that will ameliorate family stress should be supplemented by advice giving. Or advice giving can lead to counseling or counseling to in-depth psychotherapy. Practitioners must therefore develop flexible ground plans that can be modified, sometimes rather quickly.

Doing Differently

Does practice with aging families differ in any substantial ways from practice with other families? A health crisis for a younger family may also benefit from help in decision making. Care at home for a disabled adolescent may also warrant counseling. Ethnosensitivity and sensitivity to gay and lesbian issues is important regardless of the ages of clients. Also independent of age, characteristics of individuals and families may dictate treatment strategies. Socioeconomic status and gender always influence treatment, as do capacity for insight and absence, as well as extent, of psychopathology. But stage in the life course of individuals and of families must always be considered. Married couples at the birth of a first child are different from couples at mid-life and couples in advanced old age. Parent-child interactions differ when children are youngsters, are middle aged, and are in their younger-old years, when their parents are likely to be 85 or over. The aging of the family as a unit has a counterpart in the aging of individuals, which is most clear when the oldest family members are in advanced old age. The task in advanced old age is to preserve the self when age-associated losses of others and of health can corrode the self. As discussed earlier, control in everyday life (which feeds inflated beliefs that the world is controllable), hastiness, and even functional paranoia can be helpful to preservation of the self but can cause difficulties to families. Thus when very old persons are clients, whether they are seen face-to-face or are simply the people for whom assistance is sought, the therapeutic encounter must incorporate the psychology of the very old.

One possible component of this psychology is Butler's (1963) life review, which he described as an inevitable return to consciousness of reminiscences as death approaches at the end of the life cycle. Reconstructing reminiscence is the norm for clients, as past experiences become their illustrations of actions or reasons for current behaviors or, in turn, are elicited by practitioners so that practitioners and clients can come to a better understanding of causes for behaviors. Cicirelli (Chapter 3, this volume) mentions the inevitability of sharing reminiscences when siblings are in counseling. Although one's life history, one's personal narrative, is continually being rewritten to meet current adaptive demands, the life review as posited by Butler can allow more than modifications that facilitate adaptation. The pushing into consciousness of reminiscence can allow practitioners a window of opportunity to help clients to make a whole life narrative coherent, and it also provides for the possibility of resolving intrapsychic conflicts.

The incapacities of advanced age create a complexity of emotional and practical needs that require significant others in families to adopt what Silverstone and Burack-Weiss (1983) have called "an auxiliary role," a role in which support is provided for as long as needed. The role contains not only emotional and instrumental tasks but also articulation with the formal service system so that care is shared informally by family members and by providers of nonfamily formal supports. The practitioner becomes a link in the chain, sometimes advising family members in how to carry out the auxiliary function and at other times adopting the auxiliary function by obtaining essential extrafamilial services for them.

Thus the clearest difference between direct practice with aging families and with other families is evident when working with or for persons of advanced age. How practice should be modified when working with aging families, as it should be when working with aging individuals (Tobin & Gustafson, 1987), is a concern that is only in its infancy. It is hoped that this volume will assist in its development as ways to enable the diversity of aging families are considered.

12

Preventive Approaches
to Building Competencies

GREGORY C. SMITH

Families at each stage of the family life cycle vary according to the degree to which they are adversely affected by normative and nonnormative events that challenge them. L'Abate (1990), for example, has suggested that families can be placed into three categories regarding potential disruption from major life events, transitions, or crises:

1. Families are *at risk* when it is likely they will eventually be affected by a threatening situation.
2. They are *in need* when the situation has already been encountered, but it has not seriously damaged family equilibrium.
3. Families are *in crisis* when the situation has resulted in considerable trouble for family members or the family system as a whole.

One illustration of how this categorization is applicable to aging families is elder abuse. Kosberg and Garcia (Chapter 4) note that any family is at risk for potential abuse or neglect of an elderly relative from extreme caregiving demands, work and family pressures, family poverty, and so on. A family in need is exemplified by sporadic episodes of maltreatment, such as verbally abusive arguments with an older parent, but the situation has not yet reached catastrophic proportions. Finally, a family is in crisis when persistent abuse or neglect, such as when a grandchild with a drug addiction depletes the finances of a cognitively impaired elder, seriously and continually jeopardizes the elder's physical or emotional well-being.

The distinction among aging families as being at risk, in need, or in crisis is critical because it alerts practitioners to how families heading toward crises may escape serious trouble if appropriate preventive steps are initiated. Indeed family practitioners have identified three levels of prevention that correspond to the family's functional state (L'Abate, 1990; Mace, 1983):

1. Primary prevention is the use of early interventions to enable families to avoid serious difficulties.
2. Secondary prevention is used appropriately for families who are having difficulties, but without the occurrence of major crises.
3. Tertiary prevention is applicable to situations in which a major crisis has already developed within the family.

Although primary prevention obviously represents the ideal, all three levels of prevention share the same fundamental goal of building family competencies in aging families. Another similarity is that each level of intervention includes two basic strategies: imparting information and skills through educational programs and engineering the societal environment on behalf of families (L'Abate, 1990; Mace, 1983). In some ways, then, the boundaries between the three types of prevention are more imagined than real (L'Abate, 1990).

Although prevention has received increased recognition in the general family practice literature, little attention has been given to its relevance in later stages of the family life cycle. The purpose of the present chapter, therefore, is to describe the use of preventive interventions for increasing competencies within aging families. Four questions will be addressed: What is meant by competency in aging families? What specific preventive interventions are useful with aging families? What factors make prevention work with aging families? And, how does prevention interface with family counseling and therapy, as well as with family policy? Examples from other chapters in this volume will be used to illustrate responses to these important questions.

Defining Competency in Aging Families

Because the fundamental goal of all preventive interventions is to build family competency, it is imperative to define this construct in a manner that clarifies the objectives of prevention efforts for aging families. Fortuitously, Kuypers and Bengston (1984) have proposed three ways of conceptualizing competence in aging families that suggest meaningful outcome goals for family prevention with this target population: effective social role performance, the ability to cope, and experienced mastery.

Competence in Social Role Performance. According to Kuypers and Bengston (1984), individuals should competently enact the duties and expectations of their roles within the aging family. However, some duties and expectations may be inappropriate if they persist from earlier stages of the family life cycle. Smith, Tobin, and Fullmer (Chapter 5), for instance, discuss how older parents of adults with lifelong disabilities often stubbornly hold on to parenting behaviors and expectations that are no longer appropriate to the developmental stage of their son or daughter with a disability. Similarly, Whitbourne and Cassidy (Chapter 9) comment that some older couples are unable to redefine intimacy after age-related physical, cognitive, and emotional changes have been experienced by one or both partners.

Competence as Ability to Cope. Family competence as coping encompasses three major concerns (Kuypers & Bengston, 1984):

1. How flexible the family can be to seek out alternatives and new responses to challenges
2. How integrated these responses are with supports and resources outside the family
3. How clearly and accurately the family can assess the meaning of change and challenge

An excellent example of these issues is provided by Johnson (Chapter 10), who describes how ethnic and cultural forces can substantially affect the manner in which the older family defines new challenges and then uses or does not use available supports outside the family in response to these challenges.

Competence as Experienced Mastery. A final aspect of competence identified by Kuypers and Bengston (1984) involves feelings that members of aging families have about their ability to influence important outcomes. An example of this kind of competence is presented by Tobin (Chapter 2) who notes that relatives of the institutionalized elderly often achieve a sense of mastery in ensuring high-quality care for their elder, for instance, by engaging in such activities as sharing caregiving responsibilities with nursing home staff and participating in family councils.

Preventive Strategies for Aging Families

To achieve these three kinds of competencies in aging families, educational programming and social-environmental engineering may be applied to either primary, secondary, or tertiary prevention (L'Abate, 1990). The interface of family prevention with both counseling and policy will be addressed at the conclusion of this chapter.

EDUCATION TO ASSIST AGING FAMILIES

In various ways the competency of individual family members or the entire family system can be enhanced through education as new skills are developed, new attitudes are formed, new insights occur, or new knowledge is obtained. Educational interventions are thought to be especially appropriate for aging family members because they offer an approach to life's problems that is free from the labeling and stigmatization that is dreaded by today's older cohorts (Brubaker & Roberto, 1993; Giordano & Beckman, 1985). In this section, four types of preventive educational programs are described for use with aging families: psychoeducational support groups, family life education, guided family reminiscence, and structured family enrichment.

Psychoeducational Support Groups. These groups provide a blend of information and therapy where the main objectives are enabling participants to develop new coping skills, cognitively reappraise the stressful family situation, ventilate negative affects regarding stressors, and obtain relevant information. Thus in addition to learning factual information related to important family events, psychoeducational support groups attempt personal change in participants concerning their affective and behavioral response to demanding family situations. In this sense, these interventions are generally more appropriate for family members who are either in need or in crisis than they are for families at risk.

The gerontological literature is already replete with reports of the use of psychoeducational programs for family caregivers to the frail elderly. However, a major drawback has been that extant programs have focused almost exclusively on the older parent-adult child relationship, while overlooking the impact of caregiving on other family members (Couper & Sheehan, 1987). As discussed by Toseland, Smith, and McCallion (Chapter 1), many specific objectives of psychoeducational support groups for primary caregivers may be easily modified to include a family systems perspective. Thus even though it may not be feasible for the entire family to attend psychoeducational support groups, issues pertaining to all relevant family members should be addressed.

Family Life Education. Although definitions of family life education vary widely in the literature, there appears to be consensus that this is a primarily cognitive activity designed to provide useful information to participants about relevant content and skill areas (Hoopes, Fisher, & Barlow, 1984). As such, these programs may be targeted for either individual family members, family subsystems, or the entire family. Whereas family life education in the past had focused chiefly on the concerns of younger families (e.g., parent education), there is now a growing belief that people of all ages need to learn about the many aspects of family life and that opportunities exist for family life education at each developmental phase (see, for discussion, Hennon & Arcus, 1993).

Brubaker and Roberto (1993) offer two particular advantages associated with family life education for older adults. First, it provides a means of assisting a cohort who is often reluctant to become involved with either formal services or affectively oriented support groups. Second, family life education can encompass diverse methods of presenting information to later-life families, including workshops, seminars, brochures, pamphlets, and mass media. This range of modalities is important given the physical and financial limitations commonly experienced by older family members.

The value of educational formats for aging families who resist formal services is evident in Chapter 5, in which it was noted that, although many older parents of adults with lifelong disabilities refuse assistance from professionals regarding the making of future plans for their offspring, these parents do seem willing to attend workshops and other educational programs on this important family issue. Another example of the use of family life education is given by Tobin (Chapter 2), who asserts that family life education can be invaluable in helping families to learn strategies for having more meaningful visits with their elders in nursing homes. Bata and Power (Chapter 8) describe the im- portance of learning about living wills, guardianship, and conservatorship.

Three important characteristics of older adults must be kept in mind when developing family life education programs for them and their families. First, the great heterogeneity among elderly persons must be addressed (Brubaker & Roberto, 1993), including such factors as urban versus rural participants, and differences in functional abilities, financial status, marital status, and ethnicity (see Johnson, Chapter 10). Second, because family life intervention is primarily a cognitive activity, it must be realized that age-related changes in cognition may affect the older adult's ability to retain and process new information (Hennon & Arcus, 1993). Finally, because older individuals have such a lengthy history as family members, it is important to recognize the influence of their past on current family functioning when developing a family-based curriculum (Brubaker & Roberto, 1993).

Some major drawbacks of family life education must also be noted. One is that the generic nature of family life education programs does not permit each participant's needs to be addressed the way other, more intensive, individual or family interventions can (Couper & Sheehan, 1987; Gold & Gwyther, 1989). Another pitfall has to do with the difficulty in designing and implementing prevention programs focused on sensitive areas like elder abuse (Kosberg and Garcia, Chapter 4) or aging among gay and lesbian families (Fullmer, Chapter 6). Many families who would otherwise benefit from family life education programs are unlikely to risk unwanted stigmatization by attending public classes (Gold & Gwyther, 1989). More anonymous, albeit less direct, means of disseminating information (such as mass media, brochures, and videotapes) may be used to offset this difficulty (Hennon & Arcus, 1993).

Guided Family Reminiscence. De Vries, Birren, and Deutchmann (1990) have proposed a guided family reminiscence approach that they describe as "an educational process of bringing up one's understanding of the past into the present in order to integrate the experiences of a lifetime" (p. 4). The specific purposes of this intervention, which include putting the contradictions of life into perspective, reaffirming one's abilities to meet life's challenges, restoring one's sense of self-sufficiency and personal identity, and educating families about shifting roles, seem particularly useful for aging families. Although they apparently have not yet tested their guided reminiscence procedure with actual aging families, its potential value is revealed by several authors in the present volume. In Chapter 2, for example, Tobin maintains that two significant contributions that family members of institutionalized elders can make is to provide biographical information to staff and to help their older relative maintain a sense of their selfhood. Indeed, these two objectives could be met simultaneously if nursing homes were to make a guided reminiscence program available to families. The merit of guided family reminiscence is also indicated by Cicirelli (Chapter 3), who notes how older siblings may benefit from shared life review, and by Whitbourne and Cassidy (Chapter 10, this volume), who regard life review as an important means of enhancing intimacy in late-life marriages.

Structured Family Enrichment. These programs are based on a belief that couples and families have strengths and resources that can be used as the basis of experiences to enhance growth and development within the family (Hennon & Arcus, 1993). For the most part, then, they are aimed at couples and families who are fairly functional and are interested in improving their relationships. The major focus is on assisting the family to identify issues and potential problem areas by helping family members to generate alternatives for dealing with issues and offering opportunities for experimenting with new behavior patterns. Simply put, the intention of structured enrichment programs is to increase the overall quality and intimacy of family life. This goal is accomplished through programmed instruction dealing with interpersonal relations between and among family members. This process emphasizes the systematic arrangement of exercises and lessons in a gradual sequence that is intended to help the family or specific family members (L'Abate & Weinstein, 1987). Structured family enrichment therefore differs from family life education in two significant ways: Structured family enrichment is experiential rather than cognitive in nature; and it requires the participation of the entire relevant family unit to facilitate new insights into the family's (or couple's) interpersonal dynamics.

It has been said that structured family enrichment can cover a wide range of marital and family issues and that if a program has not yet been written to cover a particular topic, it can be written (L'Abate & Weinstein, 1987). Yet descriptions of the use of these interventions with aging families have been virtually absent to date. However, one obvious use of structured enrichment in aging families is apparent in Whitbourne and Cassidy's discussion in Chapter 9 on intimacy in later-life marriages. In fact, they maintain that a defining trait of "mutually intimate" older couples is the desire to achieve even higher levels of intimacy in their marriage. Structured enrichment programs designed to help such couples to enhance their relationship in light of age-related changes would apparently be well-received by them. Appropriate enrichment goals listed by these authors include identification of qualities to be strengthened in the relationship, learning to cope with the effects of physical illness and economic hardship, and enhancing sexuality. Similarly, Cicirelli (Chapter 3) maintains that many siblings become open to enriching their relationship in the later years when other competing demands (such as work and childrearing) have subsided.

SOCIAL-ENVIRONMENTAL
ENGINEERING FOR AGING FAMILIES

In addition to the educational programs described above, family prevention involves the creation of conditions, settings, and physical arrangements and facilities that reduce family stress (L'Abate, 1990). Two major categories of social-environmental engineering described in the family prevention literature (see, for example, Mace, 1983) are relevant to aging families: family support services and advocacy.

Family Support Services. These may be defined as formal services that offer instrumental support to families in meeting the basic responsibilities of family living. They are preventive in nature because they provide resources to reduce stressors that may otherwise exceed the family's ability to cope. The salience of family support services in reducing stress within aging families is widely documented throughout this book. In Chapter 1, Toseland et al. discuss the importance of respite care and case management for family caregivers of the frail elderly. In turn, Kosberg and Garcia (Chapter 4) discuss how these support services are often essential in reducing family stress in order to prevent potential abuse or neglect from occurring in aging families. Similarly, Smith et al. note in Chapter 5 that older parents caring for an offspring who has chronic disability often require support services (such as homemaker services and day programs) in order to maintain family stability. They also point out that it is often difficult for these parents to plan for their offspring's future because acceptable residential alternatives are frequently unavailable for them to choose from. In her chapter on the family life of older gays and lesbians, Fullmer (Chapter 6) stresses the importance of community programs that frequently provide ersatz family circumstances for these men and women. Bata and Power (Chapter 8) discuss the need for health care providers to spend time in family conferences that include oldest family members and to be aware of resources that assist families.

Perhaps the most critical and consistent issue regarding support services for aging families is that so few families use these services, and those that do often fail to use them effectively. Stephens (1993) has compiled a list of possible reasons for this underuse of formal services by aging families, a list that includes insufficient knowledge of services, unfamiliarity with accessing them, prohibitive cost, the perception of not needing services, discomfort and embarrassment over family circumstances, fear of criticism from others, discomfort over making decisions for other family members in need, and negative attitudes toward service providers. Moreover, Johnson observes that many of these influences are particularly true among various ethnic and racial groups. Until this lack of service use is better understood and confronted by professionals, many aging families will needlessly experience oppressive levels of strain and discomfort.

Advocacy. In this context, advocacy consists of promoting attitudes, values, and knowledge within the broader society that are in the best interests of aging families. Indeed until society acknowledges the unique needs and circumstances of aging families, neither the desire nor the resources necessary to develop the programs and services described above will be forthcoming. It is equally necessary for society to recognize and appreciate the tremendous diversity that exists among aging families if the needs of special populations are to be met sufficiently. Thus it is essential for gerontological and family-oriented professionals to serve as advocates, as well as counselors and educators for older families.

The need for advocacy on behalf of aging families is well illustrated by Kosberg and Garcia, who consider several environmental modifications that foster the prevention of elder abuse. Community awareness of elder abuse and greater professional collaboration, for example, can promote early detection before abuse leads to tragedy. The elimination of such precipitating conditions as ageism, societal violence, poverty, and employment were also mentioned by these authors as important social-environmental changes toward reducing the incidence of elder abuse in our society.

Making Prevention
Work for Aging Families

Understanding the fundamental objectives of prevention with aging families and becoming aware of pertinent preventive interventions, in and of themselves, are not sufficient to assure successful practice with this target population. Practitioners must also be cognizant of a number of guidelines and considerations that are pertinent to the development of effective programs. Bond and Wagner (1988b) have identified four general orientations that typify successful family prevention programs: (a) emphasis on the promotion of competence; (b) empowerment of individuals and groups; (c) a multisystem, multilevel perspective; and (d) sensitivity to developmental processes. Each of these orientations is discussed in this section for its particular relevance to aging families.

An Emphasis on Competence. Although it was stated earlier in this chapter that the ultimate goal of all preventive programs is to build competencies in aging families with respect to the areas of role performance, coping skills, and sense of mastery, these objectives are all too easily overlooked in reality. L'Abate (1990), for example, cautioned that even the provision of instrumental family support services should be augmented with efforts to increase family competence.

A clear example of the failure by service providers to address the issue of competence in aging families is referred to by Toseland et al., who note the controversy in gerontology regarding the value of respite programs for family caregivers to the elderly. Although these programs seem to be well received by most caregiving families, investigators have found them to be ineffective in reducing emotional distress in this target population (see, for review, Chappell, 1990). A likely explanation is that respite programs, which provide short-term relief from caregiving responsibilities, do not typically address the educational and psychosocial needs of the families they serve. Consequently, the reduction of family stress is limited to the actual duration of the respite period and does not persist in the absence of enhanced coping or new insights of family members.

By no means is the above example meant to suggest that all family support services (e.g., respite, day care, homemakers, home health aides, etc.) should include an elaborate psychoeducational component. Clearly this would exceed the resources of most family support service agencies. Nonetheless it does seem appropriate for family support services to disseminate pamphlets, brochures, newsletters, and other written materials that present information about such relevant matters as becoming involved with family support groups, recognizing emotional and physical symptoms of caregiver distress, understanding public entitlements such as Medicaid, and accessing additional resources available to aging families. Activities of this sort fall plainly within the definition of family life education presented above.

Family Empowerment. This orientation is based on the belief that the expert-helper model should be replaced by one in which program participants are empowered to deal with family challenges by providing them with opportunities for growth without continued reliance on professional helpers (Bond & Wagner, 1988b). A superb example of this empowerment orientation is Marsha Seltzer's program (as cited by Smith et al., Chapter 5), designed to train older family members to act as case managers for a relative with mental retardation. Not only did this program offset the reluctance of many aging families to have their family affairs managed by strangers, but it also reduced the caseloads of professionals, helped to ensure continuity of care, and increased the family's sense of mastery.

The concept of empowerment also implies that members of aging families should be instrumental in the development, presentation, and evaluation of prevention programs intended for them. Along these lines, Brubaker and Roberto (1993) have suggested that older adults should be viewed as resources who can serve in such roles as program planners, discussion leaders, or as case examples. When families have played a role in conceptualizing or implementing a program, they will likely have a greater commitment to it (Bond & Wagner, 1988b).

A Multisystem, Multilevel Perspective. According to Bond and Wagner (1988b), effective family prevention programs are based on the assumption that individual family members are an integral part of hierarchies of overlapping systems that include both dyads and the entire family system, which in turn are embedded in subcultures and communities that compose even larger and more complex social, political, and legal systems. Furthermore, they commented that "ideally, a prevention program would target as many levels of influence as possible in identifying and targeting agents for change, monitoring program implementation, and evaluating program effects" (p. 344). This not only explains why family advocacy (as described above) is such an important component of prevention, but it also indicates that family support services and prevention-oriented educational programs must address issues that extend beyond the boundaries of the immediate family. Successful family life education programs for family caregivers to the elderly, for example, should inform family members regarding such issues as the availability of community resources, how to manage job responsibilities in light of caregiving demands, and the legal ramifications of family caregiving (Couper & Sheehan, 1987).

The importance of a multilevel, multisystem perspective to prevention is also indicated by Fullmer (Chapter 6), who suggests that family interventions for older gays and lesbians must go beyond the immediate family to include the attitudes of the local community toward homo- sexuality, the orientation of the legal system to gays and lesbians, and the perspectives of clergy, as well as changing the course of opinion of society at large.

Sensitivity to Developmental Processes. Bond and Wagner (1988b) have proposed that effective family prevention programs demonstrate sensitivity with respect to three important aspects of family development: (a) the chronological age of participants, (b) an awareness of the point of evolution in the family system, and (c) the family's current position with respect to the transition or event at hand. Attention to each of these developmental concerns is especially important for prevention activities with aging families.

With respect to chronological age, it has already been mentioned that age-related changes in older adults may influence their ability to participate in prevention programs. Physical adversities often jeopardize attendance at programs outside the home, and normative changes in learning and memory may make it difficult for older adults to comprehend or retain the didactic information presented in educational programs. It has also been pointed out that today's oldest cohorts are often reluctant to use family support services or to attend group-oriented programs. However, these concerns are not insurmountable. Family practitioners may address them, for example, by arranging transportation for elderly participants, being willing to conduct programs within the family's own home, and developing educational curriculum that are sensitive to the limitations of older learners.

Awareness of the family's evolutionary phase is important because four-generation and even five-generation families are becoming increasingly common (Power, Chapter 7). Accompanying this trend is the need for family prevention programs to encompass a multigenerational perspective (Brubaker & Roberto, 1993). A program for middle-aged caregivers, for example, should provide information on how teenage children may be affected by the care being provided to a grandparent (Toseland et al., Chapter 1). It is also important to realize that interventions presented early in the family life cycle should be structured to yield dividends in the later years. Cicirelli (Chapter 3), for example, notes that the best way to ensure quality sibling relationships in old age is to enrich them during childhood and adolescence.

A final issue regarding developmental processes concerns the family's present position in the transition or event under consideration. L'Abate and Weinstein (1987) have argued that the ideal time for prevention is just before a family life event occurs. The issues at this time are real enough to warrant the family's attention, yet still distant enough for family members to remain objective in their outlook toward the future. This "anticipatory stage" may be especially helpful in enabling family members to accept new roles or to realize modifications in existing roles.

As an illustration, many of the problems commonly experienced by aging families after an elder enters a nursing home (Tobin) may be avoided by educational programs presented prior to this event. Through such efforts family members would discover that their role as caregivers will not end as they fear, but instead will be transformed to include a partnership with nursing home staff. Thus, rather than dreading an eventual abandonment of their loved one to strangers, family members can perceive the move as a new experience in which they will be able to retain considerable mastery.

The Interface of Family
Prevention With Other Interventions

FAMILY PREVENTION AND COUNSELING

As previously noted, the boundaries between primary, secondary, and tertiary prevention are often more imagined than real. Even when aging families are in crisis, for example, they may benefit from primary or secondary prevention that either deters further disruption from occurring or restores the family's previous level of functioning (L' Abate, 1990; Mace, 1983). For many of these families, preventive strategies can also be used in conjunction with the family counseling approaches described by Tobin and Power (Chapter 11). It must also be recognized that some families may prefer the private and personalized attention that is offered by family counseling and therapy.

FAMILY PREVENTION AND POLICY

Three important policy issues are worth noting with respect to prevention for aging families. First, although the number of aging families at risk or in need is far greater than the number of families in crisis, there are much fewer professionals trained in primary and secondary prevention than those trained as counselors or therapists (L'Abate, 1990). Until our society begins to favor a developmental model over a medical model of serving aging families, an emphasis on treatment will prevail over an emphasis on prevention.

Second, among those family prevention programs that have been developed so far, the overwhelming emphasis has been on families of young children. This is not surprising in view of the fact that no modern nation has interpreted family policy to include the aged as well as children (Neiderhardt & Allen, 1993). Until older adults are no longer seen as competitors with younger families, prevention activities that promote interactions among older and younger generations will suffer.

Finally, a major theme of this book has been to demonstrate the tremendous diversity that exists among aging families. Not only do these families differ greatly in how they respond to normative family challenges, but some aging families clearly fall outside of society's expectations of normal family life. As reported in this book, some families abuse or neglect their elders (Kosberg and Garcia, Chapter 4), others consist of same-sex partners who grow old together (Fullmer, Chapter 6), and still others appear different because of their unique cultural or ethnic values (Johnson, Chapter 9). Family prevention programs that do not recognize the uniqueness found among aging families are destined to fail.

13

☒

Critical Policy Issues

ELLIE BRUBAKER

TIMOTHY H. BRUBAKER

☒

As the older population in the United States expands, policies, programs, and services affecting that population take on an increased importance in the minds of policymakers and service providers. The expansion of the aging population, initiated by the aging of the baby boom cohort (Brubaker & Brubaker, 1992), will continue to increase into the 21st century. Whereas 12.4% of individuals were aged 65 and older by the end of the last decade (U.S. Bureau of the Census, 1990), it is expected that this will increase to 14% by 2010 and to 21.8% by 2030 (U.S. Bureau of the Census, 1988).

Given the current and projected increase in the elderly population, particularly the increase in individuals over the age of 75, long-term care has become a major policy issue that influences older families. In the United States, there are currently almost 7 million elders who require long-term care. That number is expected to expand to approximately 9 million by the year 2000 and to nearly 12 million by the year 2020 (U.S. Senate Special Committee on Aging et al., 1991). These projections are based on a definition of long-term care that refers not only to nursing home care, but to care in the community as well.

Issues related to the care of the elderly in later life are influenced not only by older persons as individuals but also by their family members.

Consequently these issues become family issues. Family members of various ages are providing assistance to the elderly in extraordinary ways. Research demonstrates that family members regularly interact with and provide support and care to their older members (Brubaker, 1990b; Gatz, Bengtson, & Blum, 1990), both in the community and in nursing homes. Consequently families are extensively involved in the long-term care of their elders, and policies directed toward needs of older persons should also focus on the needs of families.

Future projections underscore increasing needs of later-life families. For example, as the aging population expands, the numbers of families dealing with the needs of the elderly increase. Correspondingly the needs of relatives and other caregivers will grow. Thus there is little doubt that families are directly and indirectly influenced by the policies affecting their aged members, and later-life families should be considered as the policies are formulated.

Given some of the changes in the family during the past several decades, it is likely that the family needs are changing. Although family responsibilities and services are on the rise, family members will find themselves less able to successfully provide those services than did families in previous generations. Family size has decreased (U.S. Bureau of the Census, 1988), causing the number of potential family caregivers to decrease. Among those potential caregivers, the increased employment of women, who provide the majority of care to elderly family members (Brody, 1990), will further interfere with family support.

Policies that direct programs and services for older citizens and their families have an impact on older individuals and their families, medical and social service professions, the economy, and the larger society. It may be useful to view older individuals and family caregivers as partners in the caregiving process, and policies directed toward the needs of the elderly should recognize this relationship. Therefore, the saliency of the family should not be underestimated in the development of policy for older individuals.

Policy and Aging Families

POLICY FOR CONTINUED FAMILY INVOLVEMENT

To ensure the continuation and success of older family relationships, policies should direct attention to the need for programs and services that provide support to older individuals so that families can continue to provide support and care to their older members. Numerous policies are structured so that families are facilitated as they do this. For example, Title III of the Older Americans Act provides for Meals on Wheels programs, nutritional sites for older individuals, and homemaker/home health aide programs, among others, which are structured to maintain older individuals in the community. Families who are also caregivers are aided in the care they provide to their elderly members through these services. Policies that can specifically address themselves to family caregiving will be more likely to provide services beneficial to both their elderly clients and family caregivers. It is essential that policies continue to attend to both the needs of elders and their families.

PROVIDING SUPPORT TO ELDERS

There are several areas related to support for older recipients of care in which policy issues exist. First, policies that provide for the coordination of formal services with services provided by family members can help reduce gaps and overlaps in services. Second, coordination of services can, at times, be most successfully provided by case management carried out by family caregivers. Such policies can often facilitate the success of provision of services to individuals and their families. Third, policies that call for programs to determine the individual needs and desires of older recipients and their families, as well as the needs of the older population at large, will most likely achieve their goals. Finally, policies are needed to deal with the long-term care needs of older individuals and the support of families for extensive periods of time.

It is important to question whether policies provide for coordination of formal services with the services provided by family members. The types of services provided by formal and informal caregivers are often different. Formal services are those carried by professional or paraprofessional service providers. Individuals providing formal services receive training necessary for the completion of their work. Informal services are provided by those who have some type of relationship with the recipient of the services. Informal services are most often given by family members.

Formal services can serve many functions, including reducing the amount of care family members provide or adding to the services already provided by family members. There is no doubt that formal services are not intended to and should not replace family services. Formal services, then, "are best seen as a complement to rather than substitute for informal caregiving" (Pillemer & Wolf, 1986, p. 294).

When families and formal practitioners are working in tandem, it is important that their involvement be coordinated. Coordination between formal and informal caregivers can strengthen the services provided and meet the specific needs of the older individual. For example, it may be extremely helpful to an older individual to have her home cleaned on a weekly basis. However, if that is an activity her daughter is already carrying out, it would be important to coordinate the service with the daughter, so that either the daughter is relieved of that responsibility or the daughter continues to clean and other, more necessary, formal services are established. Lack of coordination could result in service activities that interfere with the relationship between the older parent and her daughter, whereas coordination of services could result in providing necessary services to the elderly individual and either releasing the caregiving daughter from an unwanted responsibility or providing an expansion of services to the elderly mother.

Because family members are so involved in the care of their older relatives, human service policies that provide for services to older individuals should also provide a mechanism whereby services must be coordinated with the older client and informal caregivers prior to the delivery of services. Knowing what the older persons and their families are providing and what they need will help service providers to maximize their support. Policies that do not do this may result in an overlap of services in some areas of need and gaps in service delivery in others.

Policy can also provide for family members as case managers. Coordination of services can perhaps best be provided through case management. Case management involves the coordination of a variety of services provided to meet the complex needs of clients (Hennon, Brubaker, & Kaplan, 1991). Brody (1990) states that in the case of older clients, family members frequently carry out the role of case manager. Even with the involvement of formal services, family members continue their participation (Pillemer & Wolf, 1986). Therefore family members who are the case managers can be a resource for the coordination of services.

In order to ensure that desired services are targeted to meet actual need, family members can perhaps represent their relatives more successfully than can formal service providers. This is not to suggest that formal service provision is unnecessary, but rather, that family members who best know the wishes of the older relative and also have the most knowledge of the variety of services provided may be most able to provide coordination of services. The family member who is the informal case manager can work closely with the formal service provider to provide the needed assistance. Salzberger (1979) suggests that when an older individual is not able to determine outcome, it is often a family member who should be involved in helping to make choices. Although most older individuals can express their desires, for those who cannot (for example, those with Alzheimer's disease), family members who have known them throughout their lives could possibly make decisions that would best represent the decisions the older individual would have made if able to do so. The family case manager, then, in addition to coordinating services, may also be most able to accurately represent the older family member and thereby advocate for the older person.

Policy is most successful when it attends to the specific desires and needs of older care recipients and their families. Services may be deemed helpful by service providers but not perceived as such by the elderly recipient and family caregiver. Perception of need by the older recipient and family should play a major role in the determination of services to be provided.

Policies can benefit the individuals to whom services are directed when they establish a structure that encourages service providers to take into account the personal characteristics of the elderly recipient, the characteristics of the family caregiver, the social support available to both caregiver and recipient, the relationship between caregiver and recipient, and the characteristics of the caregiving itself (Brubaker, Gorman, & Hiestand, 1990). Although recognition of the complexity of the older person's situation may not be the most efficient way to provide services, it does enhance the delivery of services. Such a holistic approach to the provision of services supports the older person and family caregivers within their typical living situation.

Programs that serve older individuals and their families are most helpful when the specific and unique desires of the clients are considered. If, for example, an older woman wants her daughter to cook for her and wants the homemaker aide to clean her kitchen, she will be more receptive to both formal and informal services when her wishes are granted. Although it may not always be possible to meet the expectations of older individuals, family members and professionals will find service provision facilitated when they attempt to do so. When these factors are taken into consideration, the stresses experienced by both older recipient and caregiver are likely to lessen (Brubaker et al., 1990), and the services provided are most likely to achieve success.

In addition to structuring policies so that individual needs of the elderly are taken into account, policies must also attend to the needs and desires of the elderly population as a whole. Certain needs exist for all older individuals. Attention to those needs enhance the success of service delivery and the ability of older individuals to accept services. This in turn benefits family caregivers.

Selby and Schecter (1982) have suggested that the self-concept of older individuals is related to their role as consumers. The need for older individuals to carry out the role of contributor, rather than only recipient, has been documented in the gerontological literature (Brubaker, 1987). A strong self-concept involves having the ability to exert influence over what occurs in one's life (Brubaker, 1987). An individual who is merely the recipient of care lacks this sense of influence. Encouraging the involvement of older persons in the decision making process concerning caregiving reinforces their individual autonomy as discussed by Bata and Power (Chapter 8). Policies that provide some way for older individuals to reciprocate for the care they receive from formal and informal caregivers will be helpful to meet the emotional needs of older individuals.

Policies that provide older individuals with a stipend to pay for care, rather than paying the caregiver directly, could enable older people to exert influence over their lives. A stipend also provides older individuals with a choice of care, giving each the ability to "shop around" for the care he or she believes to be most beneficial. However, this raises the issue of the source of that stipend, as well as the issue of whether all older individuals should receive a stipend or just those who have been determined to require care or only those who have passed a means test.

Long-Term Care
Needs of Older Families

For those individuals who are unable to remain in their own homes, institutionalized long-term care becomes a policy issue facing older families. Although at any one time, only approximately 5% of those age 65 and older reside in nursing homes, the percentage of older individuals who will use nursing homes during their lifetimes is much greater. It has been estimated that "43 percent of people who were 65 in 1990 will use nursing homes at some time during their remaining years" (U.S. Senate Special Committee on Aging et al., 1991). As individuals age, the risk of residing in a nursing home increases. The risk of being in a nursing home is six times greater for someone in the 75 to 84 age range than for someone between ages 65 and 74. That risk is 22 times greater for someone over age 85 than for someone between ages 65 and 74 (U.S. Senate Special Committee on Aging et al., 1991). The implications of these statistics are great for older individuals and their families, particularly in the area of health insurance. Although more than 99% of individuals age 65 and older have health insurance for acute care conditions, the "vast majority of elderly lack public or private insurance coverage for long-term care" (U.S. Senate Special Committee on Aging et al., 1991, p. 131). Older individuals and families not prepared for long-term care would benefit from policies that would protect them in the event long-term care is required. The Ford Foundation, in its project to address social welfare, has made several policy recommendations concerning long-term care. These include: public subsidies that would help individuals to invest in private insurance for long-term care and government monies for families with extraordinarily high costs for disabilities and chronic illnesses (Ford Foundation, 1989). The costs of long-term care to older individuals, families, and society cannot be ignored.

Policies should also take into account that the majority of older individuals prefer to live in their own homes and not in age-segregated communities. Facilitating this is "not only socially desirable, . . . it is economically desirable as well. . . . [A policy that enables older people to remain in their homes with family help] will usually be cheaper than institutional care" (Selby & Schecter, 1982, p. 183).

Policy Addressing
the Needs of Family Caregivers

Policies and services have traditionally been targeted toward meeting the needs of older recipients, with the latent function of supporting family caregivers. A need exists for increased programs and services providing support to family caregivers. Support for family involvement in caregiving is important within a community setting (as noted in Toseland, Smith, and McCallion, Chapter 1) as well as within an institutional setting (as explicated by Tobin, Chapter 2). First, policies need to take into consideration the differential needs of informal caregivers, as well as the variety of individuals who provide family care. In addition, policies must direct their attention toward the stressors that family caregivers experience, both from providing informal services and from historical family disagreements. Family caregivers experience different types of needs. In addition, older family members have different backgrounds and may occupy a variety of roles. Do policies that relate to older families take into account the cultural and ethnic issues that influence those families' responses to services? Frequently they do not. As Johnson (Chapter 10) notes, ethnic differences need to be recognized and ethnic integrity should be respected. Therefore policies need to provide for programs and services that are culturally sensitive and flexible to the ethnic backgrounds of older families.

Primary caregivers in older families are most frequently wives and daughters (Brody, 1990; Brubaker, 1985). Husbands, sons, nieces and nephews, and siblings, although less frequently than wives and daughters, provide care for older family members. Of caregivers to noninstitutionalized elderly, 72% are women (23% wives and 29% daughters) and 23% are siblings and nieces. Of husbands who provide care, 42% are age 75 or older (U.S. Senate Special Committee on Aging et al., 1991). Although women seem to have a caregiving career within the family (Brody, 1990), male caregivers should not be overlooked (Kaye & Applegate, 1990a). The variety of caregivers illustrates the different needs and relationships of later-life families.

For all of these individuals, caregiving may interfere with relationships with other family members. For example, as Whitbourne and Cassidy (Chapter 9) explain, intimacy of marital partners is important in later life, and such intimacy can either hinder or enhance the caregiving situation. The marital relationship of the caregiver may be affected by the responsibilities associated with caregiving. A daughter or daughter-in-law who is providing primary care to an older parent may experience stress within her marriage because of the caregiving demands. Similarly, employment and leisure activities may be interrupted by the caregiving experience. Although sibling relationships are secondary (as noted by Cicirelli, Chapter 3), caregiving can affect these important relationships for elderly persons. The varying needs of caregivers and the effect of services on their relationship with older family members, as well as with other family members, are issues that influence policy effectiveness.

Policy must take into consideration and provide programs to prevent and alleviate the stress experienced by older families. Family members who provide care to their elderly relatives may experience a variety of stressors that not only interfere with the effectiveness of the care they provide but also with other aspects of their lives. For example, a daughter providing care may experience tension between needing to spend time with her teenage children after work and needing to visit her mother's home each day to make sure she is well. A wife may have to cope with her impending sense of loss while caring for her husband following his stroke. A policy that provides respite care will help reduce the stress experienced by the daughter in trying to fulfill numerous responsibilities. Policy that is translated into providing a support group for the older wife will allow her to care more successfully for her ill husband. Policies that generate information and referral and education sources for families help to meet their needs as they struggle to give care to their older family members.

Family members caring for an older relative with Alzheimer's disease may find themselves particularly frustrated in their ability to meet that individual's needs while functioning successfully in other areas of their lives. Older individuals with mental disorders make up 15% to 25% of the older population, with Alzheimer's disease being the leading cause of mental disorders (U.S. Senate Special Committee on Aging et al., 1991). Cohen and Eisdorfer (1988) note that family members who care for older individuals with Alzheimer's are more likely to experience depression and physical problems.

For some older families, stress presents itself in the form of physical and/or emotional abuse of the older family member. Numerous situations contribute to abuse of an older family member. Among those is the situation in which the family is caring for an older person with dementia. In this situation, the constant need for the caregiver's presence and active involvement may be overwhelming to the caregiver.

In addition, the demented parent offers the child few of the rewards gained in a normal human relationship. The adult child's affection may not be returned, there are no longer shared memories, and so on. Under these circumstances, it is difficult for adult children to maintain the commitment to continue giving care, and the elderly parent becomes highly vulnerable to neglect and abuse (Pillemer & Wolf, 1986).

As Kosberg and Garcia (Chapter 4) note, a number of strategies are needed to lessen the heightening of stress to levels of abuse. Prevention of abuse can be enhanced through counseling of caregivers and the development of detection protocols to identify abuse at the earliest time. Support for education and intervention programs that help family caregivers deal with their emotions (e.g., anger, guilt, frustration) will likely reduce the amount of elder abuse.

It has also been suggested that families, who provide the majority of care to those older individuals with dementia, be provided with indirect care as incentives to continue to provide care to their older member (Kane, 1990). Kane stresses the possible problems with policies that would provide direct financial resources to those family caregivers, including the possibility of "exploitation" and the fact that most families would provide care whether or not they are paid. The question of whether social provisions should be in cash or in the form of services is widely debated. However, payment to family caregivers may help families meet other responsibilities so that they can better care for their elders. In addition, aid to families provided through formal service agencies would lessen the burden experienced and allow those individuals to continue their help to older relatives and carry out other life tasks as well.

Stress experienced by family caregivers could be reduced and to some extent prevented through education of family members about dementia. Families who do not understand why their older relatives are functioning differently than they did previously could benefit from having been educated about dementia, as well as about resources available to them and their relatives. Policies that provide for education to families, physicians, and the public can enable family members to work more successfully with their older relatives (Brubaker & Roberto, 1993; Fogel, Gottlieb, & Furino, 1990).

As Smith, Tobin, and Fullmer (Chapter 5) illustrate, lifelong disabilities of family members may also contribute to stress in later-life families. For example, older families who have an adult child with mental retardation may experience a good deal of stress as both parent and child grow older. In these situations, the older parent is often the caregiver for the adult child. The caregiving situation has been long established; however, as older parents age, their ability to provide care for their adult child may decrease. Stress derives from the parent's concerns about his or her ability to continue care for the child as he or she grows older, as well as about who will care for the adult child after the parent dies.

Another form of stress in older families is conflict that may have been experienced between members over the years. History of family interactions is particularly important when examining the stress within the caregiving relationship. Often the past helps to define the present feelings associated with caregiving (Brubaker, 1990a). In some families, conflict may have existed years earlier, but due to the lack of close interaction, it has been dormant. Families reunited due to the needs of an older member may renew the conflicts they experienced at an earlier time. Programs that provide education for older families as they encounter new/old conflicts, as well as therapy for those who are unable to resolve those differences on their own, facilitate families as they attempt to support one another.

Policy is needed to enable older families to deal with these situations in a way that provides continuity of care for the adult child and support for the older parent. Older families would benefit from policies that provide for family life education for the adult children. Such education would be particularly useful in helping the adult children to develop friendship skills that will aid them when their parents can no longer provide the social interaction they need. Support groups for older parents would also help to alleviate their concerns about the future (Brubaker & Brubaker, 1993).

Future Policy Issues

The future of policy related to older families is uncertain. Much of future policy development will be related to the needs and voting patterns of current elders and their family members. Family members, many of whom are members of the baby boom generation, make up a large portion, approximately 60%, of all voters (Boaz, 1986). Regardless of whether or not this generation votes as a bloc, their impact on policy will be important. As Caddell (Atwater, Boaz, & Caddell, 1986) notes:

> The rush [to turn out to vote] of participation of previous generations at the time they reached their thirties has still not been matched by the baby boom. But the baby boom is so big that even at lesser percentages the numbers are overwhelming in terms of impact. (p. 42)

The political views of the baby boom generation have been said to be "more conservative on economic issues than older voters, while they retain the social liberalism . . . acquired in the Sixties" (Boaz, 1986, p. 3). Fiscal conservatism may result in a preference for decentralized public programs or for private programs. Decentralized programs are fiscally conservative in terms of spending at the federal level, but they also result in differential services to individuals living in different geographic areas. Whereas one community, or state, may have comprehensive programs for older individuals and families, another state may choose to provide different programs for its citizens. The advantage is that programs can be individually tailored to the needs of the citizens of each specific area. The disadvantage of decentralized programs is that families in one area may not receive the services they require, although those same services are being provided to older families in another community. Consequently gaps in service may result.

By the same token, private programs, with little backup from public programs, will likely leave gaps in some areas of service and overlaps in others. For example, in a community in which home health aide services are provided only through private agencies, there is likely to be less communication between private agencies to determine who has or has not been served. Private programs can lack the coordination with other services more frequently provided by public agencies. The need for family members as case managers is even greater in this type of situation.

At the same time fiscal conservatism is embraced, social liberalism may result in an increase in volunteer services and an emphasis on providing services efficiently. However, with the expanded older population, the demand for services will be greater than volunteer programs and informal caregivers can meet. As more and more baby boomers become caregivers and elders, they will have smaller families than did their parents. The availability of informal caregivers will decrease. This cohort's need for services may outweigh economic conservatism, with the result that the baby boom generation becomes a political powerhouse that demands programs to meet the needs of older families.

It is imperative that future policy development be guided by research about the needs of this new, larger, older generation. The needs of older individuals and their families should be monitored. It is essential to have data on the needs and desires of this aging population and later-life families. Although a great deal of research on later-life families has been completed in the past several decades, there are many gaps (e.g., ethnic and racial differences) within the knowledge base (Brubaker, 1990b). Therefore, caution should be exercised when developing policies that affect families for which there is little empirical knowledge.

Conclusion

Policies directed toward later-life families need to provide support for both older individuals and their families. Given the extraordinary support family members provide to their elders, it is not surprising that service delivery is enhanced when the older person and his or her family is defined as the client. Policies to support the education of older persons and their families are encouraged, along with the development of a coordination of the delivery of services to the elderly. Maximizing the case management strengths of family members may result in the efficient provision of services. Older individuals and their families are partners in the challenges associated with the later years, and policies defining education and service delivery can enhance this partnership. Even though the future political situation seems to be changing, long-term care needs of older individuals and their families can be maximized through increased centralization and support from private organizations. To efficiently provide services to later-life families, policies need to recognize that older individuals and their families are resources.

The actual development of policy related to these issues will be facilitated by research of the new generation of older families. Research on the baby boom generation will provide necessary insight into the individual and family needs of this unique population.

Policy development will be dependent, to some extent, on the voting patterns of the baby boom population. This population has demonstrated its desire for fiscally conservative government that is socially liberal. Baby boomers will, because of their numbers, have an impact on the policy decisions of the future. As this population ages, its political views and impact may evolve to an orientation that will serve its interests.

References

Abramson, M. (1991). Ethical assessment of the use of influence in adult protective services. *Journal of Gerontological Social Work, 16,* 125-135.

Ackerman, N. (1972). The growing edge of therapy. In C. Sager & H. Kaplan (Eds.), *Group and family therapy* (p. 442). New York: Brunner/Mazel.

Adams, B. N. (1968). *Kinship in an urban setting.* New York: Markham.

Adebimpe, V. R. (1994). Race, racism, and epidemiological surveys. *Hospital & Community Psychiatry, 45*(1), 27-31.

Adelman, M. (1980). *Adjustment to aging and styles of being gay: A study of elderly gay men and lesbians.* Doctoral dissertation, Wright Institute.

Adelman, M. (1986). *Long time passing: Lives of older lesbians.* Boston: Alyson.

Adelman, R. D., Greene, M. G., & Charon, R. (1987). The physician-elderly patient-companion triad in the medical encounter: The development of a conceptual framework and research agenda. *The Gerontologist, 27,* 729-734.

American Association of Retired Persons. (1986). *A profile of older persons, 1986.* Washington, DC: Author.

Aronson, M. (1984, June). *And who will care for the caregiver?* Paper presented at the Conference on Alzheimer's Disease: Assessment and Treatment of Patients and Caregivers, Palo Alto, CA.

Ashworth, C., Williamson, P., & Montano, D. (1984). A scale to measure physician beliefs about psychosocial aspects of patient care. *Social Science and Medicine, 19,* 1235-1238.

Atchley, R. C., & Miller, S. J. (1986). Older people and their families. In C. Eisdorfer (Ed.), *Annual review of gerontology and geriatrics* (pp. 337-369). New York: Springer.

Atwater, L., Boaz, D., & Caddell, P. (1986). The politics of the baby boom. In D. Boaz (Ed.), *Left, right & babyboom: America's new politics* (pp. 31-58). Washington, DC: CATO Institute.

Avioli, P. S. (1989). The social support functions of siblings in later life. *American Behavioral Scientist, 33,* 45-57.

Avison, Turner, Noh, & Speechly. (1993). The impact of caregiving: Comparison of different family contexts and experiences. In S. H. Zarit, L. I. Pearlin, & K. W. Schaie (Eds.), *Caregiving systems: Informal and formal helpers* (pp. 75-105). Hillsdale, NJ: Lawrence Erlbaum.

Bahr, S. J., & Peterson, E. T. (1989). *Aging and the family.* Boston, MA: Lexington.

Baker, F. M. (1994). Psychiatric treatment of older African Americans. *Hospital & Community Psychiatry, 45*(1), 32-37.

Bank, S. P. (1988). The stolen birthright: The adult sibling in individual therapy. In M. D. Kahn & K. G. Lewis (Eds.), *Siblings in therapy: Life span and clinical issues* (pp. 341-355). New York: W. W. Norton.

Bank, S. P., & Kahn, M. D. (1982a). Intense sibling loyalties. In M. E. Lamb & B. Sutton-Smith (Eds.), *Sibling relationships: Their nature and significance across the life span* (pp. 251-266). Hillsdale, NJ: Lawrence Erlbaum.

Bank, S. P., & Kahn, M. D. (1982b). *The sibling bond.* New York: Basic Books.

Barbero, S. L. (1989, November). Community-based, day treatments for mentally retarded adults. *Social Work, 545-548.*

Barusch, A. S. (1987). Power dynamics in the aging family: A preliminary statement. *Journal of Gerontological Social Work, 11,* 43-56.

Becker, C. S. (1988). *Unbroken ties: Lesbian ex-lovers.* Boston: Alyson.

Bedford, V. H. (1989). A comparison of thematic apperceptions of sibling affiliation, conflict, and separation at two periods of adulthood. *International Journal of Aging and Human Development, 28,* 53-66.

Bedford, V. H. (1992). *Changing affect toward siblings and the transition to old age.* Paper presented at the Second International Conference on the Future of Adult Life, Leeuwenhorst, The Netherlands.

Bell, A. P., & Weinberg, M. S. (1978). *Homosexualities: A study of diversity among men and women.* New York: Simon & Schuster.

Bengtson, V., Rosenthal, C., & Burton, L. (1990). Families and aging: Diversity and heterogeneity. In R. H. Binstock & L. K. George (Eds.), *Handbook of aging and the social sciences* (3rd ed., pp. 263-287). New York: Academic Press.

Berger, R. (1982). *Gay and gray: The older homosexual man.* Boston: Alyson.

Boaz, D. (1986). Introduction. In D. Boaz (Ed.), *Left, right & babyboom: America's new politics* (pp 1-10). Washington, DC: CATO Institute.

Bond, L. A., & Wagner, B. M. (Ed.). (1988a). *Families in transition: Primary prevention programs that work.* Newbury Park, CA: Sage.

Bond, L. A., & Wagner, B. M. (1988b). What makes primary prevention programs work? In L. A. Bond & B. M. Wagner (Eds.), *Families in transition: Primary prevention programs that work* (pp. 343-354). Newbury Park, CA: Sage.

Boszormenyi-Nagy, I., & Spark, G. M. (1973). *Invisible loyalties: Reciprocity in intergenerational family therapy.* New York: Harper & Row.

Bowers, B. J. (1988). Family perceptions of care in a nursing home. *The Gerontologist, 28,* 361-368.

Boyd-Franklin, N. (1988). *Black families in therapy: A multisystems approach.* New York: Guilford.

Boyd-Franklin, N. (1993). A response to David Riess. *American Family Therapy Newsletter, 54,* 39-45.

Boyd-Franklin, N., & Aleman, J. (1990). Black, inner-city families and multigenerational issues: The impact of AIDS. *New Jersey Psychologist, 40*(3), 14-17.

Boyd-Franklin, N., & Hines, P. M. (1982). Black families. In M. McGoldrick, J. K. Pearce, & J. Giordano (Eds.), *Ethnicity and family therapy* (pp. 84-107). New York: Guilford.

Bozett, F. W. (1989). Gay fathers: A review of the literature. In F. W. Bozett (Ed.), *Homosexuality and the family* (pp. 137-162). New York: Harrington Park Press.

Brashler, R., & Hartke, R. J. (1991). The caregiving family for the disabled older adult. In R. J. Hartke (Ed.), *Psychological aspects of geriatric rehabilitation* (pp. 247-277). Gaithersburg, MD: Aspen.

Breckman, R. S., & Adelman, R. D. (1988). *Strategies for helping victims of elder mistreatment*. Newbury Park, CA: Sage.

Brody, E. M. (1985a). Parent care as a normative family stress. *The Gerontologist, 25,* 19-29.

Brody, E. M. (1985b). The role of the family in nursing homes: Implications for research and public policy. In M. S. Harper & B. Lebowitz (Eds.), *Mental illness in nursing homes: Agenda for research* (pp. 234-264). Washington, DC: U.S. Government Printing Office.

Brody, E. M. (1990). *Women in the middle: Their parent-care years.* New York: Springer.

Brody, E. M., Dempsey, N. P., & Pruchno, R. A. (1990). Mental health of sons and daughters of the institutionalized aged. *The Gerontologist, 30,* 212-219.

Brody, E. M., Hoffman, C., Kleban, M. H., & Schoonover, C. B. (1989). Caregiving daughters and their local siblings: Perceptions, strains, and interactions. *The Gerontologist, 29,* 529-538.

Brody, E. M., & Schoonover, C. B. (1986). Patterns of parent care when adult daughters work and when they do not. *The Gerontologist, 26,* 372-381.

Brody, E. M., & Spark, G. (1966). Institutionalization of the aged: A family crisis. *Family Process, 5,* 76-90.

Brubaker, E. (1987). *Working with the elderly: A social systems approach.* Newbury Park, CA: Sage.

Brubaker, E., & Brubaker, T. H. (1993). *Caring for adult children with mental retardation.* In K. A. Roberto (Ed.), *The elderly caregiver: Caring for adults with developmental disabilities* (pp. 51-60). Newbury Park, CA: Sage.

Brubaker, E., Gorman, M. A., & Hiestand, M. (1990). *Stress perceived by elderly recipients of family care.* In T. H. Brubaker (Ed.), *Family relationships in later life* (2nd ed., pp. 267-281). Newbury Park, CA: Sage.

Brubaker, T. H. (1983). *Family relationships in later life.* Beverly Hills, CA: Sage.

Brubaker, T. H. (1985). *Later life families.* Beverly Hills, CA: Sage.

Brubaker, T. H. (1990a). *A contextual approach to the development of stress associated with caregiving in later-life families.* In M. A. P. Stephens, J. H. Crowther, S. E. Hobfill, & D. L. Tennenbaum (Eds.), *Stress and coping in later-life families* (pp. 29-47). New York: Hemisphere.

Brubaker, T. H. (1990b). Families in later life: A burgeoning research area. *Journal of Marriage and the Family, 52,* 959-981.

Brubaker, T. H. (Ed.). (1990c). *Family relationships in later life* (2nd ed.). Newbury Park, CA: Sage.

Brubaker, T. H., & Brubaker, E. (1992). Caregiving and cost of health care for later life families. *Journal of Family and Economic Issues, 13,* 477-483.

Brubaker, T. H., Englehardt, J. L., Brubaker, E., & Lutzer, V. D. (1989). Gender differences of older caregivers of adults with mental retardation. *The Journal of Applied Gerontology, 8,* 183-191.

Brubaker, T. H., & Roberto, K. A. (1993). Family life education for the later years. *Family Relations, 42,* 212-221.

Bumagin, V. E., & Hirn, K. F. (1990). *Helping the aging family: A guide for professionals.* Chicago: Scott, Foresman.

Burnside, I. M. (1981). *Nursing and the aged.* New York: McGraw-Hill.

Burton, L. (Ed.). (1993). *Families and aging.* Amityville, NY: Baywood.

Butler, R. N. (1963). The life review: An interpretation of reminiscence in the aged. *Psychiatry, 26,* 63-76.

Cabaj, R. P. (1988). Homosexuality and neurosis: Considerations for psychotherapy. In M. W. Ross (Ed.), *The treatment of homosexuals with mental health disorders* (pp. 13-23). New York: Harrington Park Press.

Carroll, R. (1988). Siblings in the family business. In M. D. Kahn & K. G. Lewis (Eds.), *Siblings in therapy: Life span and clinical issues* (pp. 379-398). New York: W. W. Norton.

Carstensen, L. L. (1992). Social and emotional patterns in adulthood: Support for socioemotional selectivity theory. *Psychology and Aging, 7,* 331-338.

Caserta, M. S., Connelly, J. R., Lund, D. A., & Poulton, J. L. (1987). Older adult caregivers of developmentally disabled household members: Service needs and fulfillment. *Journal of Gerontological Social Work, 10,* 35-50.

Chappell, N. L. (1990). Aging and social care. In R. H. Binstock & L. N. George (Eds.), *Handbook of aging and the social sciences* (3rd ed., pp. 438-454). New York: Academic Press.

Chenoweth, B., & Spencer, B. (1986). Dementia: The experience of family caregivers. *The Gerontologist, 26,* 267-272.

Chodorow, N. (1978). *The reproduction of mothering: Psychoanalysis and the sociology of gender.* Los Angeles: University of California Press.

Church, M. (1986). Issues in psychological therapy with elderly people. In I. Hanley & M. Gilhooly (Eds.), *Psychological therapies for the elderly* (pp. 1-21). London: Croom Helm.

Cicirelli, V. G. (1977). Relationship of siblings to the elderly person's feelings and concerns. *Journal of Gerontology, 32,* 317-322.

Cicirelli, V. G. (1979, May). *Social services for elderly in relation to the kin network.* Washington, DC: NRTA-AARP Andrus Foundation.

Cicirelli, V. G. (1980a). Relationship of family background variables to locus of control in the elderly. *Journal of Gerontology, 35,* 108-115.

Cicirelli, V. G. (1980b). Sibling influence in adulthood: A life span perspective. In L. W. Poon (Ed.), *Aging in the 1980s* (pp. 455-462). Washington, DC: American Psychological Association.

Cicirelli, V. G. (1981). *Helping elderly parents: Role of adult children.* Boston: Auburn House.

Cicirelli, V. G. (1982). Sibling influence throughout the lifespan. In M. E. Lamb & B. Sutton-Smith (Eds.), *Sibling relationships: Their nature and significance across the lifespan* (pp. 267-284). Hillsdale, NJ: Lawrence Erlbaum.

Cicirelli, V. G. (1984). Marital disruption and adult children's perception of their sibling's help to elderly parents. *Journal of Family Relations, 33,* 613-621.

Cicirelli, V. G. (1985a). The role of siblings as family caregivers. In W. J. Sauer & R. T. Coward (Eds.), *Social support networks and the care of the elderly* (pp. 93-107). New York: Springer.

Cicirelli, V. G. (1985b). Sibling relationships throughout the life cycle. In L. L'Abate (Ed.), *The handbook of family psychology and therapy* (Vol. 1, pp. 177-214). Homewood, IL: Dorsey Press.

Cicirelli, V. G. (1988). Interpersonal relationships among elderly siblings: Implications for clinical practice. In M. D. Kahn & K. G. Lewis (Eds.), *Siblings in therapy* (pp. 435-456). New York: W. W. Norton.

Cicirelli, V. G. (1989). Feelings of attachment to siblings and well-being in later life. *Psychology and Aging, 5,* 458-66.

Cicirelli, V. G. (1990). Family support in relation to health problems of the elderly. In T. H. Brubaker (Ed.), *Family relationships in later life* (2nd ed., pp. 218-228). Newbury Park, CA: Sage.

Cicirelli, V. G. (1992a). *Family caregiving: Autonomous and paternalistic decision making.* Newbury Park, CA: Sage.

Cicirelli, V. G. (1992b). Siblings as caregivers in middle and old age. In J. E. Dwyer & R. T. Coward (Eds.), *Gender and family care of the elderly* (pp. 84-101). Newbury Park, CA: Sage.

Cicirelli, V. G. (1994). Sibling relationships in cross-cultural perspective. *Journal of Marriage and the Family, 56,* 7-20.

Cicirelli, V. G., Coward, R. T., & Dwyer, J. W. (1992). Siblings as caregivers for impaired elders. *Research on Aging, 14,* 331-350.

Clark, M., & Anderson, B. (1967). *Culture and aging: An anthropological study of older Americans.* Springfield, IL: Charles C Thomas.

Clunis, D. M., & Green, G. D. (1988). *Lesbian couples.* Seattle: Seal Press.

Coe, R. M., & Prendergast, C. G. (1985). The formation of coalitions: Interaction strategies in trials. *Sociology of Health and Illness, 1,* 236-247.

Cohen, D., & Eisdorfer, C. (1988). Depression in family members caring for a relative with Alzheimer's disease. *Journal of the American Geriatrics Society, 36,* 885-889.

Coleman, E. (1985). Developmental stages of the coming out process. In J. Gonsiorek (Ed.), *A guide to psychotherapy with gay and lesbian clients* (pp. 31-43). New York: Harrington Park Press.

Colerick, E. J., & George, L. K. (1986). Predictors of institutionalization among caregivers of patients with Alzheimer's disease. *Journal of the American Geriatrics Society, 34,* 493-498.

Connidis, I. A. (1992). Life transitions and the adult sibling tie: A qualitative study. *Journal of Marriage and the Family, 54,* 972-982.

Connidis, I. A., & Davies, L. (1990). Confidants and companions in later life. *Journal of Gerontology: Social Sciences, 45,* 141-149.

Couper, D. P., & Sheehan, N. W. (1987). Family dynamics for caregivers: An educational model. *Family Relations, 36,* 181-186.

Crutcher, D. M. (1991). Family support in the home: Home visiting and Public Law 99-457. *American Psychologist, 46*(2), 138-140.

Crystal, S. (1982). *America's old age crisis: Public policy and the two worlds of aging.* New York: Basic Books.

Cumming, E., & Henry, W. (1961). *Growing old.* New York: Basic Books.

Day, R. W., & Sparacio, R. T. (1980). Structuring the counseling process. *Personnel and Guidance Journal, 59,* 246-249.

Decker, B. (1985). Counseling gay and lesbian couples. In R. Schoenberg & R. S. Goldberg (Eds.), *Homosexuality and social work* (pp. 39-52). New York: Haworth.

Deimling, G. R., & Harel, Z. (1984). Social integration and mental health of the aged. *Research on Aging, 6,* 515-527.

Dejowski, E. F. (Ed.). (1990). Protecting judgment-impaired adults: Issues, interventions, and policies [Special issue]. *Journal of Elder Abuse and Neglect, 2.*

de Vries, B., Birren, J. E., & Deutchmann, D. E. (1990). Adult development through guided autobiography: The family context. *Family Relations, 39,* 3-7.

Dobrof, R. (1983). *Training workshops for the mentally impaired elderly.* New York: The Brookdale Center on Aging of Hunter College.

Dobrof, R. (1985). Some observations from the field of aging. In M. P. Janicki & H. M. Wisniewski (Eds.), *Aging and developmental disabilities: Issues and approaches* (pp. 411-415). Baltimore: Paul Brooks.

Doherty, W. J., & Baird, M. A. (1983). *Family therapy and family medicine.* New York: Guilford.

Doty, P. (1986). Family care of the elderly: The role of public policy. *The Milbank Quarterly, 67,* 485-506.

Duffy, M. (1986). The techniques and contexts of multigenerational therapy. In T. L. Brink (Ed.), *Clinical gerontology—A guide to assessment and intervention.* New York: Haworth.

Dunn, J. (1984). Sibling studies and the developmental impact of critical incidents. In P. B. Baltes & O. G. Brim, Jr. (Eds.), *Life-span development and behavior* (Vol. 6, pp. 335-353). San Diego: Academic Press.

Dunn, J. (1985). *Sisters and brothers.* Cambridge, MA: Harvard University Press.

Dunn, J., & Kendrick, C. (1982). *Siblings: Love, envy, and understanding.* Cambridge, MA: Harvard University Press.

Edelson, J. S., & Lyons, W. (1985). *Institutional care of the mentally impaired elderly.* New York: Van Nostrand Reinhold.

Edwards, J. N., & Brauburger, M. B. (1973). Exchange and parent-youth conflict. *Journal of Marriage and the Family, 35,* 101-107.

Eisenberg, H. B. (1991). Combatting elder abuse through the legal process. *Journal of Elder Abuse and Neglect, 3,* 65-96.

Engelhardt, J., Brubaker, T. H., & Lutzer, V. (1988). Older caregivers of adults with mental retardation: Service utilization. *Mental Retardation, 26,* 191-195.

Erikson, E. H. (1963). *Childhood and society* (2nd ed.). New York: Norton.

Falicov, C. J., & Karrer, B. M. (1980). Cultural variations in the family life cycle: The Mexican-American family. In E. A. Carter & M. McGoldrick (Eds.), *The family life cycle: A framework for family therapy* (pp. 383-424). New York: Gardner.

Fandetti, C. V., & Gelfand, D. E. (1976). Care of the aged: Attitudes of white ethnic families. *The Gerontologist, 16,* 544-549.

Feil, N. (1993). *The validation breakthrough: Simple techniques for communicating with people with "Alzheimer's type dementia."* Baltimore: Health Professional Press.

Ferris, S. H., Steinberg, G., Shulman, E., Kahn, R., & Reisberg, B. (1987). Institutionalization of Alzheimer's disease patients: Reducing precipitating factors through family counseling. *Home Health Care Services Quarterly, 8,* 23-51.

Flynn, M. L. (1993). The policy and program planning base for family therapy with aging persons. In E. R. Neiderhardt & J. A. Allen (Eds.), *Family therapy with the elderly* (pp. 159-177). Newbury Park, CA: Sage.

Fogel, B. S., Gottlieb, G. L., & Furino, A. (1990). *Present and future solutions.* In B. S. Furino & G. L. Gottlieb (Eds.), *Mental health policy for older Americans: Protecting minds at risk* (pp. 257-278). Washington, DC: American Psychiatric Press.

Foner, N. (1993). Troubled aides at "Crescent Nursing Home." *Aging Today: The Bimonthly Newspaper of the American Society on Aging, 14,* 6.

Ford Foundation Project on Social Welfare and the American Future. (1989). *The common good: Social welfare and the American future.* New York: Author.

Fullmer, E. M., & Eastland, L. J. (1993). *Community adaption and intergenerational communication among lesbians and gay men.* Paper presented at the annual scientific meetings of the Gerontological Society of America, New Orleans, LA.

Fulmer, T. T. (1990). The debate over dependency as a relevant predisposing factor in elder abuse and neglect. *Journal of Elder Abuse and Neglect, 2,* 51-58.

Gallagher, D. E. (1988). Intervention strategies to assist caregivers of frail elders: Current research status and future research directions. In M. P. Lawton & G. L. Maddox (Eds.), *Annual review of gerontology and geriatrics* (pp. 249-282). New York: Springer.

Garbarino, J. (1977). The human ecology of child maltreatment: A conceptual model for research. *Journal of Marriage and the Family, 39,* 721-735.

Garcia, J. L., & Kosberg, J. I. (1992). Understanding anger: Implications for formal and informal caregivers. *Journal of Elder Abuse and Neglect, 4,* 87-98.

Garcia, J. L., & Kosberg, J. I. (1994). Family caregiving to the elderly. In *Directions in marriage and family therapy* (Vol. 2, pp. 1-14). New York: Hatherleigh.

Garcia-Preto, N. (1982). Puerto Rican families. In M. McGoldrick, J. K. Pearce, & J. Giordano (Eds.), *Ethnicity and family therapy* (pp. 164-186). New York: Guilford.

Gartner, A., & Riessman, F. (1981). Self-help organizations. In W. H. Silverman (Ed.), *Community mental health.* New York: Praeger.

Gatz, M., Bengtson, V. L., & Blum, M. J. (1990). Caregiving families. In J. E. Birren & K. W. Schaie (Eds.), *Handbook of psychology of aging* (3rd ed., pp. 404-426). San Diego: Academic Press.

Gelfand, D. E., & Kutzik, A. J. (Eds.). (1979). *Ethnicity and aging.* New York: Springer.

George, L. K. (1984). *The burden of caregiving* (Center Reports on Advances in Research No. 8). Durham, NC: Duke University Center for the Study of Aging and Human Development.

George, L. K. (1986). Caregiver burden: Conflict between norms of reciprocity and solidarity. In K. Pillemer & R. Wolf (Eds.), *Elder abuse: Conflict in the family* (pp. 67-92). Boston: Auburn House.

George, L. K., & Gwyther, L. P. (1984, November). *The dynamics of caregiver burden: Changes in caregiver well-being overtime.* Paper presented at the annual scientific meeting of the Gerontological Society of America, San Antonio, TX.

Gevalnik, J. M., & Simonsick, E. M. (1993). Physical disability in older Americans. *The Journal of Gerontology, 48,* 3-10.

Giordano, J. A., & Beckman, K. (1985). The aged within a family context: Relationships, roles, and events. In L. L'Abate (Ed.), *The handbook of family psychology and therapy* (Vol. 1, pp. 284-320). Homewood, IL: Dorsey Press.

Goetting, A. (1986). The development tasks of siblingship over the life cycle. *Journal of Marriage and the Family, 48,* 703-714.

Gold, D. T. (1986). *Sibling relationships in retrospect: A study of reminiscence in old age.* Unpublished doctoral dissertation, Northwestern University, Evanston, IL.

Gold, D. T. (1989). Generational solidarity. *American Behavioral Scientist, 33,* 19-32.

Gold, D. T., & Gwyther, L. P. (1989). The prevention of elder abuse: An educational model. *Family Relations, 38,* 8-14.

Goodman, D. M. (1978). Parenting an adult mentally retarded offspring. *Smith College Studies in Social Work, 48,* 209-234.

Grant, G. (1986). Older carers, interdependence and care of mentally handicapped adults. *Ageing and Society, 6,* 333-351.

Greeley, A. M. (1969). *Why can't they be like us?* New York: Institute of Human Relations Press.

Greenberg, J. R., McKibben, M., & Raymond, J. A. (1990). Dependent adult children and elder abuse. *Journal of Elder Abuse and Neglect, 2,* 73-86.

Greenberg, J. S., Seltzer, M. M., & Greenley, J. R. (1993). Aging parents of adults with disabilities: The gratifications and frustrations of later-life caregiving. *The Gerontologist, 33,* 542-550.

Greene, M. G., Adelman, R. D., Charon, R., & Hoffman, S. (1986). Ageism in the medical encounter: An exploratory study of the doctor-elderly patient relationship. *Language and Communication, 6,* 113-124.

Greene, M. G., Hoffman, S., Charon, R., & Adelman, R. (1987). Psychosocial concerns in the medical encounter: A comparison of the interactions of doctors with their old and young patients. *The Gerontologist, 27,* 164-168.

Greene, R. (1989). A life-systems approach to understanding parent-child relationships in aging families. *Journal of Psychotherapy and the Family, 5,* 57-69.

Grier, W., & Cobbs, P. (1968). *Black rage.* New York: Basic Books.

Hansen, S. S., Patterson, M. A., & Wilson, R. W. (1988). Family involvement on a dementia unit: The resident enrichment and activity program. *The Gerontologist, 28,* 508-510.

Hansson, R. O., Nelson, R. E., Carver, M. D., Neesmith, D. H., Dowling, E. M., Fletcher, W. L., & Suhr, P. (1990). Adult children with frail elderly parents: When to intervene. *Family Relations, 39,* 153-158.

Hargrave, T. D., & Anderson, W. T. (1992). *Finishing well: Aging and reparation in the intergenerational family.* New York: Brunner/Mazel.

Harris, E. G. (1988). My brother's keeper: Siblings of chronic patients as allies in family treatment. In M. D. Kahn & K. G. Lewis (Eds.), *Siblings in therapy: Life span and clinical issues* (pp. 315-340). New York: W. W. Norton.

Harry, J., & Devall, W. (1978). Age and sexual culture among homosexually oriented males. *Archives of Sexual Behavior, 7*(3), 199-209.

Harshbarger, S. (1993). From protection to prevention: A proactive approach. *Journal of Elder Abuse and Neglect, 5,* 41-55.

Hartman, A., & Laird, J. (1983). *Family centered social work practice.* New York: Free Press.

Haug, M., & Ory, M. (1986, August). *Issues in elderly patient-provider interactions.* Paper presented at the annual meeting of the American Sociological Association, New York.

Hazler, R. J., & Roberts, G. (1984, March). Decision making in vocational theory. *Personnel and Guidance Journal,* 408-410.

Heifetz, M. D. (1978). Ethics in human biology. In C. A. Garfield (Ed.), *Psychosocial care of the dying patient* (pp. 304-316). New York: McGraw-Hill.

Heiselman, T., & Noelker, L. S. (1991). Enhancing mutual respect among nursing assistants, residents and residents' families. *The Gerontologist, 31,* 552-555.

Heller, T. (1985). Residential relocation and reactions of elderly mentally retarded persons. In M. P. Janicki & H. M. Wisniewski (Eds.), *Aging and developmental disabilities: Issues and approaches* (pp. 379-389). Baltimore: Paul Brooks.

Heller, T., & Factor, A. (1987, November). *Elderly parents caring for disabled adult offspring: Issues in permanency planning.* Paper presented at the 40th annual scientific meeting of the Gerontological Society of America, Washington, DC.

Heller, T., & Factor, A. (1991). Permanency planning for adults with mental retardation living with family caregivers. *American Journal of Mental Retardation, 96,* 163-176.

Heller, T., & Factor, A. (1993). Support systems, well-being, and placement decision-making among older parents and their adult children with developmental disabilities. In E. Sutton, A. R. Factor, B. A. Hawkins, T. Heller, & G. B. Seltzer (Eds.), *Older adults with developmental disabilities: Optimizing choice and change* (pp. 107-122). Baltimore: Paul Brooks.

256 STRENGTHENING AGING FAMILIES

Henderson, M. (1990). Beyond the living will. *The Gerontologist, 30,* 480-485.

Hennon, C. B., & Arcus, M. (1993). Life-span family life education. In T. H. Brubaker (Ed.), *Family relations: Challenges for the future* (pp. 181-210). Newbury Park, CA: Sage.

Hennon, C. B., Brubaker, E., & Kaplan, L. (1991). Health, housing, and aging: Families as case managers. *Journal of Home Economics, 8,* 54-62.

Hernandez, G. G. (1991). Not so benign neglect. Researchers ignore ethnicity in defining family caregiver burden and recommending services. *The Gerontologist, 31*(2), 271-272.

Herr, J. J., & Weakland, J. H. (1979). *Counseling elders and their families: Practical techniques for applied gerontology.* New York: Springer.

Hess, B. B., & Soldo, B. J. (1985). Husband and wife networks. In W. J. Sauer & R. T. Coward (Eds.), *Social support networks and the care of the elderly* (pp. 67-92). New York: Springer.

Hines, P. M. (1989). The family life cycle of poor black families. In E. Carter & M. McGoldrick (Eds.). *The changing family life cycle: A framework for family therapy* (2nd ed.). Boston: Allyn & Bacon.

Hines, P. M. (1990). African-American mothers. *Journal of Feminist Family Therapy, 2*(2), 23-32.

Holmes, T. H., & Rahe, R. (1967). The social readjustment rating scale. *Journal of Psychosomatic Research, 11,* 213-218.

Hoopes, M. H., Fisher, B. L., & Barlow, S. H. (1984). *Structured family facilitation programs: Enrichment, education and treatment.* Rockville, MD: Aspen.

Hooyman, N. R., & Kiyak, H. A. (1993). *Social gerontology.* Needham Heights, MA: Allyn & Bacon.

Hooyman, N. R., & Lustbader, W. (1986). *Taking care: Supporting older people and their families.* New York: Free Press.

Horne, M. (1989). Identifying a "hidden" population of older adults with mental handicap: Outreach in the U.K., Australia and New Zealand. *Journal of Developmental Disabilities, 15,* 207-218.

Hoyt, D. R., & Babchuk, N. (1983). Adult kinship-networks: The selective formation of intimate ties with kin. *Social Forces, 62,* 84-101.

Hughston, G. A., Christopherson, V. A., & Bonjean, M. J. (Eds.). (1989). *Aging and family therapy: Practitioner perspectives on golden pond.* New York: Haworth.

Humphreys, R. A. L. (1970). *The tearoom trade: Impersonal sex in public places.* Chicago: Aldine.

Hunt, M., & Hunt, B. (1977). *The divorce experience.* New York: McGraw-Hill.

Iris, M. A. (1990). Uses of guardianship as a protective intervention for frail, older adults. *Journal of Elder Abuse and Neglect, 2,* 57-71.

Janicki, M. P. (1988). Symposium overview—The new challenge. *Mental Retardation, 26,* 177-180.

Janicki, M. P., Otis, J. P., Puccio, P. S., Rettig, J. H., & Jacobson, J. W. (1985). Service needs among older developmentally disabled persons. In M. P. Janicki & H. M. Wisniewski (Eds.), *Aging and developmental disabilities: Issues and approaches* (pp. 289-304). Baltimore: Paul Brooks.

Janicki, M. P., & Wisniewski, H. M. (Eds.). (1985). *Aging and developmental disabilities: Issues and approaches.* Baltimore: Paul Brooks.

Jecker, N. S. (1990). The role of intimate others in medical decision making. *The Gerontologist, 30,* 65-71.

Jennings, J. (1987). Elderly parents as caregivers for their adult dependent children. *Social Work, 32,* 430-433.

Johnson, C. L. (1982). Sibling solidarity: Its origins and functioning in Italian-American families. *Journal of Marriage and the Family, 44,* 155-167.

Johnson, C. L., & Catalano, D. J. (1981). Childless elderly and their family supports. *The Gerontologist, 21,* 610-618.

Johnson, H. C. (1986, July/August). Emerging concerns in family therapy. *Social Work,* 299-306.

Justice, B., & Duncan, D. (1976). Life crisis as a precursor to child abuse. *Public Health Reports, 91,* 110-115.

Kahn, M. D. (1983). Sibling relationships in later life. *Medical Aspects of Human Sexuality, 17*(2), 94-103.

Kahn, M. D., & Bank, S. (1981). In pursuit of sisterhood. *Family Process, 20*(1), 85-95.

Kane, R. A., & Kane, R. L. (1982). *Values and long-term care.* Lexington, MA: Lexington.

Kane, R. A., & Penrod, J. D. (1993). Family caregiving policies: Insights from an intensive longitudinal study. In S. H. Zarit, L. I. Pearlin, & K. W. Schaie (Eds.), *Caregiving systems: Informal and formal helpers* (pp. 273-292). Hillsdale, NJ: Lawrence Erlbaum.

Kane, R. A., & Reinardy, J. (1989). Family caregiving in home care. In C. Zuckerman, N. N. Dubler, & B. Callopy (Eds.), *Home health care options: A guide for older persons and concerned families.* New York: Plenum.

Kane, R. L. (1990). Testing new models of service delivery. In B. S. Fogel, A. Furino, & G. L. Gottlieb (Eds.), *Mental health policy for Americans: Protecting minds at risk* (pp. 179-200). Washington, DC: American Psychiatric Press.

Kapp, M. (1991). Health care decision making by the elderly: I get by with a little help from my family. *The Gerontologist, 11*(5), 619-623.

Kaufman, A. V., Adams, J. P., & Campbell, V. A. (1991). Permanency planning by older parents who care for adult children with mental retardation. *Mental Retardation, 5,* 293-300.

Kaufman, A. V., DeWeaver, K., & Glicken, M. (1989). The mentally retarded aged: Implications for social work practice. *Journal of Gerontological Social Work, 14,* 93-110.

Kaye, L. W., & Applegate, J. S. (1990a). *Men as caregivers to the elderly: Understanding and aiding unrecognized family support.* Lexington, MA: Lexington.

Kaye, L. W., & Applegate, J. S. (1990b). Men as elder caregivers: A response to changing families. *American Journal of Orthopsychiatry, 60,* 86-95.

Kazak, A. E., & Marvin, R. S. (1984). Differences, difficulties and adaption: Stress and social networks in families with a handicapped child. *Family Relations, 33,* 67-77.

Kehoe, M. (1989). *Lesbians over sixty speak for themselves.* New York: Haworth.

Keith, P. M., & Wacker, R. R. (1991) Guardianship reform: Does revised legislation make a difference in outcomes for proposed wards? *Journal of Aging and Social Policy, 4*(3-4), 139-155.

Kelley, H. H., Berscheid, E., Christensen, A., Harvey, J. H., Huston, T. L., Levinger, G., McClintock, G., Peplau, L. A., & Peterson, D. R. (1983). *Close relationships.* New York: W. H. Freeman.

Kemp, J. T. (1984, January). Learning from clients: Counseling the frail and dying elderly. *Personnel and Guidance Journal,* 270-272.

Kimmel, D. C. (1992, Summer). The families of older gay men and lesbians. *Generations,* 37-38.

Kirschner, C. (1985). Social work practice with the aged and their families: A systems approach. In G. S. Getzel & M. J. Mellor (Eds.), *Gerontological social work practice in the community* (pp. 55-69). New York: Haworth.

Kivett, V. R. (1985). Consanguinity and kin level: Their relative importance to the helping networks of older adults. *Journal of Gerontology: Social Sciences, 40,* 228-234.

Kleban, M. H., Brody, E. M., Schoonover, C. B., & Hoffman, C. (1989). Family help to the elderly: Perceptions of sons-in-law regarding parent care. *Journal of Marriage and the Family, 51,* 303-312.

Kosberg, J. I. (1988). Preventing elder abuse: Identification of high risk factors prior to placement. *The Gerontologist, 28,* 43-50.

Kosberg, J. I. (1990). Assistance to crime and abuse victims. In A. Monk (Ed.), *Handbook of gerontological services* (2nd ed., pp. 450-473). New York: Columbia University Press.

Kosberg, J. I., & Cairl, R. C. (1986). The cost of care index: A case management tool for screening informal care providers. *The Gerontologist, 26,* 273-278.

Krauss, M. W. (1993, June). *Role variation among adult siblings of persons with mental retardation.* Paper presented at the 117th annual meeting of the American Association on Mental Retardation, Washington, DC.

Krauss, M. W., & Seltzer, M. M. (1993). Current well-being and future plans of older caregiving mothers. *Irish Journal of Psychology, 14,* 48-63.

Krauss, M. W., Seltzer, M. M., & Goodman, S. J. (1992). Social support networks of adults with mental retardation at home. *American Journal of Mental Retardation, 96,* 432-441.

Krumboltz, J. D. (1983). *Private rules in career decision making.* Columbus, OH: The National Center for Research in Vocational Education.

Kurdeck, L. A., & Schmitt, J. P. (1986). Relationship quality of partners in heterosexual married, heterosexual cohabitating, and gay and lesbian relationships. *Journal of Personality and Social Psychology, 51,* 711-720.

Kushner, T. (1992). *Angels in America, part one: Millenium approaches.* New York: TGC.

Kuypers, J. A., & Bengston, V. L. (1984). Perspectives on the older family. In W. H. Quinn & G. A. Hughston (Eds.), *Interdependent aging: Family and social systems perspectives* (pp. 2-21). Rockville, MD: Aspen.

L'Abate, L. (1978). *Enrichment: Structured interventions with couples, families, and groups.* Washington, DC: University Press of America.

L' Abate, L. (Ed.). (1985). *The handbook of family psychology and therapy, Vol. 1.* Homewood, IL: Dorsey Press.

L'Abate, L. (1990). *Building family competence: Primary and secondary prevention strategies.* Newbury Park, CA: Sage.

L' Abate, L. (Ed.). (1994). *Handbook of developmental family psychology and psychopathology.* New York: John Wiley.

L'Abate, L., & Weinstein, S. E. (Eds.). (1987). *Structured enrichment programs for couples and families.* New York: Brunner/Mazel.

Lang, K. M., & Brody, E. M. (1983). Characteristics of middle-aged daughters and help to their elderly mothers. *Journal of Marriage and the Family, 45,* 193-202.

Langer, E. J. (1989). *Mindfulness.* New York: Addison-Wesley.

Langer, E., & Rodin, J. (1976). The effects of choice and enhanced personal responsibility for the aged: A field experiment in an institutional setting. *Journal of Personality and Social Psychology, 34,* 191-198.

Lawton, M. P., Brody, E. M., & Saperstein, A. R. (1989). A controlled study of respite services for caregivers of Alzheimer's patients. *The Gerontologist, 29,* 8-16.

Lawton, M. P., Kleban, M. H., Moss, M., Rovine, M., & Glicksman, A. (1989). Measuring caregiver appraisal. *Journal of Gerontology, 44*, 61-71.

Lazarus, L. W., Stafford, B., Cooper, K., Cohler, B., & Dysken, M. (1981). A pilot study of an Alzheimer patients' relative discussion group. *The Gerontologist, 21*(4), 353-359.

Lee, G. (1988). Marital satisfaction in later life: The effects of nonmarital roles. *Journal of Marriage and the Family, 50*, 775-783.

Lee, G. R., & Ihinger-Tallman, M. (1980). Sibling interactions and morale. *Research on Aging, 2*, 367-391.

Lee, J. A. (1988). Invisible lives of Canada's gray gays. In V. Marshall (Ed.), *Aging in Canada* (pp. 138-155). Toronto: Fitzhenry & Whiteside.

Lefly, H. P. (1987). Aging parents as caregivers of mentally ill adult children: An emerging social problem. *Hospital and Community Psychiatry, 38*, 1063-1070.

Levin, I., & Trost, J. (1992). Understanding the concept of family. *Family Relations, 41*, 348-351.

Levinger, G. (1980). Toward the analysis of close relationships. *Journal of Experimental Social Psychology, 16*, 510-544.

Lieberman, M. A., & Tobin, S. S. (1983). *The experience of old age: Stress, coping and survival.* New York: Basic Books.

Lipman, A. (1986). Homosexual relationships. *Generations, 10*(4), 51-54.

Lippman, L., & Loberg, D. E. (1985). An overview of developmental disabilities. In M. P. Janicki & H. M. Wisniewski (Eds.), *Aging and developmental disabilities: Issues and approaches* (pp. 41-58). Baltimore: Paul Brooks.

Litwak, E. (1965). Extended kin relations in an industrial democratic society. In E. Shanas & G. Streib (Eds.), *Social structure and the family.* Englewood Cliffs, NJ: Prentice Hall.

Lopata, H. (1973). *Widowhood in an American city.* Cambridge, MA: Schenkman.

Loulan, J. (1984). *Lesbian sex.* San Francisco: Spinsters\aunt lute.

Lubin, R. A., & Kiely, M. (1985). Epidemiology of aging in developmental disabilities. In M. P. Janicki & H. M. Wisniewski (Eds.), *Aging and developmental disabilities: Issues and approaches* (pp. 95-113). Baltimore: Paul Brooks.

Lyon, P., & Martin, D. (1979). The older lesbian. In B. Berzon & R. Leijhton (Eds.), *Positively gay* (pp. 134-145). Millbrae, CA: Celestial Arts Press.

Lystad, M. (1975). Violence at home: A review of the literature. *American Journal of Orthopsychiatry, 45*, 328-345.

Mace, D. R. (Ed.). (1983). *Prevention in family services: Approaches to family wellness.* Beverly Hills, CA: Sage.

Maddox, G. L., & Lawton, M. P. (Eds.). (1993). *Annual review of gerontology and geriatrics: Focus on kinship, aging, and social change, Vol. 13.* New York: Springer.

Maguire, L. (1983). *Understanding social networks.* Beverly Hills, CA: Sage.

Margolies, L., Becker, M., & Jackson-Brewer, K. (1987). *Internalized homophobia: Identifying and treating the oppressor within.* Chicago: University of Illinois Press.

Martico-Greenfield, E. (1986). *CONNECT (Communication Used Not Ever Cease Totally): A communication enriched project for families at the Jewish Home and Hospital for the Aged.* Unpublished manuscript.

Masciocchi, C., Thomas, A., & Moeller, T. (1984). Support for the impaired elderly: A challenge for family care-givers. In W. H. Quinn & G. A. Hughston (Eds.), *Independent aging* (pp. 115-132). Rockville, MD: Aspen.

Matthews, S. H. (1987). Provision of care to older parents. *Research on Aging, 9*, 45-60.

Matthews, S. H., Delaney, P. J., & Adamek, M. E. (1989). Male kinship ties: Bonds between adult brothers. *American Behavioral Scientist, 33,* 58-69.

McAdoo, H. P. (Ed.). (1993). *Family ethnicity: Strength in diversity.* Newbury Park, CA: Sage.

McCandlish, B. M. (1985). Therapeutic issues with lesbian couples. In J. C. Gonsiorek (Ed.), *A guide to psychotherapy with gay and lesbian clients* (pp. 71-78). New York: Harrington Park Press.

McCubbin, H. I., & Patterson, J. M. (1982). Family adaptation to crises. In H. I. McCubbin, A. E. Cauble, & J. M. Patterson (Eds.), *Family stress, coping and social support* (pp. 26-47). Springfield, IL: Charles C Thomas.

McCullough, C. B., Wilson, N. C., Teasdale, T. A., Kolpakchi, A. L., & Skelly, J. R. (1993). Mapping personal, familial, and professional values in long-term care decisions. *The Gerontologist, 33*(3), 324-332.

McGhee, J. L. (1985). The effect of siblings on the life satisfaction of the rural elderly. *Journal of Marriage and the Family, 47,* 85-91.

McGill, D., & Pearce, J. K. (1982). British families. In M. McGoldrick, J. K. Pearce, & J. Giordano (Eds.), *Ethnicity and family therapy* (pp. 457-479). New York: Guilford.

McGoldrick, M. (1982). Ethnicity and family therapy: An overview. In M. McGoldrick, J. K. Pearce, & J. Giordano (Eds.), *Ethnicity and family therapy* (pp. 3-30). New York: Guilford.

McGoldrick, M. (1989). Ethnicity and the family life cycle. In E. Carter & M. McGoldrick (Eds.), *The changing family life cycle: A framework for family therapy* (2nd ed., pp. 69-90). Boston: Allyn & Bacon.

McGoldrick, M. (1990). Irish mothers. *Journal of Feminist Family Therapy, 2*(2), 3-8.

McGoldrick, M., Pearce, J. K., & Giordano, J. (Eds.). (1982). *Ethnicity and family therapy.* New York: Guilford.

McWhirter, D. P., & Mattison, A. M. (1984). *The male couple: How relationships develop.* Englewood Cliffs, NJ: Prentice Hall.

Michaud, T. G. (1990). Italian mothers. *Journal of Feminist Family Therapy, 2*(2), 53-58.

Mindel, C. H. (1983). The elderly in minority families. In T. H. Brubaker (Ed.), *Family relationships in later life* (pp. 193-208). Beverly Hills, CA: Sage.

Minuchin, S. (1974). *Families and family therapy.* Cambridge, MA: Harvard University Press.

Minuchin, S., Rosman, B., & Baker, L. (1978). *Psychosomatic families: Anorexia nervosa in context.* Cambridge, MA: Harvard University Press.

Molinari, V., & Reichlin, R. E. (1985). Life review reminiscence in the elderly: A review of the literature. *International Journal of Aging and Human Development, 230*(2), 81-92.

Montgomery, R. J. V. (1982). Impact of institutional care policies on family integration. *The Gerontologist, 22,* 54-58.

Montgomery, R. J. V. (1983). Staff-family relations and institutional care policies. *Journal of Gerontological Social Work, 6,* 25-38.

Montgomery, R. J. V., & Datwyler, M. M. (1990). Women and men in the caregiving role. *Generations, 14,* 34-38.

Montgomery, R. J. V., & Kosloski, K. (1994). A longitudinal analysis of nursing home placement for dependent elders cared for by spouses vs. adult children. *Journal of Gerontology, 49,* S62-S74.

Moody, H. R. (1988). From informed consent to negotiated consent. *The Gerontologist, 28* 64-70.

Moody, H. R. (1992). *Ethics in an aging society.* Baltimore, MD: Johns Hopkins University Press.

Moore, S. T. (1987). The capacity to care: A family focused approach to social work practice with the disabled elderly. *Journal of Gerontological Social Work, 12,* 79-97.

Morycz, R. K. (1985). Caregiving strain and the desire to institutionalize family members with Alzheimer's disease. *Research on Aging, 7,* 329-361.

Moses, A. E., & Hawkins, R. O. (1982). *Counseling lesbian women and gay men: A life-issues approach.* St. Louis: C. V. Mosby.

Moss, M. S., & Kurland, P. (1979). Family visiting with institutionalized mentally impaired aged. *Journal of Gerontological Social Work, 1,* 271-278.

Nadler, A., Lewinstein, E., & Rahav, G. (1991). Acceptance of mental retardation and help-seeking by mothers and fathers of children with mental retardation. *Mental Retardation, 29,* 17-23.

Neiderhardt, E. R., & Allen, J. A. (1993). *Family therapy with the elderly.* Newbury Park, CA: Sage.

Noelker, L. S., & Bass, D. M. (1989). Home care for elderly persons: Linkages between formal and informal caregivers. *Journal of Gerontology, 44,* 563-570.

Nuland, S. B. (1994). *How we die.* New York: Knopf.

O'Brien, C. R., Johnson, J. L., & Miller, B. (1979, February). Counseling the aging: Some practical considerations. *Personnel and Guidance Journal,* 288-291.

Office of the Inspector General. (1990). *Resident abuse in nursing homes: Understanding and preventing abuse* (OEI-06-88-00360). Washington, DC: U.S. Department of Health and Human Services.

Office of Special Education and Rehabilitative Services. (1984). *Disability and families: A family systems approach* (Vol. 7). Washington, DC: U.S. Department of Education.

Okun, B. F. (1987). *Effective helping: Interviewing and counseling techniques.* Monterey, CA: Brooks/Cole.

Orlofsky, J. L., Marcia, J. E., & Lesser, I. M. (1973). Ego identity status and the intimacy versus isolation crisis of young adulthood. *Journal of Personality and Social Psychology, 27,* 211-219.

Osgood, N. J. (1985). *Suicide in the elderly: A practitioner's guide to diagnosis and mental health intervention.* Rockville, MD: Aspen.

Pagel, M. D., Becker, J., & Coppel, D. B. (1985). Loss of control, self-blame, and depression: An investigation of spouse caregivers of Alzheimer's disease patients. *Journal of Abnormal Psychology, 94,* 169-182.

Palazzoli, M. S. (1985). The problem of the sibling as the referring person. *Journal of Marital and Family Therapy, 11,* 21-34.

Parsons, R. J., & Cox, E. O. (1989). Family mediation in elder care decisions: An empowerment intervention. *Social Work, 34,* 122-126.

Pelaez, M., & David, D. (1991). Training professionals to enhance autonomy in long-term care. *The Gerontologist, 31,* 71.

Peplau, L. (1981). What homosexuals want in relationships. *Psychology Today, 15*(3), 28-38.

Pepper, C. (1989). Guardianship: Friend or foe of America's frail and elderly? *Journal of Elder Abuse and Neglect, 1,* 65-74.

Petersen, S. (1990). Dealing with the difficult patient-family and remaining sane. *Caring, 9,* 23-25.

Pietrukowicz, M. E., & Johnson, M. M. S. (1991). Using life histories to individualize nursing home staff attitudes toward residents. *The Gerontologist, 31,* 102-106.

Pillemer, K. (1985). The dangers of dependence: New findings on domestic violence against the elderly. *Social Problems, 33,* 146-158.

Pillemer, K., & Bachman, R. (1991). Helping and hurting: Predictors of maltreatment of patients in nursing homes. *Research on Aging, 13,* 74-95.

Pillemer, K., & Finkelhor, D. (1988). The prevalence of elder abuse: A random sample survey. *The Gerontologist, 28,* 51-57.

Pillemer, K., & Hudson, B. (1993). A model abuse prevention program for nursing assistants. *The Gerontologist, 33,* 128-131.

Pillemer, K., & Moore, D. W. (1989). Abuse of patients in nursing homes: Findings from a survey of staff. *The Gerontologist, 29,* 314-320.

Pillemer, K., & Moore, D. W. (1990). Highlights from a study of abuse of patients in nursing homes. *Journal of Elder Abuse and Neglect, 2,* 5-29.

Pillemer, K. A., & Wolf, R. S. (1986). *Elder abuse: Conflict in the family.* Dover, MA: Auburn House.

Podnieks, E. (1992). National survey on abuse of the elderly in Canada. *Journal of Elder Abuse and Neglect, 4,* 5-58.

Poggi, R. C., & Berland, D. I. (1985). The therapist's reactions to the elderly. *The Gerontologist, 25,* 508-513.

Poor, M. (1982). The older lesbian. In M. Cruikshank (Ed.), *Lesbian studies* (pp. 165-173). Old Westbury, NY: Feminist Press.

Power, P. W. (1988). An assessment approach to family intervention. In P. W. Power, A. E. Dell Orto, & M. B. Gibbons (Eds.), *Family interventions throughout chronic illness and disability* (pp. 5-24). New York: Springer.

Power, P. W., & Dell Orto, A. E. (1980). *Role of the family in the rehabilitation of the physically disabled.* Austin, TX: Pro-Ed.

Power, P. W., Dell Orto, A. E., & Gibbons, M. B. (Eds.). (1988). *Family interventions throughout chronic illness and disability.* New York: Springer.

Pratt, C. C., Schmall, V. L., Wright, S., & Cleland, M. (1985). Burden and coping strategies of caregivers to Alzheimer's patients. *Family Relations, 34,* 27-33.

Pruchno, R., & Kleban, M. H. (1993). Caring for an institutionalized person: The role of coping strategies. *Psychology and Aging, 8,* 18-25.

Qualls, S. H. (1991). Resistance of older families to therapeutic interventions. *Clinical Gerontologist, 11*(1), 59-68.

Qualls, S. H. (1992). *Clinical interventions research with older families: Review and recommendations.* Paper presented at the annual meeting of the Gerontological Society of America, Washington, DC.

Quinn, M. J., & Tomita, S. K. (1986). *Elder abuse and neglect: Causes, diagnosis, and intervention strategies.* New York: Springer.

Rankin, E. D. (1990). Caregiver stress and the elderly: A familial perspective. *Journal of Gerontological Social Work, 15,* 57-73.

Rankin, E. D., Haut, M. W., & Keefover, R. W. (1992). Clinical assessment of family caregivers in dementia. *The Gerontologist, 32,* 813-821.

Rape, R. N., Bush, J. P., & Slavin, L. A. (1992). Toward a conceptualization of the family's adaptation to a member's head injury: A critique of developmental stage models. *Rehabilitation Psychology, 37*(1), 3-22.

Rathbone-McCuan, E. (1991). Family counseling: An emerging approach in clinical gerontology. In P. K. Kim (Ed.), *Serving the elderly: Skills for practice.* New York: Aldine de Gruyter.

Reedy, M., Birren, J. E., & Schaie, K. W. (1981). Age and sex differences in satisfying love relationships across the adult life span. *Human Development, 24,* 52-66.

Regan, J. J. (1983). Protective services for the elderly: Benefits or threat. In J. I. Kosberg (Ed.), *Abuse and maltreatment of the elderly: Causes and interventions* (pp. 279-291). Boston: John Wright-PSG.

Rhyne, D. (1981). Bases of marital satisfaction among men and women. *Journal of Marriage and the Family, 43,* 941-955.

Riess, D. (1993). Chronicle of a Euro-American researcher directing a study of African-American families. *American Family Therapy Academy Newsletter, 54,* 30-39.

Ritchie, M. H. (1986). Counseling the involuntary client. *Journal of Counseling and Development, 64,* 516-518.

Roberto, K. A. (1988). *Caring for aging developmentally disabled adults: Perspectives and needs of older parents* [Final report presented to the Colorado Developmental Disabilities Planning Council]. Greeley: Department of Human Services, University of Northern Colorado.

Roberts, R. N., Wasik, B. H., Casto, G., & Ramey, C. T. (1991). Family support in the home. *American Psychologist, 46,* 131-137.

Robischon, P., & Smith, J. (1977). Family assessment. In A. Rheinhardt & M. Quinn (Eds.), *Current practice in family-centered community nursing* (pp. 85-100). St. Louis: C. V. Mosby.

Rodin, J. (1980). Managing the stress of aging: The role of control and coping. In H. Orsin & S. Levine (Eds.), *Coping and health.* New York: Academic Press.

Rodin, J., & Langer, E. (1977). Long-term effects of a control-reliquent intervention with the institutionalized aged. *Journal of Personality and Social Psychology, 35,* 897-902.

Rose, L., Finestone, K., & Bass, J. (1985). Group support for the families of psychiatric patients. *Journal of Psychosocial Nursing, 23*(12), 24-29.

Rose, T., & Ansello, E. F. (1987). *Aging and developmental disabilities: Research and planning.* College Park: University of Maryland, Center on Aging.

Rosenberg, G. S., & Anspach, D. F. (1973). Sibling solidarity in the working class. *Journal of Marriage and the Family, 35,* 108-113.

Rosenthal, C. J. (1986). Family supports in later life: Does ethnicity make a difference? *The Gerontologist, 26*(1), 19-24.

Rosner, S. (1985). On the place of siblings in psychoanalysis. *Psychoanalytic Review, 72,* 457-477.

Rosow, I. (1981). Coalitions in geriatric medicine. In M. Haug (Ed.), *Elderly patients and their doctors.* New York: Springer.

Ross, H. G., & Milgram, J. I. (1982). Important variables in adult sibling relationships: A qualitative study. In M. E. Lamb & B. Sutton-Smith (Eds.), *Sibling relationships: Their nature and significance across the lifespan* (pp. 225-249). Hillsdale, NJ: Lawrence Erlbaum.

Rotunno, M., & McGoldrick, M. (1982). Italian families. In M. McGoldrick, J. K. Pearce, & J. Giordano (Eds.), *Ethnicity and family therapy* (pp. 340-363). New York: Guilford.

Rubin, A., & Shuttlesworth, G. E. (1983). Engaging families as support resources in nursing home care: Ambiguity in the subdivision of tasks. *The Gerontologist, 23,* 632-636.

Safford, I. (1980). A program for families of the mentally impaired elderly. *The Gerontologist, 20,* 3-11.

Salzberger, R. (1979). Casework and the client's right to self-determination. *Social Work, 24,* 398-400.

264 STRENGTHENING AGING FAMILIES

Sanborn, B., & Bould, S. (1991). Intergenerational caregivers of the oldest old. In S. K. Pfeifer & M. B. Sussman (Eds.), *Families: Intergenerational and generational connections* (pp. 125-142). New York: Haworth.

Satir, V. (1967). *Conjoint family therapy*. Palo Alto, CA: Science and Behavior Books.

Schmidt, W. C. (1993). Accountability of lawyers in serving vulnerable, elderly clients. *Journal of Elder Abuse and Neglect, 5,* 39-50.

Schoonover, C. B., Brody, E. M., Hoffman, C., & Kleban, M. H. (1988). Parent care and geographically distant children. *Research on Aging, 10,* 472-492.

Schulz, R., & Williamson, G. M. (1991). A 2-year longitudinal study of depression among Alzheimer's caregivers. *Psychology and Aging, 6,* 569-578.

Schwartz, A. N., & Vogel, M. E. (1990). Nursing home staff and residents' families role expectations. *The Gerontologist, 30,* 49-53.

Scott, J. P. (1983). Siblings and other kin. In T. H. Brubaker (Ed.), *Family relationships in later life* (pp. 47-62). Beverly Hills, CA: Sage.

Scott, J. P. (1990). Sibling interaction in later life. In T. H. Brubaker (Ed.), *Family relationships in later life* (2nd ed., pp. 86-99). Newbury Park, CA: Sage.

Selby, P., & Schecter, M. (1982). *Aging 2000: A challenge for society*. Lancaster, England: MTP Press Limited.

Seltzer, G., Begun, A. L., Seltzer, M. M., & Krauss, M. W. (1991). Adults with mental retardation and their aging mothers: Impacts on siblings. *Family Relations, 40,* 310-317.

Seltzer, M. M. (1992). Training families to be case managers for elders with developmental disabilities. *Generations, 16,* 65-70.

Seltzer, M. M. (1993, June). *Siblings of adults with retardation: Current and future patterns of support.* Paper presented at the 117th annual meeting of the American Association on Mental Retardation, Washington, DC.

Seltzer, M. M., & Krauss, M. W. (1989). Aging parents with mentally retarded children: Family risk factors and sources of support. *American Journal on Mental Retardation, 94,* 303-312.

Seltzer, M. M., & Krauss, M. W. (in press). Aging parents with co-resident adult children: The impact of lifelong caregiving. In M. M. Seltzer, M. W. Krauss, & M. P. Janicki (Eds.), *Life course perspectives in adulthood and old age* (pp. 3-18). Washington, DC: American Association on Mental Retardation.

Seltzer, M. M., Krauss, M. W., Choi, S. C., & Hong, J. (in press). Mid-life and later life parenting of adult children with mental retardation. In C. Ryff & M. Seltzer (Eds.), *The parental experience in midlife*. Chicago: University of Chicago Press.

Seltzer, M. M., Krauss, M. W., & Heller, T. (1991). Family caregiving over the life course. In M. P. Janicki & M. M. Seltzer (Eds.), *Aging and developmental disabilities: Challenges for the 1990s* (pp. 3-24). Washington, DC: Special Interest Group on Aging, American Association on Mental Retardation.

Seltzer, M. M., & Ryff, C. (in press). Parenting across the lifespan: The normative and nonnormative cases. In D. L. Featherman, R. M. Lerner, & M. Perlmutter (Eds.), *Life-span development and behavior,* (Vol. 12). Hillsdale, NJ: Lawrence Erlbaum.

Seltzer, M. M., & Seltzer, G. (1985). The elderly mentally retarded: A group in need of service. *Journal of Gerontological Social Work, 8,* 99-119.

Shanas, E. (1968). *Old people in three industrial societies*. New York: Atherton.

Shanas, E., Townsend, P., Wedderburn, D., Friis, H., Milhoj, D., & Stehouwer, J. (1968). *Older people in three industrial societies*. New York: Atherton.

Shon, S. P., & Ja, D. Y. (1982). Asian families. In M. McGoldrick, J. K. Pearce, & J. Giordano (Eds.), *Ethnicity and family therapy* (pp. 208-228). New York: Guilford.

Shuttlesworth, G., Rubin, A., & Duffy, M. (1982). Families versus institutions: Incongruent role expectations in the nursing home. *The Gerontologist, 22,* 200-208.

Silverstone, B., & Burack-Weiss, A. (1983). *Social work practice with frail elderly and their families: The auxilliary function model.* Springfield, IL: Charles C Thomas.

Sison, G. F. P., & Cotten, P. D. (1989). The elderly mentally retarded person: Current perspectives and future directions. *The Journal of Applied Gerontology, 8,* 151-167.

Slater, M. A., & Wikler, L. (1986). "Normalized" family resources for families with a developmentally disabled child. *Social Work, 31,* 385-389.

Smith, G. C., Fullmer, E. M., & Tobin, S. S. (1994). Living outside the system: An exploration of older families who do not use day programs. In M. M. Seltzer, M. W. Krauss, & M. P. Janicki (Eds.), *Life course perspectives in adulthood and old age* (pp. 17-38). Washington, DC: American Association on Mental Retardation.

Smith, G. C., & Kirchner, N. (1994, June). *Psychoeducational support groups for aging parents: A case study.* Paper presented at the 118th annual meeting, American Association on Mental Retardation, Boston, MA.

Smith, G. C., & McClenny, B. D. (1994, November). *Aging parents of offspring with lifelong disabilities: Still at home vs. living away.* Paper presented at the 47th annual scientific meeting of the Gerontological Society of America, Atlanta, GA.

Smith, G. C., Smith, M. F., & Toseland, R. W. (1991). Problems identified by family caregivers in counseling. *The Gerontologist, 31,* 377-382.

Smith, G. C., & Tobin, S. S. (1989). Permanency planning among older parents of adults with lifelong disabilities. *Journal of Gerontological Social Work, 14,* 35-59.

Smith, G. C., & Tobin, S. S. (1993a). Case managers' perceptions of practice with older parents of adults with developmental disabilities. In K. A. Roberto (Ed.), *The elderly caregiver: Caring for adults with developmental disabilities* (pp. 146-172). Newbury Park, CA: Sage.

Smith, G. C., & Tobin, S. S. (1993b, June). *Older mothers of adults with mental retardation: Antecedents and consequences of subjective burden.* Paper presented at the 117th annual meeting of the American Association on Mental Retardation, Washington, DC.

Smith, G. C., & Tobin, S. S. (1993c). Practice with older parents of developmentally disabled adults. *Clinical Gerontologist, 14,* 59-77.

Smith, G. C., Tobin, S. S., & Fullmer, E. M. (1995). Assisting older families of adults with lifelong disabilities. In G. C. Smith, S. S. Tobin, E. A. Robertson-Tchabo, & P. W. Power (Eds.), *Strengthening aging families: Diversity in practice and policy.* Thousand Oaks, CA: Sage.

Smith, G. C., Tobin, S. S., & Fullmer, E. M. (in press). Elderly mothers caring at home for offspring with mental retardation: A model of permanency planning. *American Journal on Mental Retardation.*

Smith, K. F., & Bengtson, V. L. (1979). Positive consequences of institutionalization: Solidarity between elderly parents and their middle-aged children. *The Gerontologist, 19,* 438-447.

Soldo, B. J., & Agree, E. M. (1988). America's elderly. *Psychological Bulletin, 43,* 1-51.

Spark, G., & Brody, E. M. (1970). The aged are family members. *Family Process, 9,* 195-210.

Spencer, B. (1991). Partners in care: The role of families in dementia care units. In D. H. Coons (Ed.), *Specialized dementia care units* (pp. 189-204). Baltimore: Johns Hopkins University Press.

266 STRENGTHENING AGING FAMILIES

Springer, D., & Brubaker, T. H. (1984). *Family caregivers and dependent elderly: Minimizing stress and maximizing independence.* Beverly Hills, CA: Sage.

Stein, K. F. (1991). *Elder abuse and neglect: A national research agenda.* Washington, DC: National Aging Resource Centre on Elder Abuse.

Stein, T. S. (1988). Theoretical considerations in psychotherapy with gay men and lesbians. In M. W. Ross, (Ed.). *The treatment of homosexuals with mental health disorders* (pp. 75-95). New York: Harrington Park Press.

Stephens, M. A. P. (1993). Understanding barriers to caregivers's use of formal services: The caregiver's perspective. In S. H. Zarit, L. I. Pearlin, & K. W. Schaie (Eds.), *Caregiving systems: Informal and formal helpers* (pp. 261-272). Hillsdale, NJ: Lawrence Erlbaum.

Stephens, M. A. P., Bridges, A. M., Ogrocki, P. K., Kinney, J. M., & Norris, V. K. (1988, November). *Daily stressors for family caregivers to institutionalized Alzheimer's disease patients.* Paper presented at the annual meeting of the Gerontological Society of America, San Francisco.

Stephens, M. A. P., Kinney, J. M., & Ogracki, P. K. (1981). Stressors and well-being among caregivers: The in home-versus nursing home experience. *The Gerontologist, 31,* 217-223.

Sternberg, R. (1986). A triangular theory of love. *Psychological Review, 93,* 119-135.

Steur, J. L., & Clark, E. O. (1982). Family support groups within a research project on dementia. *Clinical Gerontologist, 1*(1), 87-95.

Stone, R., Cafferata, G. S., & Sangl, J. (1987). Caregivers of the frail elderly: A national profile. *The Gerontologist, 27,* 616-626.

Stone, R. I., & Kemper, P. (1989). Spouses and children of disabled elders: How large a constituency for long-term care reform. *The Milbank Quarterly, 64,* 485-506.

Strawbridge, W. J., & Wallhagan, M. I. (1991). Impact of family conflict on adult child caregivers. *The Gerontologist, 31,* 770-777.

Strommen, E. F. (1989). You're a what?: Family member reactions to the disclosure of homosexuality. In F. W. Bozett (Ed.), *Homosexuality and the family* (pp. 37-58). New York: Harrington Park Press.

Sutton, E., Heller, T., Sterns, H. L., Factor, A., & Miklos, S. (1994). *Person-centered planning for later life: A curriculum for adults with mental retardation.* Akron, OH: RRTC on Aging with Mental Retardation, University of Illinois at Chicago, University of Akron.

Sutton, E., Sterns, H. L., Schwartz, L., & Roberts, R. (1992). The training of a specialist in developmental disabilities and aging. *Generations, 16,* 71-74.

Swensen, C. H. (1994). Older individuals in the family. In L. L'Abate (Ed.), *Handbook of developmental family psychology and psychopathology* (pp. 202-217). New York: John Wiley.

Swensen, C. H., Eskew, R. W., & Kohlhepp, K. A. (1981). Stage of family life cycle, ego development, and the marriage relationship. *Journal of Marriage and the Family, 43,* 841-853.

Swensen, C. H., & Trauhaug, G. (1985). Commitment and the long-term marriage relationship. *Journal of Marriage and the Family, 47,* 939-945.

Tan, A. (1989). *The joy luck club.* New York: Ivy.

Tanenbaum, S. J. (1993). Kinship and family policy in an aging society. In G. L. Maddox & M. P. Lawton (Eds.), *Annual review of gerontology and geriatrics: Focus on kinship, aging, and social change* (Vol. 13, pp. 239-258). New York: Springer.

Tellis-Nayak, V., & Tellis-Nayak, M. (1989). Quality of care and the burden of two cultures: When the world of the nurse's aide enters the world of the nursing home. *The Gerontologist, 29,* 307-313.

Tesch, S. A., & Whitbourne, S. K. (1982). Intimacy and identity status in young adults. *Journal of Personality and Social Psychology, 43,* 1041-1051.

Thompson, E., Futterman, A., Gallagher-Thompson, D., Rose, J., & Lovett, S. (1993). Social support and caregiving burden in family caregivers of frail elders. *Journal of Gerontology, 48,* S245-S254.

Thornton, J. F., Plummer, E., & Seeman, M. B. (1981). Schizophrenia: Group support for relatives. *Canadian Journal of Psychiatry, 26,* 341-344.

Tiedeman, D. V. (1961). Decision and vocational development: A paradigm and its implication. *Personnel and Guidance Journal, 40,* 15-21.

Tobin, S. S. (1991). *Personhood in advanced old age: Implications for practice.* New York: Springer.

Tobin, S. S., Fullmer, E. M., & Smith, G. C. (in press). Fear of death and religiosity in nonnormative aging. In E. Thomas & S. Eisenhandler (Eds.), *Handbook of religion, spirituality, and aging.* Westport, CN: Auburn House.

Tobin, S. S., & Gustafson, J. (1987). What do we do differently with aging clients. *Journal of Gerontological Social Work, 6,* 29-46.

Tobin, S. S., & Lieberman, M. A. (1976). *Last home for the aged: Critical implications of institutionalization.* San Francisco: Jossey-Bass.

Todd, S., Shearn, J., Beyer, S., & Felce, D. (1993). Careers in caring: The changing situations of parents caring for an offspring with learning difficulties. *Irish Journal of Psychology, 14,* 130-153.

Tonti, M. (1988). Relationships among adult siblings who care for their aged paretns. In M. D. Kahn & K. G. Lewis (Eds.), *Siblings in therapy: Lifespan and clinical issues* (pp. 417-434). New York: Columbia University Press.

Toseland, R. W., & Rossiter, C. (1989). Group interventions to support family caregivers: A review and analysis. *The Gerontologist, 29,* 438-448.

Toseland, R. W., & Smith, G. C. (1990). Effectiveness of individual counseling by professional and peer helpers for family caregivers of the elderly. *Psychology & Aging, 5,* 256-263.

Toseland, R. W., & Smith, G. C. (1991). Family caregivers of the frail elderly. In A. Gitterman (Ed.), *Handbook of social work practice with vulnerable populations* (pp. 549-583). New York: Columbia University Press.

Townsend, A. L. (1993). Methodological issues confronting research and service use among caregiving families. In S. H. Zarit, L. I. Pearlin, & K. W. Schaie (Eds.), *Caregiving systems: Informal and formal helpers* (pp. 293-301). Hillsdale, NJ: Lawrence Erlbaum.

Townsend, A. L., & Noelker, L. S. (1987). The impact of family relationships on perceived caregiving effectiveness. In T. H. Brubaker (Ed.), *Aging, health, and family* (pp. 80-99). Newbury Park, CA: Sage.

Troll, L. E. (Ed.). (1986). *Family issues in current gerontology.* New York: Springer.

Troll, L. E., Miller, S., & Atchley, R. (1978). *Families of later life.* Belmont, CA: Wadsworth.

Turner, B. F., Tobin, S. S., & Lieberman, M. A. (1972). Personality traits as predictors of institutional adaptation among the aged. *Journal of Gerontology, 27,* 61-68.

Turner, P. H., Scadden, L., & Harris, M. B. (1985, March). *Parenting in gay and lesbian families.* Paper presented at the First Annual Future of Parenting Symposium, Chicago.

Tymchuk, A. J. (1983). Interventions with parents of the mentally retarded. In J. L. Matson & J. A. Mulick (Eds.), *Handbook of mental retardation* (pp. 369-380). New York: Pergamon.

U.S. Bureau of the Census. (1988). *Who's helping out?: Support networks among American families* (Current Populations Reports Series P-70, No. 13). Washington, DC: U.S. Government Printing Office.

U.S. Bureau of the Census. (1990). *Statistical abstracts of the United States* (110th ed.). Washington, DC: U.S. Government Printing Office.

U.S. Congress, House Select Committee on Aging. (1980). *Elder abuse: The hidden problem.* Washington, DC: U.S. Government Printing Office.

U.S. House of Representatives. (1992, April 9). *Congressional record,* H 2606.

U.S. Senate Special Committee on Aging, the American Association of Retired Persons, the Federal Council on the Aging, and the U.S. Administration on Aging. (1991). *Aging America: Trends and projections.* Washington, DC: U.S. Department of Health and Human Services.

Walls, C. T., & Zarit, S. H. (1991). Informal support from black churches and the well-being of elderly blacks. *The Gerontologist, 31*(4), 490-495.

Walz, T., Harper, D., & Wilson, J. (1986). The aging developmentally disabled person. *The Gerontologist, 26,* 622-629.

Ware, L. A., & Carper, M. (1982). Living with Alzheimer disease patients: Family stresses and coping mechanisms. *Psychotherapy: Theory, Research, and Practice, 19*(4), 472-481.

Watzlawick, P., & Weakland, J. H. (Eds.). (1977). *The interactional view.* New York: Norton.

Weishaus, S., & Field, D. (1988). A half century of marriage: Continuity or change? *Journal of Marriage and the Family, 50,* 763-774.

Whitbourne, S. K. (1986). *Adult development.* New York: Praeger.

Whitbourne, S. K. (1987). Personality development in adulthood and old age: Relationships among identity style, health, and well-being. In K. W. Schaie (Ed.), *Annual review of gerontology and geriatrics* (pp. 189-216). New York: Springer.

Whitbourne, S. K., & Ebmeyer, J. B. (1990). *Identity and intimacy in adulthood: A study of couples.* New York: Springer Verlag.

Whitbourne, S. K., & Tesch, S. A. (1985). A comparison of identity and intimacy statuses in college students and alumni. *Developmental Psychology, 21,* 1039-1044.

White, L. K., & Riedmann, A. (1992). When the Brady bunch grows up: Step/half- and full sibling relations in adulthood. *Journal of Marriage and Family, 54,* 197-208.

Wilkin, D. (1979). *Caring for the mentally handicapped child.* London: Croom Helm.

Winbush, G. B. (1993). Family caregiving programs: A new look at the premises on which they are based. In L. Burton (Ed.), *Families and aging* (pp. 129-133). Amityville, NY: Baywood.

Wood, J. B., & Skiles, L. L. (1992). Planning for the transfer of care. *Generations, 16,* 61-62.

Worden, J. W. (1982). *Grief counseling and grief therapy.* New York: Springer.

Wright, L. K. (1991). The impact of Alzheimer's disease on the marital relationship. *The Gerontologist, 31,* 224-237.

Yalom, I. D. (1989). *Love's executioner & other tales of psychotherapy.* New York: Basic Books.

York, J. L., & Calsyn, R. J. (1977). Family involvement in nursing homes. *The Gerontologist, 17,* 500-505.

Zarit, S. H., & Pearlin, L. I. (1993). Family caregiving: Integrating informal and formal systems for care. In S. H. Zarit, L. I. Pearlin, & K. W. Schaie (Eds.) *Caregiving systems: Informal and formal helpers* (pp. 290-316). Hillsdale, NJ: Lawrence Erlbaum.

Zarit, S. H., Reever, K. E., & Bach-Peterson, J. (1980). Relatives of the impaired elderly: Correlates of feelings of burden. *The Gerontologist, 20,* 649-655.

Zarit, S. H., & Teri, L. (1991). Intervention and services for family caregivers. In K. W. Schaie (Ed.), *Annual review of gerontology and geriatrics* (Vol. 2, pp. 287-310). New York: Springer.

Zarit, S. H., & Whitlach, C. J. (1992). Institutional placement: Phases of the transition. *The Gerontologist, 32,* 665-672.

Zborowski, M. (1969). *People in pain.* San Francisco: Jossey-Bass.

Zimny, G. H., & Diamond, J. A. (1993). Judicial evaluation of recommendations for improving monitoring of guardians. *Journal of Elder Abuse and Neglect, 5,* 51-68.

Zola, I. K. (1966). Culture and symptoms: An analysis of patients presenting complaints. *American Sociological Review, 5,* 141-155.

Author Index

Abramson, M., 73
Ackerman, N., 130
Adamek, M. E., 49
Adams, B. N., 48
Adams, J. P., 87, 88, 96
Adebimpe, V. R., 192
Adelman, M., 100, 113
Adelman, R., 147
Adelman, R. D., 66, 76, 149, 150
Agree, E. M., 164
Aleman, J., 184, 189
Allen, J. A., ix, 234
American Association of Retired Persons
    (AARP), 4, 235, 240-243
Anderson, B., 47
Anderson, W. T., ix, 123, 124, 130, 172
Ansello, E. F., 91
Anspach, D. F., 48
Applegate, J. S., 5, 242
Arcus, M., 225, 226, 227
Aronson, M., 127
Ashworth, C., 147
Atchley, R., 48
Atchley, R. C., 4
Atwater, L., 245
Avioli, P. S., 51
Avison, 85

Babchuk, N., 50
Bachman, R., 38
Bach-Peterson, J., 8

Bahr, S. J., 123, 124
Baird, M. A., 126, 128, 131, 134
Baker, F. M., 184, 190
Baker, L., 130
Bank, S., 57
Bank, S. P., 53, 57
Barbero, S. L., 93
Barlow, S. H., 225
Barusch, A. S., 70
Bass, D. M., 15, 18
Bass, J., 127
Becker, C. S., 107
Becker, J., 27
Becker, M., 116
Beckman, K., 125, 127, 224
Bedford, V. H., 48, 49, 53, 55
Begun, A. L., 85, 86, 90
Bell, A. P., 101, 106
Bengtson, V., x
Bengtson, V. L., 3, 5-7, 11, 15-16, 19, 27,
    223-224, 236
Berger, R., 101, 106, 110-111, 113
Berland, D. I., 209
Berscheid, E., 160
Beyer, S., 85, 88
Birren, J. E., 164, 226
Blum, M. J., 3, 5-7, 11, 15-16, 19, 236
Boaz, D., 245
Bond, L. A., xi, 230, 231, 232
Bonjean, M. J., ix
Boszormenyi-Nagy, I., 136
Bould, S., 3, 5

Bowers, B. J., 27
Boyd-Franklin, N., 177, 180, 181, 184,
    189, 192, 196-197
Bozett, F. W., 110, 111
Brashler, R., 145, 148
Brauburger, M. B., 70
Breckman, R. S., 66, 76
Bridges, A. M., 28
Brody, E. M., 3, 4, 5, 7, 8, 9, 12, 27, 236,
    238, 242
Brubaker, E., ix, 85, 235, 238, 239, 240,
    245
Brubaker, T. H., x, 15, 77, 83, 85, 164,
    165, 171-172, 224-226, 231, 233-
    236, 242-246
Bumagin, V. E., ix
Burack-Weiss, A., 219
Burnside, I. M., 35
Burton, L., ix, x
Bush, J. P., 130
Butler, R. N., 57, 219

Cabaj, R. P., 115
Caddell, P., 245
Cafferata, G. S., 4, 5
Cairl, R. C., 74
Calsyn, R. J., 25
Campbell, V. A., 87, 88, 96
Carper, M., 125, 128
Carroll, R., 54
Carstensen, L. L., 164
Carver, M. D., 11, 12
Caserta, M. S., 96
Casto, G., 139
Catalano, D. J., 50
Chappell, N. L., 230
Charon, R., 147, 149, 150
Chenoweth, B., 25
Chodorow, N., 102
Choi, S. C., 85
Christensen, A., 160
Christopherson, V. A., ix
Church, M., 57
Cicirelli, V. G., 7, 46-48, 50-51, 55-57,
    144, 147-148
Clark, E. O., 128
Clark, M., 47

Cleland, M., 27
Clunis, D. M., 100, 105, 108
Cobbs, P., 178, 192
Coe, R. M., 149
Cohen, D., 243
Cohler, B., 128
Coleman, E., 104
Colerick, E. J., 27
Connelly, J. R., 96
Connidis, I. A., 49, 53, 55
Cooper, K., 128
Coppel, D. B., 27
Cotten, P. D., 91
Couper, D. P., 11, 15-17, 19, 225-226, 232
Coward, R. T., 51
Cox, E. O., 6
Crutcher, D. M., 133
Crystal, S., 5
Cumming, E., 50

Datwyler, M. M., 6
David, D., 145
Davies, L., 49
Day, R. W., 135
Decker, B., 102, 105, 114, 116
Deimling, G. R., 163
Dejowski, E. F., 73
Delaney, P. J., 49
Dell Orto, A. E., 133, 135, 136, 148
Dempsey, N. P., 27
Deutchmann, D. E., 226
Devall, W., 106
de Vries, B., 226
DeWeaver, K., 91, 94
Diamond, J. A., 73
Dobrof, R., 38, 90, 91
Doherty, W. J., 126, 128, 131, 134
Doty, P., 3
Dowling, E. M., 11, 12
Duffy, M., 27, 35, 123, 131, 133, 138
Duncan, D., 68, 69
Dunn, J., 51, 53, 56
Dwyer, J. W., 51
Dysken, M., 128

Eastland, L. J., 102, 106

Ebmeyer, J. B., 159, 161, 169
Edelson, J. S., 36
Edwards, J. N., 70
Eisdorfer, C., 243
Eisenberg, H. B., 76
Engelhardt, J., 83
Englehardt, J. L., 85
Erikson, E. H., 159, 160
Eskew, R. W., 167

Factor, A., 82, 85, 87-92, 95-97
Falicov, C. J., 181, 183, 191
Fandetti, C. V., 183
Federal Council on the Aging, 235, 240-243
Feil, N., 36
Felce, D., 85, 88
Ferris, S. H., 6
Field, D., 165
Finestone, K., 127
Finkelhor, D., 66
Fisher, B. L., 225
Fletcher, W. L., 11, 12
Flynn, M. L., 139
Fogel, B. S., 244
Foner, N., 38
Ford Foundation, 241
Friis, H., 47, 48
Fullmer, E. M., 84-85, 87, 89-91, 93-94, 102, 106
Fulmer, T. T., 69
Furino, A., 244
Futterman, A., 11

Gallagher, D. E., 125, 127-128
Gallagher-Thompson, D., 11
Garbarino, J., 64, 70, 71
Garcia, J. L., 75-77
Garcia-Preto, N., 192
Gartner, A., 127
Gatz, M., 3, 5, 6, 7, 11, 15, 16, 19, 236
Gelfand, D. E., 177, 183
George, L. K., 8, 27
Gevalnik, J. M., 4
Gibbons, M. B., 136
Giordano, J., 177
Giordano, J. A., 125, 127, 224

Glazer, J., vii
Glicken, M., 91, 94
Glicksman, A., 5
Goetting, A., 50, 51
Gold, D. T., 48-52, 55, 57, 226
Goodman, D. M., 91
Goodman, S. J., 82
Gorman, M. A., 239
Gottlieb, G. L., 244
Grant, G., 85, 87, 94
Greeley, A. M., 176
Green, G. D., 100, 105, 108
Greenberg, J. R., 70
Greenberg, J. S., 82, 86, 94
Greene, M. G., 147, 149, 150
Greene, R., 16, 124, 131-132, 134, 137-138
Greenley, J. R., 82, 86, 94
Grier, W., 178, 192
Gustafson, J., 220
Gwyther, L. P., 27, 226

Hansen, S. S., 37
Hansson, R. O., 11, 12
Harel, Z., 163
Hargrave, T. D., ix, 123, 124, 130, 172
Harper, D., 81
Harris, E. G., 57
Harris, M. B., 101, 110
Harry, J., 106
Harshbarger, S., 67
Hartke, R. J., 145, 148
Hartman, A., xi
Harvey, J. H., 160
Haug, M., 149
Haut, M. W., 13
Hawkins, R. O., 104
Hazler, R. J., 152
Heifetz, M. D., 146
Heiselman, T., 38
Heller, T., 82, 84-92, 95-96, 97
Henderson, M., 147
Hennon, C. B., 225-227, 238
Henry, W., 50
Hernandez, G. G., 199
Herr, J. J., ix, 57, 124, 128
Hess, B. B., 6
Hiestand, M., 239

Hines, P. M., 180, 181, 184, 188, 192, 196, 197
Hirn, K. F., ix
Hoffman, C., 3-5, 7-9, 12
Hoffman, S., 147, 149
Holmes, T. H., 69
Hong, J., 85
Hoopes, M. H., 225
Hooyman, N. R., 7, 9, 10, 12, 147
Horne, M., 82
Hoyt, D. R., 50
Hudson, B., 39
Hughston, G. A., ix
Humphreys, R. A. L., 101
Hunt, B., 109
Hunt, M., 109
Huston, T. L., 160

Ihinger-Tallman, M., 50
Iris, M. A., 73

Ja, D. Y., 180
Jackson-Brewer, K., 116
Jacobson, J. W., 93
Janicki, M. P., 82, 83, 88, 93
Jecker, N. S., 151
Jennings, J., 80, 81, 82, 96
Johnson, C. L., 48, 50
Johnson, H. C., 129, 130
Johnson, J. L., 133, 135
Johnson, M. M. S., 36
Justice, B., 68, 69

Kahn, M. D., 53, 57
Kahn, R., 6
Kane, R. A., 3, 17, 18, 145, 244
Kaplan, L., 238
Kapp, M., 145, 147, 151
Karrer, B. M., 181, 183, 191
Kaufman, A. V., 87, 88, 91, 94, 96
Kaye, L. W., 5, 242
Kazak, A. E., 101
Keefover, R. W., 13
Kehoe, M., 100-101, 104, 106, 110-111
Keith, P. M., 151

Kelley, H. H., 160
Kemp, J. T., 135
Kemper, P., 4
Kendrick, C., 53
Kiely, M., 81
Kimmel, D. C., 101, 109
Kinney, J. M., 27, 28
Kirchner, N., 95
Kirschner, C., 9, 11
Kivett, V. R., 50
Kiyak, H. A., 147
Kleban, M. H., 3-5, 7-9, 12, 28
Kohlhepp, K. A., 167
Kolpakchi, A. L., 145
Kosberg, J. I., 66-68, 74-77
Kosloski, K., 6
Krauss, M. W., 82, 84-87, 90-92, 96
Krumboltz, J. D., 149
Kurdeck, L. A., 105
Kurland, P., 25
Kushner, T., 176
Kutzik, A. J., 177
Kuypers, J. A., 223, 224

L'Abate, L., x, 127, 221-222, 224, 227-228, 230, 233-234
Laird, J., xi
Lang, K. M., 5
Langer, E., 31
Langer, E. J., 31
Lawton, M. P., ix, 5
Lazarus, L. W., 128
Lee, G., 165
Lee, G. R., 50
Lee, J. A., 106
Lefly, H. P., 80, 82
Lesser, I. M., 159
Levin, I., x
Levinger, G., 160
Lewinstein, E., 83
Lieberman, M. A., 29, 30
Lipman, A., 108
Lippman, L., 81, 83
Litwak, E., 11
Loberg, D. E., 81, 83
Lopata, H., 50
Loulan, J., 116

Lovett, S., 11
Lubin, R. A., 81
Lund, D. A., 96
Lustbader, W., 7, 9, 10, 12
Lutzer, V., 83
Lutzer, V. D., 85
Lyon, P., 105, 106
Lyons, W., 36
Lystad, M., 69

Mace, D. R., 222, 228, 233
Maddox, G. L., ix
Maguire, L., 113
Marcia, J. E., 159
Margolies, L., 116
Martico-Greenfield, E., 35
Martin, D., 105, 106
Marvin, R. S., 101
Masciocchi, C., 11, 15
Matthews, S. H., 7, 49
Mattison, A. M., 115
McAdoo, H. P., 177
McCandlish, B. M., 102, 106
McClenny, B. D., 82
McClintock, G., 160
McCubbin, H. I., 89
McCullough, C. B., 145
McGhee, J. L., 50
McGill, D., 182
McGoldrick, M., 176-177, 179-185, 187,
    189-193, 200
McKibben, M., 70
McWhirter, D. P., 115
Michaud, T. G., 183, 192
Miklos, S., 97
Milgram, J. I., 48, 57
Milhoj, D., 47, 48
Miller, B., 133, 135
Miller, S., 48
Miller, S. J., 4
Mindel, C. H., 177, 183, 184
Minuchin, S., 130
Moeller, T., 11, 15
Molinari, V., 57
Montano, D., 147
Montgomery, R. J. V., 6, 33

Moody, H. R., 73, 148
Moore, D. W., 38
Moore, S. T., 11
Morycz, R. K., 25
Moses, A. E., 104
Moss, M., 5
Moss, M. S., 25

Nadler, A., 83
Neesmith, D. H., 11, 12
Neidhardt, E. R., ix, 234
Nelson, R. E., 11, 12
Noelker, L. S., 4, 6, 7, 12, 15, 18, 38
Noh, 85
Norris, V. K., 28
Nuland, S. B., 148

O'Brien, C. R., 133, 135
Office of Special Education and
    Rehabilitative Services, 128, 130
Office of the Inspector General, 38
Ogracki, P. K., 27, 28
Ogrocki, P. K., 28
Okun, B. F., 133
Orlofsky, J. L., 159
Ory, M., 149
Osgood, N. J., 57
Otis, J. P., 93

Pagel, M. D., 27
Palazzoli, M. S., 57
Parsons, R. J., 6
Patterson, J. M., 89
Patterson, M. A., 37
Pearce, J. K., 177, 182
Pearlin, L. I., 18
Pelaez, M., 145
Penrod, J. D., 17, 18
Peplau, L., 102
Peplau, L. A., 160
Pepper, C., 73
Petersen, S., 135
Peterson, D. R., 160
Peterson, E. T., 123, 124

Pietrukowicz, M. E., 36
Pillemer, K., 38, 39, 66, 70
Pillemer, K. A., 238, 243
Plummer, E., 127
Podnieks, E., 66
Poggi, R. C., 209
Poor, M., 106
Poulton, J. L., 96
Power, P. W., 133, 135-138, 148
Pratt, C. C., 27
Prendergast, C. G., 149
Pruchno, R., 28
Pruchno, R. A., 27
Puccio, P. S., 93

Rose, L., 127
Rose, T., 91
Rosenberg, G. S., 48
Rosenthal, C., x
Rosenthal, C. J., 177, 178
Rosman, B., 130
Rosner, S., 57
Rosow, I., 149
Ross, H. G., 48, 57
Rossiter, C., 16
Rotunno, M., 180, 183, 192
Rovine, M., 5
Rubin, A., 27, 35
Ryff, C., 85

Qualls, S. H., 17, 24, 130, 135
Quinn, M. J., 68, 74, 75, 76

Rahav, G., 83
Rahe, R., 69
Ramey, C. T., 139
Rankin, E. D., 3, 13
Rape, R. N., 130
Rathbone-McCuan, E., 125-126, 128, 139
Raymond, J. A., 70
Reedy, M., 164
Reever, K. E., 8
Regan, J. J., 72
Reichlin, R. E., 57
Reinardy, J., 3
Reisberg, B., 6
Rettig, J. H., 93
Rhyne, D., 164
Riedmann, A., 48, 50, 52
Riess, D., 177, 184
Riessman, F., 127
Ritchie, M. H., 135
Roberto, K. A., 15, 87, 164-165, 172, 224-226, 231, 233, 244
Roberts, G., 152
Roberts, R., 92
Roberts, R. N., 139
Robischon, P., x
Rodin, J., 31, 153
Rose, J., 11

Safford, I., 35
Salzberger, R., 239
Sanborn, B., 3, 5
Sangl, J., 4, 5
Saperstein, A. R., 5
Satir, V., 129
Scadden, L., 101, 110
Schaie, K. W., 164
Schecter, M., 240, 241
Schmall, V. L., 27
Schmidt, W. C., 73
Schmitt, J. P., 105
Schoonover, C. B., 3-5, 7-9, 12
Schulz, R., 168
Schwartz, A. N., 35
Schwartz, L., 92
Scott, J. P., 48, 49, 50, 52
Seeman, M. B., 127
Selby, P., 240, 241
Seltzer, G., 83, 85-86, 88, 90, 96
Seltzer, M. M., 82-92, 94, 96
Shanas, E., 4, 47, 48
Shearn, J., 85, 88
Sheehan, N. W., 11, 15-17, 19, 225-226, 232
Shon, S. P., 180
Shulman, E., 6
Shuttlesworth, G., 27, 35
Shuttlesworth, G. E., 27
Silverstone, B., 219
Simonsick, E. M., 4
Sison, G. F. P., 91

Skelly, J. R., 145
Skiles, L. L., 85, 87, 88, 90
Slater, M. A., 91, 92
Slavin, L. A., 130
Smith, G. C., 5, 10, 12, 80, 82-95
Smith, J., x
Smith, K. F., 27
Smith, M. F., 10, 12
Soldo, B. J., 6, 164
Sparacio, R. T., 135
Spark, G., 27
Spark, G. M., 136
Speechly, P., 85
Spencer, B., 25, 36
Springer, D., 77
Stafford, B., 128
Stehouwer, J., 47, 48
Stein, K. F., 64, 66
Stein, T. S., 114
Steinberg, G., 6
Stephens, M. A. P., 27, 28, 229
Sternberg, R., 162
Sterns, H. L., 92, 97
Steur, J. L., 128
Stone, R., 4, 5
Stone, R. I., 4
Strawbridge, W. J., 6, 10
Strommen, E. F., 109
Suhr, P., 11, 12
Sutton, E., 92, 97
Swensen, C. H., xii, 167

Tan, A., 186
Tanenbaum, S. J., xiii
Teasdale, T. A., 145
Tellis-Nayak, M., 38
Tellis-Nayak, V., 38
Teri, L., 15, 16
Tesch, S. A., 159
Thomas, A., 11, 15
Thompson, E., 11
Thornton, J. F., 127
Tiedeman, D. V., 152
Tobin, S. S., 29-30, 36, 80, 82-95, 212-213, 220
Todd, S., 85, 88

Tomita, S. K., 68, 74-76
Tonti, M., 4, 7, 8
Toseland, R. W., 5, 10, 12, 16
Townsend, A. L., 4, 6-7, 12, 16, 19
Townsend, P., 47, 48
Trauhaug, G., 167
Troll, L. E., ix, 48
Trost, J., x
Turner, 85
Turner, B. F., 30
Turner, P. H., 101, 110
Tymchuk, A. J., 83

U.S. Administration on Aging, 66, 235, 240-243
U.S. Bureau of the Census, 183, 235, 236
U.S. Congress, House Select Committee on Aging, 66
U.S. House of Representatives, 92
U.S. Senate Special Committee on Aging, 235, 240-243

Vogel, M. E., 35

Wacker, R. R., 151
Wagner, B. M., xi, 230, 231, 232
Wallhagan, M. I., 6, 10
Walls, C. T., 184, 192, 198
Walz, T., 81
Ware, L. A., 125, 128
Wasik, B. H., 139
Watzlawick, P., 128
Weakland, J. H., ix, 57, 124, 128
Wedderburn, D., 47, 48
Weinberg, M. S., 101, 106
Weinstin, S. E., 227, 233
Weishaus, S., 165
Whitbourne, S. K., 159-161, 163, 169
White, L. K., 48, 50, 52
Whitlach, C. J., 27
Wikler, L., 91, 92
Wilkin, D., 101
Williamson, G. M., 168
Williamson, P., 147

Wilson, J., 81
Wilson, N. C., 145
Wilson, R. W., 37
Winbush, G. B., 18, 19
Wisniewski, H. M., 82
Wolf, R. S., 238, 243
Wood, J. B., 85, 87, 88, 90
Worden, J. W., 115
Wright, L. K., 164
Wright, S., 27

Yalom, I. D., 169
York, J. L., 25

Zarit, S. H., 8, 15-16, 18, 27, 184, 192, 198
Zborowski, M., 190
Zimny, G. H., 73
Zola, I. K., 190

Subject Index

Acute care, 145
Adults with lifelong disabilities, older
    families of, 61, 210-211, 213, 218
age-associated decrements among, 82
assisting, 80-98
case management services for, 94-95
chronic sorrow among, 82
cohort influences on, 83-84
day services for, 93-94
demographic trends and, 84
educational programs for, 93, 95-96
family counseling for, 93, 96-97
family interventions for, 93-97
family support services for, 93-95, 228
future planning as family task for, 88-91
impact on offspring with lifelong dis-
    ability, 87-88
impact on older mothers, 84-86
impact on siblings, 86-87
permanency planning by, 88-91, 92, 95,
    98
permanency planning workshops for,
    95-96
perpetual parenthood of, 82, 85
policy concerning, 92-93, 244
potential stressors facing, 82
psychoeducational support groups for, 95
salience of family-based care and, 82
unavailability of formal resources for, 82
African American families:
and myth of Black superwoman, 188-189
attitudes about help seeking in, 192

attitudes toward death in, 190-191
clinical treatment of, 194-197
conceptualization of illness in, 190
construct of family in, 180, 181
family roles and responsibilities in, 184
fictive kin in, 177, 180
healthy cultural paranoia and, 178, 196
Aging:
as interpersonal process, 124
as intrapersonal process, 124
problems/challenges associated with,
    124
Aging couples:
challenges pertaining to, 163-165
exit and reentry of children of, 164
physical changes in, 163-164
retirement in lives of, 164-165
sexuality in, 164
Aging families:
assisting with normative concerns, 1-60
clients of, 213-214
critical policy issues concerned with,
    203, 235-247
defining, x-xi
diversity among, x
facilitating health care decisions
    within, 121-122, 143-157
issues confronting, xi-xii
long-term care needs of, 240-241
making prevention work for, 230-233
practice and policy concerning, xii-xiii,
    12-19, 32-41, 54-58, 74-77, 91-97,

111-117, 132-139, 152-154, 169-172,
192-194, 235-247
problems and needs experienced by,
124-125
synthesis of interventions for, 203-247
understanding intergenerational issues
in, 121, 123-142
Aging families, utilizing culture in work
with, 122, 175-201, 211, 212, 218
clinical considerations in, 193
clinical treatment, 193-194
nonclinical services and, 197-198
professional as cultural broker in, 193-
194, 197, 198
research and policy and, 199
Alzheimer's disease, 152, 163, 239, 243
institutionalization of family members
with, 25-26, 28, 32, 34, 42
prevalence of, 209

Caregiver burden, 27
Caregiving families:
conflicts in, 11
high resistance to change in, 11
impact on from strain on primary
caregiver, 11
limited resources in, 11
poor communication skills in, 11
poor parent-child relationships in, 11
Case management activities, 14
Case management services, 13, 14, 15,
228, 239, 247
for older families of adults with lifelong disabilities, 94-95
limitations of, 94-95
Chinese American families:
construct of family in, 180
healthy cultural paranoia and, 178
intergenerational strain in, 186
Competencies, preventive approaches to
building, 203, 221-234
educational programming, 224
education to assist aging families, 224-
228
primary, 222
secondary, 222

social-environmental engineering, 224,
228-229
tertiary, 222
Competency:
as ability to cope, 223
as experienced mastery, 224
defining in aging families, 223-224
in social role performance, 223
Conservatorship, 151, 226
Cultural relativism and understanding
variations in definitions of family, 182
Culture:
and clinical treatment of aging families,
193-194
utilizing in work with aging families,
122, 175-201
See also Ethnicity
Cultures of violence, 69

Death:
acceptance of by elderly, 213
attitudes toward in African American
families, 190-191
attitudes toward in Irish American families, 190-191
attitudes toward in Mexican American
families, 191
counseling for elderly, 213
practitioner fear of, 209
Decision-making styles, family, 144
Developmental disabilities:
definitions of, 81
diagnostic categories of, 81
Direct practice with aging families, 214-
218
advice giving, 205, 206, 214, 218
assessment in, 210, 214-215, 218
counseling, 205, 206, 214, 218
diversity of, 203, 205-220
intervention, choice of, 215-218
limitations of, 218
modifying, 210
process and outcome in, 210
psychotherapy, 205, 206, 214, 218
scope of, 209-210
short-term counseling, 216-217

stages in family life cycle and, 210-213
variety of clients and, 210
versus practice with other families, 218-220
See also Intervention programs for caregiving families
Double ABC-X model of family adaptation, 19
residency planning for adults with lifelong disabilities and, 89, 90
Drexel Home for the Aged (Chicago), 28, 33-35, 39, 41

Education programs for aging families, 93, 95-96, 232, 233, 246
family life education, 12, 15, 32, 75, 77, 127, 152-153, 197, 224, 225-226, 232
guided family reminiscence, 224, 226-227
psychoeducational support groups, 224-225
structured family enrichment, 224, 227-228
types of, 224-228
Elder abuse, family member, 61, 211, 215-216
active neglect, 65
and empowerment of older individuals, 61
as growing problem, 77-78
caregiver incompetence and, 70
causes of, 68-70, 221
confronting, 63-79
definitions of, 64-66
dependency and, 69-70
detection of, 75
family responsibility and, 71
family therapy and, 71
human ecological view of, 70
intergenerational conflict and, 69
intervention in cases of, 75-77
invisibility of, 66-68
legal/clinical issues and, 70-74
life crisis model and, 68-69
material/financial misappropriation, 65
passive neglect, 64-65
pathological caregivers and, 68

physical abuse, 65
prevention of, 74-75, 243
professional help for, 71-73
psychological abuse, 65
reasons for, 64
self-abuse, 65-66
socialization of aggression and, 69
violation of rights, 65
Elder abuser, family, 63
pathological caregivers, 68
Elder care, 1
as normative family stress, 3
supporting family in, 3-24
Ethnicity:
and attitudes about help seeking, 191-192
and conceptualization of illness, 179, 189-191
and construct of family, 179-182
and familial identity, 175
and family roles and responsibilities, 179, 182-186
and intergenerational strain, 179, 186-189
as determinant of social equality or minority status, 178
as expression of culture, 178
as indicator of traditional ways of thinking and behaving, 178

Families, aging. *See* Aging families
Families with special concerns, helping, 61-119
Family:
definitions of, x-xi
goal of, 129
transactional patterns in, 130
Family advocacy, 228, 229, 231
Family assessment, 12-13
Family caregivers:
daughters, 4, 6-7, 50, 242
daughters-in-law, 4, 6-7
demographic trends and, 4-5
grandchildren, 4, 9-10
number of, 4
policy addressing needs of, 241-245
siblings, 4, 7-8, 50-51
sons, 4, 50

spouses, 4, 6, 50, 242
Family caregiving:
 adverse consequences of, 74
 as positive experience, 5, 19
 as stressful experience, 5, 19
 impact of on family functioning, 6
 impact of on family system, 10-12
 impact of on individual family members, 6-10
 impact of on spouse of adult daughter caregiver, 8-9
 See also Family caregivers
Family caregiving arrangements:
 prevalence of, 4
 types of, 4
Family counseling/therapy, 12, 16-17, 32, 75-76, 93, 114-117, 127, 128, 153-154
 behavior therapy, 17
 family systems theory and, 17
 psychoanalysis, 17
 structural therapy, 17
Family dynamics:
 family decision making, 121, 143-157
 impact of ethnicity on family life, 121
 intimacy among family members, 121
 recognizing select, 121-201
Family empowerment, 12, 230, 231
Family life cycle:
 effect of migration on, 181-182
Family policy, 17-19
 diversity among caregiving families and, 18-19
 family/formal services interface and, 18, 237-240
 family systems theory and, 19
 model of family functioning and, 19
 philosophies of, 17-18
 problems of developing, 18-19
Family prevention:
 and counseling, 233-234
 and policy, 234
Family prevention programs, successful:
 emphasis on promotion of competence, 230-231
 empowerment of individuals and groups, 230, 231
 interface of with other interventions, 233-234

multisystem, multilevel perspective, 230, 231-232
 sensitivity to developmental processes, 230, 232-233
Family relationships, interlocking pathology in, 130-131. *See also* Sibling relationships, adult
Family structure:
 definition of, 130
 role definitions as part of, 130
Family system, subsystems of, 128
Family systems perspective:
 and engaging the family, 134
 and family policy, 19
 core assumptions about families in, 128-129
 in family counseling/therapy, 17
 in family counseling/therapy for older gays and lesbians, 114-115
 informal caregiving and, 1
Fictive kin, 177, 179, 181
 in African American families, 177, 180
 in Italian American families, 180
"First-month syndrome," 28, 31
Friends of Drexel Home, 41

Gay and lesbian communities:
 defining family within, 100-105
 most typical family types within, 101
Gays and lesbians, older, 61-62, 211, 213, 218, 232
 biological family and, 108-109
 challenging biases against families of, 62, 99-119
 community interventions for, 113-114
 family counseling and therapy interventions for, 114-117
 hospital policy and, 107
 housing and, 106
 influences on families of, 103-105
 inheritance and, 107
 legal and policy interventions with, 111-113
 legal issues affecting, 106, 232
 long-term committed relationships among, 105-108
 relationships of with children, 109-113

retirement income and, 106
services for, 100, 229
social bonds/support systems for, 107-
    108
Greek American families, conceptualiza-
    tion of illness in, 189
Guardianship, 145, 151, 226

Health care decisions within aging fami-
    lies, 143-157, 211, 213
autonomy versus paternalism in family
    system and, 145, 147-148
choosing family spokesperson and, 146
communication problems with health
    providers and, 149-150
decision making within family system
    and, 145, 146-147
dysfunctional communication patterns
    and, 148
ethical considerations and, 151
family decision-making styles and, 144
financial impact of, 145
identifying issues and, 145-146
interventions to facilitate, 152-154
lack of competence and, 149
lack of knowledge and, 149
lack of trust and, 150
moral conflicts and, 151
obstacles to, 148
problems generated by, 145-151
resources and, 150
values and, 151

Informal caregiving to elderly family mem-
    bers, 1, 237
Institutional care of elderly, 2, 212
as last resort, 25
continued identification with facility
    and, 41
costs of, 27
elder's adaptation to, 29
elder's passivity and, 29-30, 31, 212
enriching family visitation and, 34-35
facilitating family-staff interaction in,
    37-40

family sharing in, 35-37
"first-month syndrome" and, 28, 31
fostering family involvement in, 25-44
impact of on elder, 28-32
impact of on family, 27-28
interventions designed to foster family
    involvement in, 32-41
major cause of, 26
providing biographical information
    and, 36
recognizing important role of nursing
    assistants in, 37-40
reducing family apprehension and, 32-34
Intergenerational issues in aging families,
    121, 123-142, 211
engaging the family and, 132-136
family cooperation, 133-134
family resistance, 135
intervention approaches, 127-132,
    137-138
loyalty, 136-137
problem assessment and, 136-137, 215
social policy and, 139
use of formal services, 126, 137-138
Intervention programs for caregiving
    families:
categorical disease self-help groups, 127
community-based services, 12, 15-16,
    75, 76-77, 113-114, 197, 217-218
educational programs, 93, 95-96
family counseling/therapy, 12, 16-17,
    32, 75-76, 93, 114-117, 127, 128,
    153-154
family-life educational programs, 12,
    15, 32, 75, 77, 127, 152-153, 197
family role maintenance services, 127
family support services, 93-95, 228, 232
financial aid, 137
financial planning, 127
goals of, 19
home care services, 127
housing services, 197
peer support groups, 137, 245
planning, 75
policies addressing concerns of at socie-
    tal level, 12, 75
professional education and, 75

psychoeducational support groups, 12, 16, 32, 127-128
public policy formulation, 127
purpose of, xiii
respite care, 127, 137
social/recreational opportunities, 197
social service entitlement services, 197
special short-term groups, 127
synthesis of, 203-247
types of, 15-17
Intimacy:
concept of in adult relationships, 159-161
definition of, 158
versus isolation crisis, 159
Intimacy status(es), 159-160
during adult years, 161-163
isolate, 160
measuring, 159
merger, 160
mutual, 160
pseudointimate, 160
Irish American families:
attitudes toward death in, 190-191
conceptualization of illness in, 189, 190
construct of family in, 181
Italian American families:
attitudes about help seeking in, 191
conceptualization of illness in, 189, 190
construct of family in, 179-180
family roles and responsibilities in, 183, 184-186
fictive kin in, 180

Jewish American families, conceptualization of illness in, 189, 190

Late-life marriages, 211
achieving intimacy in, 122, 158-174
applying intimacy status model to assisting, 169-172, 215
challenges to intimacy in, 165-169, 242
challenges to intimacy in merger couples in, 167-169
challenges to intimacy in mutually intimate couples in, 165-166, 170

challenges to intimacy in pseudointimate couples in, 167, 170
using life review techniques to assist, 172
Life expectancy, increased:
change in family relationships and, 123
Life review process:
in late-life marriages, 172
reminiscence therapy in, 57, 217, 219
Living wills, 147, 226
Long-term care, 145
as major policy issue, 235, 240-241
health insurance and, 241
number of elderly requiring, 235
Long-term care facilities:
chances of living in, 212
impersonal medicalized care in, 26
importance of sense of control in, 31
psychosocial qualities of facilitating resident survival, 30
See also Nursing homes

Meals on Wheels programs, 237
Merger couples, 162-163
Mexican American families:
attitudes toward death in, 191
construct of family in, 181
family roles and responsibilities in, 183, 184
Migration, family:
effect of on family life cycle, 181-182
intergenerational strain and, 187
Multi-infarct dementia and institutionalization of elderly family members, 42
Mutually intimate couples, 161-162, 228

National Long Term Care Survey, 51
Nursing homes, 2, 26, 27, 29, 35, 213, 233, 240-241. *See also* Institutional care of elderly family members; Long-term care facilities

Older Americans Act of 1965:
proposed 1992 amendments to, 92
Title III of, 237

Parents and Friends of Lesbian and Gays
  (PFLAG), 109
Policy and practice concerning aging
  families:
  adults with lifelong disabilities and
    elderly parents, 91-97
  critical issues, 235-247
  culture/ethnicity, 192-194
  diversity of, xii-xiii
  elder abuse, 74-77
  elder care, 12-19
  for continued family involvement,
    236-237
  future of, 245-246
  health care decisions, 152-154
  institutional care, 32-41
  intergenerational issues, 132-139
  intimacy in late-life marriages, 169-172
  older gays and lesbians, 111-117
  preventive approaches to building
    competencies, 236-240
  providing support to elders, 237-240
  sibling relationships, 54-58
Power of attorney, 145
Practitioner roles with aging families, 13-
  14
  care manager, 13, 14
  consultant, 13
  coordinator, 13, 14
  counselor/therapist, 13, 14
  cultural broker, 193-194, 195, 197, 198,
    206
Practitioners:
  fears of death in, 209
  fears of dependency in, 206, 208-209
  fears of disability, 209
  feelings of, 206, 208-209
Project CONNECT, 35
  goals of, 35
Pseudointimate couples, 162, 212
Psychoeducational support groups, 12, 16
  common themes of, 16
  primary emphasis in, 16
Public Law 95-602, 81
Puerto Rican American families:
  attitudes about help seeking in, 192
  conceptualization of illness in, 189

Reminiscence therapy:
  in life review process, 57
  with older people, 57-58, 217
Renegotiations, family relations
  hip/structure:
  types of, 11-12
Respite services, 15, 127, 137, 228, 230
  policy providing, 243
Role overload, 188, 189

Sandwich generation, 211
Senile dementia, 243, 244
  Alzheimer's type (SDAT), 26
  and institutionalization of elderly
    family members, 26, 35
  See also Alzheimer's disease
Sibling help:
  in old age, 50-51, 242
  to elderly parents, 51
Sibling Information Network, 56
Sibling relationships, adult, 2
  among adoptive siblings, 46
  among fictive siblings, 46
  among half-siblings, 46
  among step-siblings, 46
  apathetic, 49, 5, 532
  congenial, 49
  effects of on well-being, 50
  existence of, 47-48
  hostile, 49, 52, 53, 211
  importance of good, 52
  indirect interventions in, 56
  intimate, 49
  loyal, 49
  meaning of, 45-47
  quality of, 48-49
  recommendations for maintaining and
    strengthening, 54-55
  sibling help in old age and, 50-51
  sibling rivalry in, 48-49, 53
  significance of, 47-52
  strengthening in later years, 45-60
  threats to good, 53-54, 55-56
  troubled, 52-54
  types of, 49
Siblings:
  as role models, 51-52

counseling/therapy with, 56-58
See also Sibling relationships, adult
Siblings and Adult Children Network, 56
Social-environmental engineering for aging families, 224, 228-229
advocacy, 228, 229, 231

family support services, 228-229

WASP families:
conceptualization of illness in, 189, 190
family roles and responsibilities in, 182-183

About the Editors

Gregory C. Smith is Assistant Professor in the Department of Human Development at the University of Maryland, College Park. As an applied geropsychologist, his research has focused on caregiving within aging families. He is a member of the Gerontological Society of America, the American Association on Mental Retardation, and the American Psychological Association. In addition to coediting the present volume, he has published numerous journal articles and book chapters on families of the frail elderly and on families of adults with lifelong disabilities.

Paul W. Power is Professor and Director of the Rehabilitation Counseling Program, University of Maryland, College Park. He has authored and co-authored several books on the family and disability, and his research has focused in the area of family adjustment to a chronic illness or the aging process. He has presented workshops both nationally and internationally on these topics. He is a Certified Rehabilitation Counselor, a National Board Certified Counselor, and a certified counselor in the State of Maryland.

Elizabeth Anne Robertson-Tchabo is Associate Professor in the Department of Human Development at the University of Maryland, College Park.

Sheldon S. Tobin is Professor in the School of Social Welfare at the Rockefeller College of Public Affairs and Policy of the State University of New York at Albany, Professor in the School of Public Health and the Department of Psychology, and Research Associate of the Ringel Institute of Gerontology in the School of Social Welfare. A former editor-in-chief of *The Gerontologist,* he has more than 100 publications, including eight books, on normative and nonnormative aging, aging families, institutionalization of the elderly, and services for the elderly.

About the Contributors

Evelyn J. Bata is an educator, a counselor in private practice, and a consultant to the national long-term care industry. Her professional involvements have included college teaching and conducting workshops and forums on dynamics of aging, gender issues, and abuse. She has been cited by the State of Maryland, the U.S. House of Representatives, and the National Conference on Christians and Jews for her work with women's organizations, mental health associations, government agencies, and business, and for her leadership in diversity issues. Her current focus is on the managed health care phenomenon and its effects on gerontological and family counseling services.

Ellie Brubaker is Professor in the Department of Family Studies and Social Work at Miami University, Oxford, Ohio. She has published numerous articles and book chapters on the topics of social service delivery and older families. She is the author of a book titled *Working With the Elderly: A Social Systems Approach.* Her research interests include social services and social policy for families in later life.

Timothy H. Brubaker is Professor in the Department of Family Studies and Social Work and Director of the Family and Child Studies Center at Miami University, Oxford, Ohio. He has authored or coauthored numerous articles and books chapters on later-life families. He is the author, co-author, or editor of eight books in the family studies field, including *Later Life Families* and *Family Relationships in Later Life.* His scholarly interests are focused on later-life families and caregiving in old age.

Erin L. Cassidy is a doctoral candidate in psychology in the Department of Psychology at the University of Massachusetts at Amherst, where she is training as a clinical geropsychologist. Her research involves looking at the interpersonal dynamics within the institutional environment, focusing on the relationships between caregivers and the elderly. She participated in a longitudinal study of relationships among multiple generations at the University of Southern California, where she served as a Research Assistant.

Victor G. Cicirelli is Professor of Developmental and Aging Psychology in the Department of Psychological Sciences at Purdue University in West Lafayette, Indiana, where he has been a faculty member since 1970. He is a Fellow of the American Psychological Association and of the Gerontological Society of America. He serves on the editorial board of the *Journal of Marriage and the Family*. His research interests include parent-child relationships in later life, sibling relationships, and family support of the elderly. He is the author of *Family Caregiving: Autonomous and Paternalistic Decision Making*, as well as numerous articles and book chapters.

Elise M. Fullmer is Assistant Professor of Social Work at the University of North Carolina, Charlotte. Her primary interest is in gerontology with a particular focus on factors that either impede or promote access to formal and informal support networks and other resources by stigmatized groups. Her current research deals primarily with intergenerational support networks within the lesbian and gay communities and on intervention strategies for dealing with bias and discrimination against older lesbians and gay men at the organizational and community level.

Juanita L. Garcia is Associate Professor in the Department of Gerontology at the University of South Florida. A psychologist, she has carried out research on culturally diverse groups of elderly in the United States and on elderly women. She has lectured on elder abuse, chaired workshops and symposia on Hispanic elderly, and written on the psychological dimensions of caregiving stress leading to abuse and maltreatment. She teaches courses on minority group elderly. She is coeditor of *Elderly Abuse in Worldwide Perspective (1995)*.

Thomas W. Johnson is Clinical Associate Professor in the Department of Psychiatry and Clinical Coordinator, Comprehensive Services on Aging, at the University of Medicine and Dentistry of New Jersey. He is also a member of the faculty at the Family Institute of New Jersey and reseearch co-coordinator of the Gay and Lesbian Family Studies Project at the Ackerman Institute in New York. He has published on family systems approaches to rehabilitating the mentally ill, on HIV risk and the mentally ill, and on treatment of gay and lesbian couples, and has presented nationally on treatment of depression in older adults, family treatment approaches in schizophrenia, and family of origin treatment of gays and lesbians. His research interests include the aging family, geriatric depression, and gay/lesbian family relationships.

Jordan I. Kosberg is Philip S. Fisher Professor in the School of Social Work and Director of The Centre for Applied Family Studies at McGill University in Montreal, Quebec. A gerontological social worker, he has been involved in research, training, and lecturing in the area of elder abuse and maltreatment since 1978. He has written many articles on elder abuse and developed the Cost of Care Index (to screen potential family caregivers) and the High Risk Assessment Form (to identify older persons who are at high risk of abuse). He is a former member of the board of the National Association for the Prevention of Elder Abuse, served on a national task force to establish a research agenda for elder abuse in the United States, and chaired a U.S. Attorney General's Task Force on Elder Abuse.

Philip McCallion is Research Associate at the Ringel Institute of Gerontology at the State University of New York at Albany. He completed his academic training in Ireland and at SUNY-Albany and also has extensive administrative and service delivery experience in Ireland and the United States, working primarily with persons with disabilities and their families. He has published in the areas of interventions with caregivers of the frail elderly, of persons with Alzheimer's disease, and of persons with disabilities and has written on management issues for the providers of services for these populations. He continues to pursue research in these areas.

Nancy K. Schlossberg is Professor at the University of Maryland, College Park, in the Department of Counseling and Personnel Services, and Acting Director of the Center of Human Services Development. Her books include *Counseling Adults in Transition, Perspectives on Counseling Adults,* and *Overwhelmed: Coping With Life's Ups and Downs,* which received the 1990 Educator's Award from Delta Kappa Gamma Society International. She also coauthored *Getting the Most Out of College, Counseling Adults in Transition,* and *Reshaping Your Dream: When the Expected*

Doesn't Happen. She is a Fellow of three divisions of the American Psychological Association, a Fellow of the Gerontological Association, and Distinguished Scholar at the University of Maryland (1983).

Ronald W. Toseland is Director of the Ringel Institute of Gerontology and a Professor in the School of Social Welfare, State University of New York at Albany. He is also a licensed clinical social worker and a consultant to social service agencies serving the elderly. He serves on a number of editorial boards, including *Gerontological Social Work, Social Work With Groups,* and *Small Group Research,* and on several social service agency boards, including the Senior Service Centers of Albany and the Retired Senior Volunteer Program of Albany County. He has written five books and over 50 articles and book chapters, many of which have focused on social work practice with the frail elderly and their families. His most recent books are *An Introduction to Group Work Practice* (1995) and *Group Work With Older Adults* (in press).

Susan Krauss Whitbourne is Professor of Psychology at the University of Masschusetts at Amherst, where she teaches courses on the psychology of aging, with a focus on clinical gerontology. She has published extensively on the topics of adult development, identity, and aging, with a focus on personality, psychosocial functioning, and adaptation. Her book *Intimacy in Marriage: A Study of Couples* examines intimate relationships in middle-aged adult couples. She is currently President of Division 20 of the American Psychological Association (Adult Development and Aging).